THE NEW POLITICS
OF RACE

THE NEW POLITICS
OF RACE
From Du Bois to the 21st Century

Edited by
Marlese Durr

PRAEGER

Westport, Connecticut
London

Library of Congress Cataloging-in-Publication Data

The new politics of race : from Du Bois to the 21st century / edited by Marlese Durr.
    p. cm.
    Includes bibliographical references and index.
    ISBN 0–275–96968–1 (alk. paper)
    1. United States—Race relations—Political aspects—History—20th century. 2. United
States—Race relations—Forecasting. 3. Race discrimination—Political aspects—United
States—History—20th century. 4. African Americans—Civil rights—History—20th century.
5. African Americans—Civil rights. 6. Minorities—Civil rights—United States. 7.
Pluralism (Social sciences)—United States. I. Durr, Marlese, 1953–
E185.61.N459   2002
305.8'00973—dc21   2001036310

British Library Cataloguing in Publication Data is available.

Library of Congress Catalog Card Number: 2001036310
ISBN: 0–275–96968–1

First published in 2002

Praeger Publishers, 88 Post Road West, Westport, CT 06881
An imprint of Greenwood Publishing Group, Inc.
www.praeger.com

Printed in the United States of America

The paper used in this book complies with the
Permanent Paper Standard issued by the National
Information Standards Organization (Z39.48–1984).

10 9 8 7 6 5 4 3 2 1

For Moses, Mary, and Monique Durr

Contents

Tables

Preface

Within the past decade or so, America's urban population has undergone a dramatic transformation. Social scientists forecast that by the year 2050, nonwhites and Hispanics will compose more than 50 percent of the population. What is clear from this forecast, is that instead of heavy immigration flows from southern and eastern Europe arriving to endanger the dominance of third- and fourth-generation white ethnics, we are more likely to see an increase in ethnocentrically biased reactions to a changing American population. Given this fact, it appears that the social, economic, and political forces of our society have begun to ready themselves for either a reversal of this trend or an incorporation of nonwhite Americans into its sociopolitical and legal structures (i.e., issues of political correctness, diversity, multiculturalism, enterprise zones, and immigration policies).

Coupled with this trend, *race politics* has changed in this new immigrant era, novel but diverse questions are being asked—like are immigrants making life harder for African Americans, or will immigrants be mistreated as yet another set of minorities, or is the progress made by some immigrants a model for African Americans to follow? Citizens' concerns around these issues have been addressed by the conservative right and once politically incorrect actions appear to have become politically correct, signaling the end of over thirty years of liberal progressive policies, fostering a new conservatism.

This new conservatism is not just an anti-immigrant backlash, but possess broader roots that have weighty implications for race politics. For example, are policy issues wrestled with during the precivil and civil rights era (e.g., affirmative action, residential segregation, entrepreneurship, education, employment opportunities, and poverty) being revisited with a refashioned, but similar criticizing tone toward indigenous African Americans and immigrating Caribbean Americans?

This manuscript provides a comprehensive overview of the intersection of race/ethnicity and gender, while examining social policy issues such as affirmative action, and inner-city entrepreneurship, providing a context for discussing the most important and hotly debated issues of today. The theoretical perspective contained within this volume provides the basis for discussion of public policy and urban social issues by administrators, community-based groups, and service practitioners. More importantly, this volume has been designed to assist students in getting a firm grasp on the current discussions surrounding race relations in the United States. Each article requires students to compare and contrast the many issues surrounding race/ethnicity in a contemporary context, which will allow them to place themselves in the current context of discussions.

Acknowledgments

This volume would not have been possible without the input of the many scholars who have written on and discussed the issue of race as part of the social fabric of this country with me from my days as a graduate student to the present. I am deeply indebted to Richard Alba, Walter Allen, Elijah Anderson, Nancy Denton, Walter Ensel, Joe Feagin, Barbara Layenette Green, Richard Hall, Hayward Derrick Horton, Cedric Herring, Nan Lin, John R. Logan, Karyn Loscocco, Gwen Moore, Aldon Morris, Scott South, and Stewart Tolnay. I would be remiss if I did not thank the members of my department for assisting me in thinking about the issues associated with race/ethnicity in the United States. They are Susan Schultheis, Marilyn Adkins, Carole Staruch. And thanks to Kristine Zamora, who reviewed and edited this manuscript. I welcome your comments, suggestions, and questions.

Introduction

Aldon Morris

It is fitting that as we approach the new millennium, the seminal ideas of W.E.B. Du Bois are taking center stage once again. At the dawn of the 20th century it was Du Bois, in the role of the prophetic scholar, who declared that "The problem of the Twentieth Century is the problem of the color-line." Although this century has confronted a plethora of problems, there is no doubt that issues of race have been paramount over the last one hundred years. As we have entered the new century, we return to the task of raising troubling questions as to what the next hundred years will hold.

Race in America and the world is one of those stubborn social facts that will not disappear. The Rodney King rebellion, the O.J. Simpson trials, church burnings, and the Million Man March are a just a few of the signposts that remind us that the new century will be rocked by issues of race. Therefore, it is no accident that we return to Du Bois for clues about what to expect on the racial front and how to navigate these stormy waters. Without such clues we feel helpless in our quest to make this a better world for our children and our children's children. In our efforts to unravel these clues, conferences are being held in the name of Du Bois and new books and articles dissecting his thoughts are rolling off the presses.

This is a good thing. Du Bois's ideas and insights are profound, and the race issue needs to be examined in depth at least every hundred years. In October 1996 a young black sociologist, Marlese Durr, then an assistant professor at Wright State University in Dayton, Ohio, organized a Du Bois conference to explore the issue of race and its meaning for the new century. It is not unimportant to note that this conference was not held at one of the leading Ivy League universities, nor was its organizer a member of an elite "dream team" of scholars. The fact that Durr could organize such a conference at her university and invite leading scholars of race, and that they showed up prepared to delve into this thorny issue, is a testament to the importance of Du Boisian thought and the centrality of racial dynamics in the contemporary world.

This volume is the result of that conference. It grapples with some of the enduring issues of race and it identifies new racial realities lurking on the horizon. With respect to enduring issues, we learn that racial discrimination and racial inequality are twin evils that are as devastating today as they were at the dawn of the 20th century. It is also clear that African Americans remain the most segregated group. While it is unequivocally clear that racial separation breeds ignorance and intolerance, there is no reason to think that this problem will be solved in the foreseeable future. White resistance to actual change, typically referred to as "white backlash," is as evident in recent affirmative action battles as it was following the reconstruction period, which culminated in the Jim Crow regime.

This work reaffirms that social activism and efforts of upward social mobility continue to be avenues through which the victims of racial oppression attempt to improve their wretched fate. Yet, both approaches have their own shortcomings. Derrick Bell, reflecting on his own activism, shows that such "altruistic" work can actually damage the victim, although he concludes that we must continue to try to do good as the alternative is worse. We also learn that empirical evidence shows that cries of self-help and other "pull yourself up by your own bootstrap" philosophies are feel-good slogans, incapable of solving the crisis of racial inequality. Moreover, in America who you know is still crucial to upward mobility, for powerful and resourceful people are the social networks constituting those bootstraps to privileges otherwise unavailable to the poor and many people of color.

These contributions alert us to the fact that the racial scene in America is dynamic and that old visions and analyses provide inadequate tools for meaningful change. Thus, early in the new millennium Hispanics will outnumber African Americans, and other minority groups are growing in size and increasingly demanding a piece of the pie. How are we to understand such racial realities if we persist in viewing the world through old black/white lenses? Then, too, we are reminded that there is a new white racism on the modern scene that even Bull Connor would be incapable of recognizing. The carriers of this new racism take a kinder/gentler approach wrapped in colorized garb. They spout the words of Martin Luther King, Jr. while pushing the nation to butcher the dream. How are we to recognize and wrestle this demon in lamb's clothing comfortably tucked away in high and low spaces?

Finally, this volume reminds us that we must expand our analytical tools and visions so that we won't detach race from other potent realities. An individual's social class, race, and gender interact in complex ways to determine that individual's character and life chances. In that sense we must become the kind of deconstructionist who can not only take Humpty Dumpty apart but put him back together as well. Only then will we be able to understand how racial, class, and gender oppression intertwine and reinforce each other. One hundred years ago Du Bois wrote in *The Philadelphia Negro* (1899):

Other centuries looking back upon the culture of the nineteenth would have a right to suppose that if, in a land of freemen, eight millions of human beings were found to be dying of disease, the nation would cry with one voice, "Heal them!" If they were staggering on in ignorance, it would cry, "Train them!" If they were harming themselves and others by crime, it would cry, "Guide them!" And such cries are heard and have been heard in the land, but it was not one voice and its volume has been ever broken by counter-cries and echoes, "Let them die!" "Train them like slaves!" Let them stagger downward!

As we look forward to the new century, a central challenge will be to embrace the noble aspirations of all races and to structure the social environment such that all these aspirations have an equal chance to bloom.

REFERENCE

Du Bois, W.E.B. 1899. *The Philadelphia Negro*. Philadelphia: University of Pennsylvania Press.

1

The Du Bois–Washington Debate in the 21st Century: Multiculturalism and the African American Community

Donald Cunnigen

> The process of men's orientation in the world involves not just the association of sense images, as for animals. It involves, above all, thought-language; that is, the possibility of the act of knowing through his praxis, by which man transforms reality. For man, this process of orientation in the world can be understood neither as a purely subjective event, nor as an objective or mechanistic one, but only as an event in which subjectivity and objectivity are united. Orientation in the world, so understood, places the question of the purpose of action at the level of critical perception of reality.
>
> (Freire 1970, p. 206)

While the quote above was written in the 1970s by a leading theorist on modern development, it provides a good contemporary interpretive reference point for the debate between W.E.B. Du Bois and Booker T. Washington (Du Bois–Washington debate). The Du Bois–Washington debate focused on a wide range of issues related to the development of the African American community in the early 1900s. Among those issues was the interest in the type of role to be played by African Americans in the production of an educated populous.

The course of action suggested by Du Bois and Washington reflected more than an intellectual exercise on the function of American educational institutions in society. It was a sociopolitical debate on the role of race and ethnicity in the modern world and the role that the construction of knowledge plays in the lives of people. Their debate was couched in their subjective orientations. The relationship of subjective reality to social action is key to the development of a knowledge base in the African American community.

Since scholars have suggested (Ladner 1973) that knowledge may be both subjective and objective, understanding the subjective realities of Du Bois and Washington provides an important tool in the construction of knowledge that objectively explores the educational needs of African Americans in the 21st century. As James A. Banks (1996, p. 65) said:

Recognizing that knowledge contains both subjective and objective elements does not mean we must abandon the quest for the construction of knowledge that is objective as possible. One's location in the social structure is based partially on relations of race, social class, and gender; these are [significant] location frames.

Banks's comment suggests that knowledge is produced within a society's economic, political, and social context. The process of analyzing and understanding the impact of the contextual location of knowledge has been labeled by scholars as positionality (Tetreault 1993). By using positionality, the Du Bois–Washington debate may be examined through the intellectual influences on their ideas.

As educational and political leaders, Du Bois and Washington had very different subjective realities that influenced their purpose of action. It was his levels of critical perception relative to reality that dictated each man's intellectual position. As African Americans face a new century, the intellectual positions of Du Bois and Washington offer an unusual vantage point for considering strategies for the educational development of the African American community. These strategies must consider the sociohistorical influences, past and present, on the American discourse about minority education.

This article examines the Du Bois–Washington debate *vis-à-vis* the influence of their world orientations by looking at the following critical issues: (1) the key themes that distinguished Du Bois's educational views from Washington's educational views; (2) the political support that Du Bois and Washington garnered for their perspectives; and (3) the contemporary discussions of John Brown Childs on the significance of world orientation in the Du Bois–Washington debate and its relationship to multicultural education in the 21st century.

EDUCATION FOR THE CHOSEN FEW—DU BOIS'S VIEWS ON AFRICAN AMERICAN EDUCATION

In 1896, Henry L. Morehouse coined the phrase the "Talented Tenth" (Anderson 1988, p. 241). Yet, most Americans associate the phrase with Du Bois because of his famous 1903 essay on the "Talented Tenth" (Banks 1996, p. 47). In this essay, Du Bois stated the African American community would be saved by its exceptional men and women. He believed the "best" of the race would guide the "mass away from the contamination and death of the worst within the race." In his opinion, the fate of the African American community rested in the hands of the enlightened intellectuals (Paschal 1971 [1903], p. 31).

Du Bois's perception of an enlightened intellectual was a sophisticated combination of his European and American training. His training helped to shape his world orientation and his views on American education. Du Bois's American educational training included a rich combination of a New England grammar and secondary schooling, Fisk University, and Harvard University. According to William Banks (1996, p. 40), his educational training helped him to project the role of all African Americans from his personal experience. His European training included two years at the University of Berlin. In Europe, his training provided a perspective that reinforced his "conviction that intellectuals were above color prejudice" (Broderick 1959, pp. 2–32; Glascoe 1996).

This combination of training focused on the development of "manhood" as the object of learning within African American schools. He used "manhood" as a universal term to apply to men and women. Du Bois's concept of manhood was a person who had "intelligence, broad sympathy, [and] knowledge of the world in relation to mankind" (Paschal 1971 [1903], p. 31). Du Bois believed the African American institutions of higher learning should strive to promote his conception of manhood. In his opinion, the promotion of manhood was a continuation of an intellectual tradition, that African Americans had maintained since the colonial period. His essay highlighted the exemplary intellectual achievements of African Americans throughout history. He identified African American intellectuals for each period such as Benjamin Banneker and Phillis Wheatley for the colonial period; Lemuel Haynes and David Walker for the revolutionary period; Sojourner Truth and Frederick Douglass for the abolitionist period; and John Mercer Langston and Richard Greener for the reconstruction period (Paschal 1971 [1903], pp. 32–35).

In his historical account, he used a broad classification for an intellectual. Du Bois's exemplars of the intellectual tradition included both college-educated and self-trained African Americans. The most important aspect of their lives was their universal values relative to mankind (Paschal 1971 [1903], pp. 32–35). Du Bois's interpretation of the African American intellectual tradition's universal values was written at a critical juncture in the changing educational patterns of African Americans. He felt the early 1900s were years filled with a wide variety of African American opinion regarding the race's direction. Yet, he thought the African American community was still being led by its exceptional personalities (Paschal 1971 [1903], p. 35).

Du Bois felt the exceptional personalities in the African American community or the "Talented Tenth" were reflected in the best and most capably trained African American youth, and felt the exceptional African American youth should attend universities (Paschal 1971 [1903], p. 36). Du Bois thought the university provided a tool "for the transmission of knowledge and culture from generation to generation," and believed in the selective university participation of African American youth. While he felt the best and most capable of African American youth should seek advanced training, he admitted that all people were not college material.

Du Bois believed American colleges and universities provided a wide range of educational experiences. While he encouraged the best and most capable within the African American community to seek university training in African American institutions with strong academic programs, he suggested that many African American colleges were not prepared adequately to train the "Talented Tenth." In addition, he said the African American student encountered high levels of racial prejudice in predominantly white institutions. The educational experience of the "Talented Tenth" was the crux of the Du Bois–Washington debate.

Much of the Du Bois–Washington debate was derived from Du Bois's view of the world as an African American from New England. He was completely enamored with the New England educational tradition of which he was a beneficiary. David Levering Lewis has suggested Du Bois's early socialization in the Berkshire village of Great Barrington, Massachusetts, remained a critical aspect of his personality, political views, and intellectual life. In this community, Du Bois excelled as a scholar; acquired the Calvinistic orthodoxy of New England Congregationalism; and gained an understanding of race relations based on a "healthy" relationship with some whites. These basic elements of Du

Bois's views were reinforced by his education at Fisk via its heavy Congregationalist and New England-influenced faculty (Lewis 1993, pp. 26–55, 59–60; Glascoe 1996).

Within recent years, scholars have explored the unique role of the New England-styled institution on the development of African American higher education. James D. Anderson conducted an investigation of African American education in the South during the period of 1860 through 1935. Anderson suggested the institutional role of African American colleges and universities was influenced strongly by an apostolic vision of a liberal cultural training. This vision was presented best by missionary philanthropists, who maintained the most successful African American colleges. Anderson described their vision in the following passage:

The missionary philanthropists rallied their colleagues to support classical liberal education for [African] Americans as a means to achieve racial equality in civil and political life. They assumed that the newly emancipated [African Americans] would move into mainstream national culture, largely free to do and become what they chose, limited only by their own intrinsic worth and effort. It was supposed . . . that the former slaves would be active participants in the republic on an equal footing with all other citizens. Education . . . was intended to prepare a college-bred [African American] leadership to uplift the [African American] masses from the legacy of slavery and the restraints of the postbellum caste system. (Anderson 1988, pp. 240–241)

The vision of the missionary philanthropists was shared by Du Bois. The "Talented Tenth" theory worked well in practice during the brief shining period of 1865 through 1900. Yet, Du Bois, the missionary philanthropists, and other African American leaders had to admit to themselves that they had fallen far short of their goal to provide a classical liberal education for the "Talented Tenth." Their failure was real. In Anderson's words, "they saw no light at the end of the tunnel" (Anderson 1988, p. 245). Despite the problems of the African American colleges and universities, Du Bois felt African Americans were trained best in the schools sponsored by the missionary philanthropists.

Anderson suggested some of the African American colleges' and universities' problems were related directly to the missionary philanthropists' vision, which had a dual focus of: (1) parternalistic tendencies to make unilateral decisions regarding the educational needs of African Americans; and (2) enthusiastic support for African American higher education (Anderson 1988, p. 241). In addition, the dual focus of the missionary philanthropists was related to their limited view of equality.

According to Anderson, the missionary philanthropic view of "equality was carefully defined as political and legal equality" (Anderson 1988, p. 241). The missionary philanthropists were in complete acceptance of economic inequality. They "shied away from questions of racial integration" because they "were convinced that [African Americans'] cultural and religious values were inferior to those of middle-class whites" (Anderson 1988, p. 241). Despite the missionary philanthropists' reservations about the African American community, they maintained a strong commitment to classical training for African Americans. Their views were in juxtaposition to the growth of industrial philanthropists, who were strongly committed to the development of manual training for African Americans. Like their missionary counterparts, they invested money in the development and maintenance of industrial schools throughout the nation. The industrial philanthropists supported racial inequality. The industrial philanthropists' view was that African-Americans "needed . . . to learn . . . the discipline of manual labor and the boundaries of their natural environment" (Anderson 1988, p. 247).

Washington was in complete agreement with the industrial philanthropists' view. According to Spivey (1978, p. 66), Washington "never intentionally did anything to upset or anger Southern whites." He was especially sensitive to the Southern and Northern white philanthropists who endorsed industrial education (Spivey 1978, pp. 71–108). Du Bois disapproved of Washington's acceptance of the industrial philanthropists' view. The differing views of Du Bois and Washington shaped the debate.

Although Du Bois and Washington shared many views in the late 1890s, Du Bois's attitudes changed dramatically in the early 1900s. His criticism of Washington marked a shift in his philosophy toward industrial education and the political participation of African Americans (Meier 1966, pp. 196–197). Du Bois believed Washington's acceptance of the industrial philanthropists' view meant relinquishing African American rights in the areas of political power, civil rights, and higher education. In Du Bois's opinion, Washington reflected "the old attitude of adjustment and submission" (Du Bois 1965 [1903], p. 246). Du Bois assessed the outcome of Washington's support of the industrial philanthropic point of view as "the disfranchisement of the [African American] the creation of a distinct status of civil inferiority for the [African American] and the steady withdrawal of aid from institutions for the higher training of [African Americans]" (Du Bois 1965 [1903], p. 247).

According to Basil Mathews, "events stung Du Bois into convictions that had for years been maturing in his mind and feeling" (Mathews

1971, p. 185). It was Du Bois's strong convictions based on years of deliberative thought regarding the race problem that led him to challenge the Washington perspective. Similarly, Mathews's comment about Washington may shed some light on Washington's orientation regarding educational activities in the African American community. According to Mathews, Washington's character and his Christian faith were the basis for his belief that "constructive cooperation between races was in accord with the meaning of the universe and with the historic process" (Mathews 1971, p. 206).

According to Meier and Rudwick (1966, p. 179), Washington's famous 1895 accommodation speech reflected his complex persona, which highlighted his interest in "accommodation, self-help, racial solidarity, acceptance of disfranchisement, economic accumulation and middle-class virtues, and industrial education." Lorini (1999, p. 53) stated that the Atlanta Cotton Exposition speech was an integral part of a public ritual by which Washington created an "idealized solution" to America's racial problem, that is, social segregation and the use of an African American labor force for the development of a local economy via African American leadership. Unlike Du Bois, Washington did not envision the remarkable impact of modern technology and urbanization on the race. According to Meier and Rudwick (1966, p. 180), Washington's views were based in "a conciliatory and gradualist philosophy." They claimed this philosophical approach was the major distinction between Du Bois and Washington. Washington's philosophical approach to race relations highlighted a conservative view, which maintained a twofold explanation: (1) African Americans suffered prejudice and discrimination as a consequence of their own poverty and ignorance and (2) prejudice and discrimination against African Americans was negligible. His views became the basic elements of the African American conservative tradition. While accepting racial self-help and solidarity as positive interests, Du Bois objected to racial caste as articulated by Washington. Thus, they had very different notions of a philosophical path for African Americans.

If one accepts Mathews's complex characterization of Du Bois's and Washington's subjective realities, the Du Bois–Washington debate becomes something more than a mere intellectual discourse on options for African American education in the late 19th and early 20th century. It becomes a tool for examining worldviews that are present in the African American community. These worldviews have been shared by many African Americans. Moreover, Du Bois and Washington used their influence to ensure support for their views.

DU BOIS AND THE ANTI-BOOKERITES

W.E.B. Du Bois and Booker T. Washington worked assiduously to cultivate followers of their differing perspectives on education. Meier looked at the followers of Du Bois and Washington in four major areas of African American life: (1) education, (2) religion, (3) journalism, and (4) law. Banks commented on Washington's influence on the African American middle-class business community.

The influence of Du Bois and Washington reflected the orientations of the men and women who followed their respective leader. According to Meier, only 1.2 percent of the African American population was comprised of professionals during the period from 1880 through 1915 (Meier 1966, p. 207). Du Bois and Washington solicited support from the small professional class who comprised the "Talented Tenth."

Lewis (1993, p. 288) claims the supporters of Du Bois were "defined by the specifics of their class background and to somewhat lesser degree, the region in which they made their living." While the majority of Washington's supporters were found among the working class African American community, middle-class businessmen, and industrial philanthropists, Du Bois found his most ardent supporters among the small group of college-educated professionals and Northern white liberals. A veritable "Who's Who" of African American society, their acceptance of the "Talented Tenth" concept coincided with their own aspirations and desires. Yet, their acceptance of the concept did not prevent some of Du Bois's supporters from acquiescing to the powerful "Tuskegee Machine" (Lewis 1993, pp. 289–90).

It is not clear whether the class views of Du Bois's supporters or their stereotyped description by Washington's supporters as "cosmopolitans" who exhibited "deracination and uppityness bred by the cities" (Lewis 1993, p. 272) led to the acerbic tensions that catapulted the Du Bois–Washington debate to the center of America's racial discourse. However, class alone was not the crux of the debate or the key to understanding the subjective realities of the two men.

Some educators who were trained in the classical liberal tradition supported Washington. They were known as Bookerites or conservatives. John Wesley Edward Bowen of Gammon Theological Seminary was an educator trained in the liberal tradition who was a Bookerite. Yet, most educators trained in the classical liberal tradition shared Du Bois's perspective. For example, John Hope of Atlanta Baptist College was a Du Bois supporter. Similarly, John Wesley Cromwell, principal of a Baltimore elementary school, was a part of a Baltimore contingent who supported Du Bois's views (Meier 1966, pp. 211–213; Du Bois Papers 1976, 2: 180–281).

Educators who were Bookerites were compelled to conformity by the strong influence of Washington. Many of the Bookerite educators were graduates of Tuskegee and Hampton Institutes. Other Bookerites were principals of industrial schools patterned after the Tuskegee and Hampton models. The industrial school presidents and principals who supported Washington included Richard Robert Wright Sr., president of the Georgia State Industrial College; William Hooper Councill, principal of the Alabama State Normal and Industrial School at Huntsville; and William Henry Holtzclaw, principal of Utica Institute in Mississippi.

In many ways, the Washington industrial school presidents and principals shared his background of early rural poverty and individual self-help such as Councill, who was a former slave like Washington. Councill held minor reconstruction political positions in Alabama; was a newspaper editor and secretary of the 1873 National Equal Rights Convention; and he competed with Washington to obtain favors from the whites who controlled the Alabama legislature and Northern philanthropy. Similarly, Holtzclaw was an 1898 Tuskegee graduate who studied at Harvard. He founded the Utica Institute after working at other institutions (Meier 1966, pp. 209–211; Washington Papers 1972, 2: 114–115, 176, 196–197, 307–308, 496–497; Washington Papers 1979, 8: 519–520; Sherer 1977, pp. 32–44; McMillen 1989, pp. 92–93).

The list of educators who supported Du Bois and Washington highlighted the influential spheres developed by the two men. The Du Bois and Washington supporters controlled the operation of institutions in the African American community. With the veil of *de jure* and *de facto* segregation in most of America, the ideas and influence of African American educational leaders had a profound impact on the African American community. These men and women could use their influence to alter the lives of hundreds of African Americans. Yet, the educational arena was only one area in which the Du Bois–Washington debate cultivated supporters.

The African American religious community was the focal point for debate on the educational direction of the African American. According to Meier (1966, p. 218), most influential religious figures followed Washington. However, in the North, there were exceptions to the strong Washington support among clerics. Benjamin Tucker Tanner of Philadelphia was one of those exceptions. Tanner served as a professor of historical theology and president at Gammon Theological Seminary. He was the founding editor of *The Voice of the Negro* (Washington Papers 1903, 3:

28–29, 166). In 1895, he wrote an effusive letter of support for Washington's Atlanta Exposition speech. Unlike their educational counterparts, the religious leaders were not prominent as anti-Bookerites. Few Southern religious leaders took a strong anti-Bookerite position. However, Henry McNeil Turner was an impressive exception to the rule. Turner was a fierce opponent to Washington (Meier 1966, p. 218).

According to William M. Banks (1996, p. 66), Washington's ideas were supported by the African American middle-class businessmen and professionals. On the other hand, Du Bois's message of a Talented Tenth was viewed by many middle-class businessmen and professionals as "naive and idealistic" for they believed the African American masses who had to survive in a racist society needed practical skills.

While previous educational training and conformity were compelling reasons for the pro-Booker supporters among educators and businessmen, social class position and Methodist and Baptist ministers' attitudes toward Washington were highly correlated in the Deep South (Meier 1966, p. 221). Du Bois's supporters were found in the "elite" denominations of Episcopalians, Presbyterians, and Congregationalists. Most of those denominational groups were strongest in urban communities, Northern and border states. Representatives of Du Bois's perspective within the community of religious leaders were Henry Hugh Proctor, Atlanta's First Congregational Church, and Du Bois's Fisk classmate; Alexander Crummel, an Episcopal cleric; and Francis James Grimke, Washington, DC's Fifteenth Street Presbyterian Church (Meier 1966, pp. 222–223; Lewis 1993, pp. 62–63, 231, 262, 336; Washington Papers 1972, 2: 395).

Most African American journalists were Bookerites. Like many of their educational and religious colleagues, the journalists' respect for Washington was "not command[ed] by an enthusias[m]" for the man; but as a result of the high regard which whites had for him and his political power (Meier 1966, p. 216). Washington used various means to dominate the press, including: (1) using his contacts with the National Negro Press Bureau in Washington, DC; (2) dissemination of news releases from Tuskegee Institute; and (3) providing monetary support for struggling magazines and newspapers. In an age when newspapers were the major method of communication, Washington's control and influence on the press was critical to the promotion of his educational ideas (Meier 1966, pp. 224–225).

Du Bois's journalistic supporters included William Monroe Trotter, editor of the Boston (Massachusetts) *Guardian*. While Trotter and Du Bois had their personal clashes, they agreed on the role of classical liberal training for African Americans. Trotter played an important role in advancing the educational views of Du Bois. Ida Wells-Barnett was an outspoken journalist who endorsed Du Bois's views. She was one of several women who shared those views, including noted women's club movement and settlement house leaders such as Lugenia Burns Hope, Mary Church Terrell, and Josephine St. Pierre Ruffin (Lewis 1993, p. 289; Rouse 1989).

Du Bois had numerous publications. Yet, his community study of Philadelphia African Americans, Atlanta University Publications, articles, and books appealed to a much smaller segment of the American population (Wolters 1975, pp. 219–386). While the Atlanta University publications influenced some social inquiry into the study of race relations, the work that had a singular impact on Du Bois's construction of the "Talented Tenth" thesis was his study of African Americans in Philadelphia, where he attempted to conduct a community study and provide the reader with a narrative description African American life. Despite its originality, Lewis claims the work failed to allow African Americans to speak in their own voice (Lewis 1993, pp. 205–210). Du Bois wrote for a biracial audience. He attributed the racial failures of African Americans to achieve as a consequence of white racism. His greatest contribution was his acknowledgement of social class structure in the African American community. This class analysis highlighted two essential aspects of the African American class structure: (1) elite African Americans led the race; and (2) the slave experiences of the African American influenced African American life. These ideas became a part of his ideological basis for a leadership class derived from an educated African American elite (Du Bois 1967 [1899], pp. 309–321).

Du Bois attempted to create journals to promote his ideas. Most of his independent publications were published for a brief period of time. With his editorship of the *Crisis* magazine, Du Bois began to have a forum as broad as the former Washington-controlled journalists. Most importantly, Du Bois spoke in a different voice. Du Bois spoke in a strident voice, which said that African Americans would not tolerate injustice. His voice was difficult for the missionary philanthropists to accept. Despite his early attempts at rapprochement, his view on education was totally unacceptable to the industrial philanthropists.

While Du Bois had limited support among African American journalists, he had strong support among Northern African American lawyers. Clement Morgan, Ferdinand Barnett, and Archibald Grimke were representative of the strong anti-Bookerites in the African American legal community (Meier 1966, pp. 236–237). Although Meier's and Banks's descriptions of the followers provided clear-cut lines of demarcation between the two groups, Lewis suggested the followers were not aligned clearly in simple opposition groups. Many straddled both groups because of the influence of either Washington or Du Bois (Lewis 1993, pp. 288–296). The lack of ideological purity was eclipsed by the subjective reality of each leader's political power. Their views reflected a vision of the modern world, which highlighted two perspectives of social thought on the future for African Americans.

THE VANGUARD AND THE MUTUALISTIC PERSPECTIVES

John Brown Childs explored the complex dimensions of African American social thought. He began his explorations into African American social thought by distinguishing two worldviews, the "vanguard perspective" and the "mutualistic perspective."

Childs's vanguard perspective offered a variation of Edward Shils's center-periphery analytical model of society. Thus, Childs suggested the followers of the vanguard perspective believed there existed within society "a dominant center from which all else flow[ed]" (Childs 1989, p. 3). The vanguard perspective was based on the idea that control of the dominant center would lead to changes in the remainder of society. In this view, the center did not accept contributions from the remainder of society. The "vanguardists' " primary goal was to develop a closed social movement that was directed by the dominant center.

Childs presented the mutualistic perspective by way of vignette. He suggested the mutualistic perspective may be understood in terms of:

many groups of people hacking their way through a dense forest from different directions, all seeking escape from oppression. They have no knowledge of one another. . . . At last they begin to hear the voices of others, indistinct at first, then clearer, as the groups chop their way through the thickets. . . . Directions are exchanged. Progress is reported. Arguments erupt. Some groups are riddled with dissension; others are harmonious. . . . [T]hey have a growing understanding of being in motion with many others. . . . As, they move, the thick brush falling before them, they create, at the very moment of meeting, a gigantic clearing. . . . [T]hey all see each other; they move to embrace; they can talk face to face. . . . In contrast to the obscurity of the forest through which they have passed, the clearing is open to the light. . . . But even as they congratulate themselves on their creation through struggle more voices are heard. Others are clearing the forest nearby. . . . Then, from off in distance, still more voices. (Childs 1989, pp. 6–7)

In this vignette, Childs suggested the mutualistic perspective stated that the various groups in a society may have a sense of "social-historical commonalties," which are communicated to groups, allowing groups to "correspond with one another" (Childs 1989, p. 7). This correspondence led to a horizontal expansion of groups in cooperative relationships, which emphasize *mutuality*.

Childs used the two worldviews as the basis for his analysis of the leading historical representatives of African American social thought. In his opinion, the Du Bois–Washington debate reflected the elite perspective of the vanguard. This perspective centered around the different ideas Washington and Du Bois had regarding the requirements for African American leadership and membership in the vanguard group. As indicated above, their perspectives on leadership were reflected in their ability to recruit supporters for their educational views. In addition, they were portents of the critical issues related to diversity in 21st-century education.

According to Childs, Washington's requirements for leadership of the African American masses included the following: (1) African Americans needed to gain the respect of white people; (2) African Americans needed to "seize economic power in the South"; (3) Through economic control, African Americans would be allowed to constrain racism (Childs 1989, pp. 15–16).

According to Childs, Washington's views were more complex than Du Bois's accusation of submissiveness and accommodation. Washington believed that America's economic system was the foundation for all aspects of society. In addition, Washington argued that African Americans should accept the "facts as they were" (Childs 1989, p. 15). The fact was simply that African Americans were at the bottom of a white-controlled American political system. The American political system was "a prisoner of the irrationality of racism" (Childs 1989, p. 15). Washington's views suggested prejudice would evaporate under the influence of African American economic independence (Childs 1989, pp. 20–21). Washington believed the economic system superseded the political system, and it was the appropriate forum for practical social action. Washington's vanguard consisted of technocrats and industrialists.

Du Bois's requirements for leadership of the African American masses included the following: (1) Through their training, African American leaders should operate in a free zone of culture in which literature, art, and philosophy would be the main principles by which action was governed; (2) African American leadership should be unique and distant from the broader African American population and from the African American elite (Childs 1989, p. 18).

Du Bois's vanguard consisted of cosmopolitans who were "free from the constrictions of any particular society" (Childs 1989, p. 18). Du Bois claimed culture transcended political influences. In Du Bois's opinion, "the exercise of cultural influence require[d] only an influential system of thought." According to Childs, Du Bois's ideas about the free zone of culture were not applicable to the "Talented Tenth." His leadership was limited to a small segment of the African American elite.

Unlike Washington, who believed racism would be eliminated by African American economic independence, Du Bois viewed racism as a phenomenon that was inextricably linked to the imperialistic advance of capitalism. Du Bois felt racism was not irrational but a functional part of the capitalist exploitation of colored people throughout the world. According to Childs, Du Bois took the "peripherality of the [African American] race . . . and transformed it into a positive location for revolution."

Childs's work provided a context in which to view the actions and ideas of Du Bois and Washington. Most importantly, it suggested African American social thought was not shaped by a pattern of sporadic statements at critical points in American history. As a consequence of its sociohistorical impact on the political discourse in minority communities, the Du Bois–Washington debate had profound implications for the 21st century. It provided telling examples of the extent to which the differing political alignments of African Americans in "conservative" and "liberal" political camps influenced public policy and social action regarding education.

While the personalities of Du Bois and Washington through their subjective realities shaped the discourse, the social conditions that dictated the methods by which African Americans acquired and utilized an education had a profound impact on the subsequent social policies of minority education for most of the 20th century. The discussion of the Du Bois–Washington debate has been oversimplified by many scholars, who have suggested their views reflected only regional and class differences related to their own socialization. In Childs's attempt to place their views in a broader perspective, he offered a response to this oversimplification. Moreover, it provided the basis for a new method of interpreting their ideas. Childs offered a view of Du Bois and Washington that spoke to contemporary issues of multiculturalism. His interpretation of the vanguard perspective highlighted their ability to view the education of African Americans from a future perspective. This perspective has particular salience with regard to the contemporary discussions on multiculturalism.

CONCLUSION—MULTICULTURAL EDUCATION AND THE AFRICAN AMERICAN COMMUNITY

As stated by James A. Banks (1996, p. 5), multicultural education is based on "values, ideologies, political positions, and human interests." Thus, multicultural education follows a direct path from the elements that shaped the Du Bois–Washington debate because it links many of the distinguishing elements of their unique perspectives.

Multicultural education suggests a form of knowledge should be imparted in the contemporary classroom for the benefit of all students. From the multicultural perspective, students should be provided an education that does not marginalize people of color and women from the curriculum (Banks 1996, pp. 3–4). It is an education designed to assist students in operating effectively as participants in a pluralistic and democratic society. Banks (1996, p. 5) has suggested the inclusion of people of color and women through multicultural education should focus on the development of five types of knowledge: (1) personal/cultural; (2) popular; (3) mainstream academic; (4) transformative academic; and (5) school. Of the five types of knowledge, he believes the transformative is the most useful for students. Unlike "mainstream academic knowledge," which places emphasis on neutrality, objectivity, and noninfluence by human interests and values, transformative knowledge suggests "that all knowledge reflects the power and social relationships within society, and that an important purpose of knowledge construction is to help people improve society" (Banks 1996, p. 16; Foucault 1972). The very nature of transformative academic knowledge is to provide alternative "concepts, paradigms, themes, and explanations" to mainstream academic knowledge. These alternatives are derived from different epistemological assumptions (Banks 1996, p. 16).

It is the transformative learning aspect of multicultural education that links it to the Du Bois–Washington debate. The Du Boisian mutuality concept suggests the shared sociohistorical knowledge of races had the potential for positive social benefits. Similarly, many proponents of multicultural education believe students of all races will derive benefits in the 21st century through implementation of effective multicultural educational programs (Thomas, Chinn, Perkins, and Carter 1994, pp. 462–463). Their primary concern has been the improper implementation of multicultural education though three "bad" approaches, that is, the missionary approach, the minstrel approach, and the tolerance approach.

According to Delpit (1986, 1988, 1992), the missionary approach fails because the educators approach the introduction of multicultural themes in the curriculum by viewing students as "culturally deprived" or economically disadvantaged. Consequently, they do not acquire useful knowledge of the diverse and complex communities that comprise minority populations.

The minstrel and tolerance approaches fail for very different reasons. The minstrel approach is unsuccessful because the educators reify stereotypical images of minority cultures. The reification often derives from biased learning tools or the popular media. In the tolerance approach, educators rely on a model of teaching students to endure uncomfortable cultural/racial/gender group encounters rather than developing a strong appreciation and understanding of the significance of different groups (Thomas et al. 1994, pp. 462–463).

The transformative knowledge base of multicultural education coincides with Childs's interpretation of the Du Boisian mutuality concept, that is, various groups sharing a sociohistorical commonality. The multiculturalists view mutuality of understanding as an essential part of minority education in the 21st century, especially for the African American community. Like Du Bois, Childs's use of a worldview suggested that African American social thought operated on a continuum that was modified and refined as the social and cultural experiences of African Americans changed in American society. It is the very flexibility of African American social thought that lends itself to the multicultural educational dynamic.

Through multicultural education, the African American community may experience education in ways that will prove beneficial to both minority and majority communities. Although race and socioeconomic background characteristics have been discovered as key factors regarding attitudes on multicultural education, a survey reported that multicultural education was viewed positively in both communities (Seltzer, Frazier, and Ricks 1995). Like the Du Bois–Washington debate over liberal arts or industrial education, the debate over multiculturalism reflects a push and pull between the old and the new regarding the role of American schools in shaping students' individual and group identities via a national curriculum. By providing all American students an opportunity to examine cultural diversity, the mutualistic perspective of Du Bois may have an impact on the 21st century as great as the 1954 *Brown* decision because it will help to remove the "psychological separation" that hampers interracial interaction (Thomas et al. 1994, p. 461). The legacy of the Du Bois–Washington debate is its contribution to a discourse on education in the minority community that suggested broader perspectives should be applied to the interpretation of African Americans' educational roles in the future.

REFERENCES

Anderson, James D. 1988. *The Education of Blacks in the South, 1860–1935.* Chapel Hill: University of North Carolina Press.

Aptheker, Herbert. 1976. *The Correspondence of W.E.B. Du Bois, Volume II, Selections 1934–1944.* Amherst: University of Massachusetts Press.

Banks, James A. 1996. *Multicultural Education, Transformative Knowledge, and Action: Historical and Contemporary Perspectives.* New York: Teachers College Press.

Banks, William M. 1996. *Black Intellectuals—Race and Responsibility in American Life.* New York: W.W. Norton.

Broderick, Francis L. 1959. *W.E.B. Du Bois—Negro Leader in a Time of Crisis.* Stanford, CA: Stanford University Press.

Childs, John Brown. 1989. *Leadership, Conflict, and Cooperation in Afro-American Social Thought.* Philadelphia, PA: Temple University Press.

Delpit, Lisa D. 1992. "Education in a Multicultural Society: Our Future's Greatest Challenge." *Journal of Negro Education* 61: 237–249.

———. 1988. "The Silenced Dialogue: Power and Pedagogy in Educating Other People's Children." *Harvard Educational Review* 58: 280–289.

———. 1986. "Skills and Other Dilemmas of a Progressive Black Educator." *Harvard Educational Review* 56: 379–385.

Du Bois, W.E.B. 1971 [1903]. "The Talented Tenth." *A W.E.B. Du Bois Reader.* Andrew G. Paschal, editor. New York: Collier Books.

———. 1967 [1899]. *The Philadelphia Negro—A Social Study.* New York: Schocken Books.

———. 1965 [1903]. *The Souls of Black Folk.* New York: Avon Books.

Foucault, M. 1972. *The Archaeology of Knowledge and Discourse on Language.* New York: Pantheon.

Freire, Paulo. 1970. "The Adult Literacy Process as Cultural Action for Freedom." *Harvard Educational Review* 40: 206.

Glascoe, Myrtle G. 1996. "W.E.B. Du Bois: His Evolving Theory of Education." *Research in Race and Ethnic Relations,* Volume 9. Greenwich, CT: JAI Press.

Green, Dan S. and Earl Smith. 1983. "W.E.B. Du Bois and the Concepts of Race and Class." *Phylon* 4: 262–272.

Harlan, Louis R., editor. 1972. *The Booker T. Washington Papers, Volume 2, 1860–1889.* Urbana: University of Illinois Press.

————. 1974. *The Booker T. Washington Papers, Volume 3, 1889–1895.* Urbana: University of Illinois Press.

Harlan, Louis R. and Raymond W. Smock, editors. 1979. *The Booker T. Washington Papers, Volume 8, 1904–1906.* Urbana: University of Illinois Press.

Ladner, Joyce A. 1973. *The Death of White Sociology.* New York: Vintage Books

Lewis, David Levering. 1993. *W.E.B. Du Bois—Biography of a Race, 1868–1919.* New York: Henry Holt.

Lorini, Alessandra. 1999. *Rituals of Race—American Public Culture and Search for Racial Democracy.* Charlottesville: University of Virginia Press.

Mathews, Basil. 1971. "The Continuing Debate: Washington vs. Du Bois." *W.E.B. Du Bois—A Profile.* Rayford W. Logan, editor. New York: Hill and Wang.

McMillen, Neil R. 1989. *Dark Journey—Black Mississipians in the Age of Jim Crow.* Urbana: University of Illinois Press.

Meier, August. 1966. *Negro Thought in America, 1880–1915.* Ann Arbor: University of Michigan.

Meier, August and Elliott M. Rudwick. 1966. *From Plantation to Ghetto—An Interpretive History of American Negroes.* New York: Hill and Wang.

Patton, June O. 1996. " 'And the Truth Shall Make You Free': Richard Robert Wright, Sr., Black Intellectual and Iconoclast, 1877–1897." *Journal of Negro History* 81, 1–4: 17–30.

Rouse, Jacqueline Anne. 1989. *Lugenia Burns Hope—Black Southern Reformer.* Athens: University of Georgia Press.

Seltzer, Richard, Michael Frazier, and Irelene Ricks. 1995. "Multiculturalism, Race, and Education." *Journal of Negro Education* 64: 124–140.

Sherer, Robert G. 1977. *Subordination or Liberation? The Development and Conflicting Theories of Black Education in Nineteenth Century Alabama.* Tuscaloosa: University of Alabama Press.

Spivey, Donald. 1978. *Schooling for the New Slavery—Black Industrial Education, 1868–1915.* Westport, CT: Greenwood Press.

Tetreault, M.K.T. 1993. "Classrooms for Diversity: Rethinking Curriculum and Pedagogy." *Multicultural Education: Issues and Perspectives.* James A. Banks and Cherry A. McGee Banks, editors. Boston: Allyn and Bacon.

Thomas, Debbie G., Phil Chinn, Fran Perkins, and David G. Carter. 1994. "Multicultural Education: Reflections on Brown at 40." *Journal of Negro Education* 63: 460–467.

Wolter, Raymond. 1975. "The NAACP in a Time of Economic Crisis." *Negroes and the Great Depression.* Westport, CT: Greenwood Press.

2

The White Backlash Against Affirmative Action: The Case of the California Civil Rights Initiative (Proposition 209)

James E. Jacob and
Miriam Ma'at-Ka-Re Monges

IN THE AFTERMATH OF THE ELECTION—THE IMPACT OF 209 ON AFFIRMATIVE ACTION IN CALIFORNIA

With the passage of Proposition 209, California became the first state in the union to forbid the use of race or gender in hiring and admissions in the public sector. The day following the election, Governor Wilson issued an executive order directing state officials to implement Proposition 209 immediately. The same day, however, opponents of 209, including the American Civil Liberties Union, filed suit in U.S. federal court challenging the issue's constitutionality. It was thus clear that despite the issue's passage in the polls, its ultimate fate would depend on the courts. Despite the temporary restraining order issued by U.S. District Court Judge Theron E. Henderson on April 8, 1997, a panel of judges from the U.S. Court of Appeals for the Ninth Circuit ruled in surprisingly clear terms that, "Proposition 209 does not violate the United States Constitution."[1] While Wilson and Connerly were jubilant, it was clear that the panel's decision opened the issue up for an appeal to the entire Ninth Circuit Court, and ultimately to the United States Supreme Court as well. When the full panel of justices of the Ninth Circuit Court of Appeals upheld 209, the action of the Supreme Court was, if anything, anticlimactic. As it turned out, the Supreme Court's review was perfunctory. It refused even to accept the question on appeal and thus affirmed the decision of the Ninth Circuit *without comment*. Yet, with Hopwood the law in the Fifth Circuit, and 209 now affirmed in the Ninth, it was clear the Supreme Court still needed to unify and complete the dismantlement of Bakke that its recent rulings on affirmative action so clearly indicated. In California, 209's supporters continued to threaten lawsuits to force its implementation in state government, and especially the state universities.

The earliest evidence of the impact of 209 on public policy came with the first admissions figures for the class that entered the University of California's Boalt Hall Law School in the Fall of 1997. Only fifteen African American students were admitted and, as it turned out, none enrolled.[2] In contrast, in 1996—the last year before restrictive affirmative action policies took effect—twenty African American students enrolled as well as fourteen Hispanics. The Regents of the University of California had voluntarily implemented these restrictions on the use of affirmative action (at the urging of Governor Wilson and Regent Connerly) even before the passage of 209.

At the same time, undergraduate admissions figures proved equally disturbing and seemed to confirm the fear of Prop. 209 opponents before the election that its passage would lead to the resegregation of the University of California system. The first statistics revealed the ethnic and racial makeup of all students admitted in the U.C. system. They also revealed that Berkeley was now the most selective public university in the United States in terms of the credentials of students admitted. According to the *New York Times*, minority students (African Americans, Mexican Americans, Hispanic Americans and American Indians) together represented 23.1 percent of the admitted freshman class at the University of California at Berkeley in 1997—the last year in which pre-209 admissions criteria were used.[3] For the class of 1998, the first under 209, the number of minority students admitted to Berkeley (not including Asians) had plummeted to 10.4 percent of all students admitted. At UCLA, they fell from 19.8 percent in 1997 to 12.7 percent for 1998.[4] These figures revealed that the number of African Americans admitted to Berkeley *declined by 66 percent. and 43 percent at UCLA*. According to the *Los Angeles Times*, "The new figures mean that fewer than 200 African Americans were among the more than 8,000 students admitted to Berkeley—the lowest number of blacks since 1981."[5]

Seven weeks later, in late May 1998, the University of California system released its figures for those students who had accepted offers of admission and who intended to enroll in Fall 1998.[6] The results confirmed the precipitous decline in minority students revealed by the earlier data on students accepted within the system. Specifically, the data on students intending to enroll in the system in fall 1998 showed the following trends. Non-Asian minorities (African Americans, Hispanics, and Native Americans) would make up 10.54 percent of the entering class at Berkeley, less than half of the 21.92 percent in the class of 1997.[7] Of these minority students enrolling at Berkeley, 98 were blacks, compared to 260 the year before.[8] At UCLA, non-Asian minorities would constitute 14.1 percent of the entering class, down from 21.8. One hundred and thirty-one would be black compared to 219 the year before.[9] Each campus experienced modest increases in their yield rates through deliberate recruitment efforts.

Systemwide, however, the total non-Asian minority enrollment declined a modest 2.4 percent, confirming predictions that more stringent admissions criteria would have a "percussive" effect by pushing students away from Berkeley and UCLA and toward other less prestigious U.C. campuses, including Santa Cruz, Santa Barbara, and Riverside, all of which experienced *increased* enrollments by African American and Hispanic students.[10] Systemwide, more Asian students were admitted than whites, a statistic that reflects the growing heterogeneity of the state's population.[11] According to Ethan Bronner, Berkeley Chancellor Robert M. Berdahl called the African American and Hispanic figures "grim" and said, "It isn't easy to put a positive light on this."[12] For UCLA Vice Chancellor Theodore R. Mitchell, "The real danger—our biggest concern—is that the University of California system will become a segregated system. If this trend continues over the next five or six years, the diversity on this campus will be seriously compromised and, with it, our greatness."[13] Mitchell's concern was echoed by one African American student at Berkeley, who stated, "This represents the resegregation of higher education. I feel uncomfortable enough [at Berkeley] right now as it is."[14] For other administrators, there was relief that the drop was no larger than it was.

For Ward Connerly, however, "This is the academic market correcting itself, with students going where they are the most competitive. We now know that for every person admitted under affirmative action, we've been turning away someone else more competitive for that slot."[15] According to the *New York Times*, "Some opponents of race-based admissions tools said they, too, were disturbed by the dropoff because they said it proved their point that the school systems had been failing to prepare black and Hispanic applicants properly and that the university system had been

discriminating against whites and Asians."[16] In another interview, Connerly argued, "If they are not ready for Berkeley or UCLA, then they
should go to a community college and get prepared so they can transfer
in. We should not be admitting people to Berkeley or UCLA who are
not ready to go."[17]

Of all the University of California campuses, Berkeley and UCLA
were the most competitive, with Berkeley accepting 27 percent of its
30,000 applicants and UCLA 33 percent of 32,600.[18] UCLA alone turned
away two-thirds of its applicants, "many of whom have 4.0 gpa's and
1,250 test scores."[19] The same declines, though to lesser degrees, were
noted at four other U.C. campuses (Davis, Irvine, San Diego, and Santa
Barbara). Yet, despite the precipitous drop in minority admissions at the
two flagship campuses of the U.C. system, two trends appeared that
nuance the impact of 209 on university admissions. The first was a
marked increase in the minority admissions rate at two other University
of California campuses, notably at U.C. Riverside where African American admittees increased 42 percent, and at Santa Cruz where Latinos
increased 7 percent. According to Gary Tudor, director of Admissions
and Outreach for the University of California at Davis, "We're thinking
that Berkeley's loss is our gain."[20]

The second trend was that, in the cases of both Berkeley and UCLA,
the number of applicants declining to identify their racial or ethnic background totaled 14.1 percent, or a one-year increase of 150 percent from
1997 to 1998.[21] UCLA cross-checked its applications with other data-
bases and concluded that 80 percent of these students were either white
or Asian.[22] For Connerly, "They are Asian and white kids who think
they are going to be disadvantaged if they reveal who they are."[23] In the
case of Asian students, in particular, if strict ethnic quotas had been
implemented at Berkeley, it would have led to sizeable numbers having
to leave. With Asian students constituting 38.3 percent of Berkeley admissions, more Asians were accepted at Berkeley for 1998, despite a far
smaller Asian population in the state as a whole. The 150 percent increase in the number of students who declined to declare their race or
ethnicity seemed to reflect the belief among these applicants that they
would be more successful being considered on the merits of their academic achievements alone.

Coming on the heels of earlier data showing that only one African
American student had accepted to attend U.C. Berkeley's prestigious
Boalt Hall Law School, these numbers prompted concern about the inequality of K-12 academic preparation across the state, and about the
nature of access to higher education.[24] As Connerly himself acknowl-

edged, "To solve the problem you have to deal with the problems in kindergarten through twelfth grade. Don't blame the university."[25] University officials began to consider a number of other strategies, including focusing on economic disadvantage (across color lines) or recruiting students from previously underserved geographic areas of the state.

At the same time that California was wrestling with the impact of 209, the University of Texas system was experiencing similar problems with implementing the Hopwood decision by the Fifth U.S. Circuit Court of Appeals. In order to avoid California's experience, the Texas legislature passed a new law mandating that the U.T. system admit any student who graduated in the top 10 percent of their high school graduating class— regardless of differences in quality among the high schools involved. Ultimately, Texas's plan led to slight increases for fall 1998 in the enrollment of both African American and Hispanic students, but less in both cases than before Hopwood.[26]

The University of Texas's plan was greeted with skepticism in California where it was felt that such a scheme risked admitting students unprepared for work at campuses like Berkeley and UCLA. Thus, little support was found for implementing a similar plan in California. In fact, the Regents of the University of California system voiced skepticism at a plan to guarantee admission to even the top *4 percent* of graduates of each high school in the state.[27] Regent Ward Connerly was most skeptical, voicing the concern that, "You're getting deep, deep concern about any dilution of quality."[28] At best, it was estimated that the change would result in black and Hispanic enrollment in the U.C. system increasing only from 11 percent to 12 percent of total enrollment. As Regent Tom Sayles put it, "I think it may cause more problems than it solves."[29]

In either case—Texas or California—the keenest competition continued to be for admission to the flagship campuses at Berkeley, Austin or UCLA. Indeed, admissions figures for the class of 1998—the first since 209's passage—seemed to partially confirm the concerns of 209 opponents that it would lead to a resegregation of public higher education in America. California's experience demonstrates that in the aftermath of 209, white and Asian students are more likely to cluster at Berkeley and UCLA. Faced with declining admissions at those campuses, African American and Hispanic applicants are shifting to second-tier U.C. campuses such as Riverside or Santa Cruz. As one University of Texas at Austin admissions official noted (in high-Texas vernacular) about why students preferred the University of Texas at Austin over the other regional U.T. campuses, "Well," he said, "they think them other dogs, they don't hunt."

CONCLUSION

Thus unfolded the campaign for passage of the California Civil Rights Initiative, Proposition 209. The issues involved in Prop. 209 touch at the very heart of pitched debates over social policy in this country, and over what kind of country we want America to be. Affirmative action was once widely accepted as a positive means to ensure the social and economic integration of all Americans into the mainstream. Today, however, there is a burgeoning literature by African American and white conservatives assailing affirmative action and its underlying premises. Opponents of affirmative action have been careful to couch their opposition to preferences by liberal references to the Constitution, the values of the Founders, Abraham Lincoln, and even the Reverend Martin Luther King, Jr.

Supporters of Proposition 209 in California stated during the campaign that they had no objection to preferences based on socioeconomic need. Gail Heriot, co-chair of the statewide CCRI campaign, asserted, "CCRI would not in any way prevent the state from considering economic disadvantage in making its decisions."[30] Indeed, Assemblyman Richter promised to introduce legislation should Prop. 209 pass to create a set of preferences based on poverty, rather than on race or gender. Richter himself has been quick to point out that the real problem lies in the nature of the inner city, including the poor quality of educational opportunity available to many minority children. For Richter, affirmative action and preferential admissions at the university level are ways to try to correct the real problem on the cheap.

With 209's passage, a whole generation of minority children may be put at risk while a new system is created, starting with improvements to primary and secondary schooling in the state. These changes are staggering and expensive. The mandate by the state to limit class sizes in K-2 to only twenty students has posed an enormous problem not only in space but in the hiring of new teachers. Los Angeles County alone announced in August 1996 that it needed to hire *ten thousand teachers* to meet the state's new mandate. At the same time, the fastest growing part of the California state budget is prison construction and corrections. The question remains whether state legislators will have the political courage to consider the kind of transformations that will be required—and their enormous costs—given the antitax and antiimmigrant mood of the California electorate.

The problem with the equity and fairness issue that is raised by supporters of CCRI is that this country has still not achieved a level socioeconomic playing field despite more than thirty years of social legislation stretching back to Lyndon Johnson's Great Society. President Lyndon Johnson provided one of the greatest arguments against the CCRI when he said in 1965 that, "You do not take a person who for years has been hobbled by chains and liberate him, bring him up to the starting line of a race and then say, you're free to compete with all the others, and justly believe that you have been completely fair."[31]

The most offensive aspect of the CCRI campaign to its opponents was the attempt of its backers to claim ownership of the legacy of Dr. Martin Luther King. This theme was recurrent in the campaign. Assemblyman Richter went so far as to argue that if King were alive today, he would "surely stand" with those supporting Prop. 209.[32] Yet, King himself noted that, "A society that has done something special against the Negro for hundreds of years must now do something special for the Negro."[33]

Roger Wilkins notes the positive impact that affirmative action has had on the minority community, even if its socioeconomic achievement lags far behind that of white Americans: "we have in fact achieved a more meritocratic society as a result of affirmative action than we have ever previously enjoyed in this country."[34] And as the *San Francisco Examiner* argued in its editorial opposing Prop. 209, "The heart of the matter is whether our society has evolved to the degree that affirmative action is no longer needed to make sure that blacks and other minority groups are treated fairly and equally."[35] In April 1998, Nathan Glazer, in an article entitled, "Why I No Longer Think Affirmative Action Is Unjust," explained his rethinking of his opposition to affirmative action that had characterized his writings on race since his book, *Affirmative Discrimination*, in 1975:

What was unforeseen and unexpected was that the gap between the educational performance of blacks and whites would persist and, in some respects, deepen despite the civil rights revolution and hugely expanded social and educational programs, that inner city schools would continue to decline and that the black family would unravel to a remarkable degree, contributing to social conditions for large number of black children far worse than those in the 1960's. In the presence of those conditions, an insistence on color-blindness means the effective exclusion today of African Americans from positions of influence, wealth and power. It is not a prospect that any of us can contemplate with equanimity. We have to rethink affirmative action.[36]

Glazer goes on to note that, despite the heady enthusiasm of similar campaigns in other states, no other state so far has passed legislation like

209.[37] Thirteen states introduced bills between 1996 and 1997 to eliminate affirmative action based on preferences.[38] *None* was passed. The next states to consider doing so will be Washington, Florida, Texas, and Michigan. President George W. Bush and a good deal of his administration, unlike the Clinton administrations, favors court supported decisions banning the use of racial preferences such as the Hopwood decision at the University of Texas, as well as the Florida and Michigan initiatives which were modeled after California's Proposition 209. This preference was echoed throughout his presidential campaign and remains one he supports. What explains why so many states and legislatures went to the brink of legislation similar to 209 only to retreat from it? According to Steven Holmes, "Advocates on both sides, as well as political analysts, say the main reason for the inability to get affirmative action bans enacted has been the ambivalence of the Republican Party."[39] There is not a Republican consensus on the issue, and more than a little fear that the perceived insensitivity surrounding this issue may damage Republican overtures to African American and Hispanic voters.

As a result, in March 1998, the Republican-dominated United States Senate failed to pass a bill ending minority and female set-asides in federal construction contracts. The next month, the Republican-dominated House of Representatives rejected the same bill and with it the opportunity to further dismantle affirmative action programs in federal practice. In May, the House rejected by a vote of 249–171 a bill to outlaw preferences based on race, gender or ethnicity in American universities.[40] Fifty-five Republicans crossed party lines to oppose the bill. This retreat on the part of the Republican majority baffled Ward Connerly. Part of the explanation was the opposition of U.S. Representative J.C. Watts, who, with Connerly, is one of the two most prominent African Americans in the Republican Party. As Watts argued, "This is not the time to eliminate the one tool we have—imperfect though it may be—to help level the playing field for many minority youth."[41] Connerly said, "Personally I have great respect for [Watts] but it has been mind-boggling to figure out where he is coming from. He says he's opposed to preferences but then he can't seem to pull the trigger."[42] Despite the fact that the issue had only recently been a holy crusade for the Republican Party, its failure to act in these cases suggested that many of its members were rethinking their stridently vocal opposition to affirmative action. It is clear that their effort to defuse the issue is a calculated political strategy. This is hardly a conversion experience, but rather a desire—having won at the polls and in the courts—to defuse the issue of some of its political volatility and minimize the backlash on Republican candidates in future elections. As such, it is an undeniable act of *realpolitik* on the part of the Republican Party.

Meanwhile, President Clinton moved to refine federal policy regarding minority set-asides in contracting. In June 1998, the White House announced that minority-owned businesses would be given an advantage in winning federal contracts, but *only* in those industries where they have been traditionally underrepresented. In a statement issued by the White House, it was announced that the new federal guidelines on affirmative action would be employed in industries accounting for about three-quarters of all money spent by the federal government in contracts with small businesses.[43] The change in policy was deliberately designed by the White House to meet the standards defined by the Supreme Court in *Adarand v. Pena*—that any affirmative action remedies be "narrowly tailored" to address specific instances of discrimination.[44]

Governor Wilson used affirmative action as a platform plank in his bid for the Republican presidential nomination in 2000, but was unsuccessful in gaining presidential nomination. It will be interesting to see how the Republicans subordinate this issue within their broader goal of furthering their inroads into the African American and Hispanic electorates. Many remember the self-imposed fate of Rep. Robert "B-1 Bob" Dornan. His outspoken support of 209 and his contemptuous treatment of the Hispanic electorate harmed the Republican Party's minority strategy nationally and doomed any future hope of reelection of himself in his losing campaign to Loretta Sanchez. So deep was his denial that he had to be asked to stop coming onto the floor of the House of Representatives, a privilege extended to former members.

With both Props. 187 and 209 coming on the heels of earlier English-language initiatives, Republican support of these issues has served to antagonize key segments of the electorate. One of the emerging trends in American elections in the 1990s was the potential of a "gender gap," as Republican women might migrate to more moderate candidates because of the Republican Party's stridency on abortion and other issues of concern to women. Similarly, 187, 209, and Dornan's campaign mobilized many Hispanic voters and led them to vote against the party and its ideologues. With estimates of as many as 500,000 new high school graduates in California in the next ten years, the size of the Hispanic electorate will continue to grow. If the Republicans have made inroads into the Hispanic middle class, it is not clear that a growing native and naturalized population will see the issue of affirmative action in the same way.

The values reflected in Prop. 209 found further expression in the June

1998 primary election where Proposition 227 proposed the essential dismantlement of bilingual education programs in the state. It called for giving non-English speaking students *one* transitional year of bilingual instruction before placing them in English-only classrooms. According to Frank Bruni in the *New York Times*, its author, businessman Ron K. Unz, succeeded in securing the support of several prominent Hispanic educators, and by focusing his arguments on educational quality, he hoped to avoid further fanning the flames of racial and cultural resentment in the state. The initiative passed with 61 percent of the vote.

It is clear that the conservative political strategy was intended to seize the moral high ground and define the legitimate side of the debate over affirmative action. In effect, the campaign for 209 was part of a broader conservative strategy to define American values and what it means to be American. The decision to lower the volume was in no way a retreat from their core values but rather an effort to calm political passions. Much of the conservative opposition to affirmative action approaches the intensity of a core political belief. Nonetheless, Republican caution combined with the failure of any of thirteen states to pass 209-type legislation has encouraged affirmative action supporters. This led NAACP Chairman Julian Bond to declare somewhat prematurely, "Despite popular thinking to the contrary, the battle to preserve affirmative action is being won, not lost."[45]

Not surprisingly, not even President Clinton's Advisory Board on Race was able to escape the issue of affirmative action. It began when Ward Connerly criticized the president's initial appointments to the panel, chaired by Professor John Hope Franklin, as excluding principled conservatives and opponents of affirmative action like himself. Over the past year, the Board has worked in the shadow of Prop. 209 and the affirmative action debate. As Larry Mamiya argues, "To some degree [the Advisory Board] has degenerated into a debate forum on affirmative action."[46] Standing above the fray, President Clinton sought to avoid engendering political ill will by partisans on either side of the issue. In the meantime, his Advisory Panel on Race founders for lack of a clear mission and charge. President Bush does not see the issue in quite the same way and in many ways pushes for the elimination of quotas based on race.

Few people will deny that racism continues to be a visible element of the life of American minorities. David Duke's insertion into the Prop. 209 debate may have outraged Connerly, Richter, and Wilson, but the former Ku Klux Klan leader saw nothing inconsistent with Prop. 209

and his call for white power in this country. Racism continues to be a visible element of American life. As Roger Wilkins argues,

The fact is that the successful public relations assault on affirmative action flows on a river of racism that is as broad, powerful and American as the Mississippi. And, like the Mississippi, racism can be violent and deadly and is a permanent part of American life. But while nobody who is sane denies the reality of the Mississippi, millions of Americans who are deemed sane—some of whom are powerful and some even thought wise—deny, wholly or in part, that racism exists.[47]

According to Theodore M. Shaw, associate director-counsel for the NAACP Legal Defense Fund, "You know, it is pretty depressing when you think that this is 30 years, almost to the day, after the assassination of Martin Luther King and we're still fighting a battle we thought we had moved beyond."[48] Ward Connerly meanwhile announced in early 1997 that he would extend his campaign against affirmative action beyond California and make it nationwide in scope. On Martin Luther King's birthday in 1997, Connerly announced that he was initiating a national antiaffirmative action campaign. Connerly justified this by asserting that "Dr. King personifies the quest for a color-blind society and I felt that it would be a great symbol to give birth to an organization that wants the nation to resume that journey on the birthday of the man who symbolizes it."[49] The fact that he deliberately chose to make his announcement on Martin Luther King, Jr.'s birthday provoked further controversy among those groups that had opposed his campaign for Prop. 209 and that were offended at Connerly's persistent effort to tie his efforts to the legacy of Dr. King. Connerly's campaign has also been challenged by the King family, which has begun its own countercampaign to challenge Connerly's use of King's legacy and to affirm the continued need for affirmative action programs. Martin Luther King, III contends that Connerly is inappropriately using his father's legacy. King believes in particular that Connerly's use of Dr. King's "I Have a Dream" speech fails to acknowledge an earlier part of the speech, which says, "America has given the Negro people a bad check; a check which has come back marked 'insufficient funds'."[50]

In 1998, Prop. 209 was implemented in California and its constitutionality has been affirmed by the refusal of the Supreme Court to hear any further appeal from its opponents. In the long run, however, the implementation of Prop. 209 and the evolving body of Supreme Court decisions will encourage other states to consider following California's lead. There is no question that the intellectual underpinnings of affirmative action are under attack as never before. As Andrew Hacker notes, "If affirmative action has a future, it will be as no more than a vestige of its former self. Politically the program never had widespread support and that lack is now glaringly apparent."[51] Connerly, who has long considered the Bakke decision to be "bad law," said, "I pray to God the Supreme Court rules on it one way or another, win, lose or draw. This is something the court needs to act on."[52] As Michael Greve noted, "As a legal matter, [Bakke] is hanging by a thread, and as a practical matter, there is no way of going back to the legal framework Bakke established.[53] In 1998, Bakke remained the law in forty-eight states. The Supreme Court's refusal to hear either Hopwood or 209 served to let stand Appellate Court rulings in those two jurisdictions. But choosing not to hear either case suggests that the Court has chosen, for now, not to dismantle Bakke in one fell swoop. Either way, Bakke's days are numbered and the weight of recent Supreme Court decisions provides a clear indication of their opposition to the historic arguments in favor of affirmative action.

The most fascinating aspect of the CCRI debate in California was that it was replete with more citations of the Constitution, Bill of Rights, Founding Fathers, Abraham Lincoln, and complex arguments based on political theory than any other citizen initiative in the state's history. Conversations with the CCRI's backers revealed a deep and sincere intellectual commitment to repealing affirmative action, which they believed to be unfair and contrary to the basic values on which this country was founded. As Andrew Sullivan, editor of *The New Republic*, argues:

Liberalism was once the creed that said you were equal before the law. Parentage, gender, race, religion: none of that mattered. The individual citizen was what counted. Now, in extending the power of government further and further, in regulating the precise percentages of racial and other minorities in a whole range of activities and places, liberalism has become the very force it was born to oppose. If liberalism is to revive, it will only do so on the ashes of affirmative action. It will revive by articulating the principles that liberalism was founded on: equality before the law, equal treatment by the state, and freedom as the guiding principle of society. It is liberalism that provides a space for individuals to achieve the success that has to be won, not provided—fought for, not fought over. . . . History's joke is that it has taken the conservatives to rediscover it.[54]

The reality is that there continues to be an underclass in this country. The particular nature of U.S. political economy has demonstrated the correlation between race, social class, and poverty. If there has been improvement in those figures, it has come, in part, as a result of affirmative action programs, which have propelled the rise of an African American middle class. To end those programs now is to insist that nothing more remains to be done.

The real victims of Prop. 209 may well be the next generation of African American children who are forced to compete with children of other colors, who realistically are coming from different worlds. As Camille DeJorna described her children's upbringing,

I considered explaining this to be a survival skill for being Black in America. Race matters in this story. It defined my children's relationship to authority and to their claims on promises of justice. I believe that the dreams of a color-blind society are earnest and sincere. Yet they fail to take into account that many still live lives where race determines where and how we live, how our children are taught, what kind of medical treatment we receive, and the extent and quality of our contacts with the criminal justice system. Hopes for equity demand that we continue to take race into account.[55]

So turns the issue of race at the beginning of the 21st century. It is clear that a nexus of similar issues (affirmative action, immigration, bilingual education) has put the California electorate at the forefront of a national debate on what it means to be an American. Though partisan passions run high on both sides of the issue, we have not yet achieved the point where race no longer matters in our society. This partisan debate involves conflicting means and alternative definitions of the American future.

Ultimately, Proposition 209 will prove to be one of many waystations along the path to a redefinition of American society. Such is the sensitivity of affirmative action that the passions it provokes are equally strong on both sides of the issue. Each side can agree that the debate is fundamentally one about fairness, and then reach *opposite* conclusions about what should be done. For Americans of color, the issue of affirmative action is about fairness, and about a set of policies that have helped to level the playing field of American social life. The arguments will continue (as they have since Americas founding) about how best to build America's "shining city on a hill." It is clear that the persistent salience of race, ethnicity, language use, and gender—and attendant socioeconomic disparities—continues to confound the emergence of one America. For that reason, race still matters in this country. With the victory of Proposition 209 at the polls, its supporters might reflect for a moment on the words of Todd Gitlin, who said simply, "People who right now are enthusiastic about the CCRI ought to look into their conscience and ask themselves, if they're White, whether they really think they would've had a happier life if they were Black.[56]

NOTES

1. Harriet Chiang, "Court Upholds Prop. 209," *San Francisco Chronicle*, April 9, 1997, p. A1. See also Ken Chavez, "Prop. 209 Ruled Constitutional," *The Sacramento Bee*, April 9, 1997, pp. A1, A12.

2. "Minority Figures Climb at Berkeley Law School," *The New York Times*, May 7, 1998, p. A26; See Ethan Bronner, "U. of California Reports Big Drop in Black Admission," *The New York Times*, April 1, 1998, pp. A1, A23.

3. Ibid.

4. Kenneth R. Weiss and Mary Curtius, "Acceptance of Blacks, Latinos to UC Plunges," *The Los Angeles Times*, April 1, 1998, pp. A1, A20; See Ethan Bronner, "Minority Enrollment at U. of California Will Dip in Fall," *The New York Times*, May 21, 1998, p. A20; Venise Wagner, "51% Drop in Some Ethnic Groups at UC-Berkeley," *San Francisco Examiner*, May 22, 1998, p. A2; Deb Kollars, "Fewer Blacks, Latinos among Fall Freshman at Cal, UCLA," *The Sacramento Bee*, May 21, 1998, pp. A1, A19.

5. Bronner, "Minority Enrollment at U. of California Will Dip in Fall," p. A20.

6. Ibid.

7. Ibid.

8. Ibid.

9. Ibid.

10. Cited in Bronner, "Minority Enrollment at U. of California Will Dip in Fall," p. A20.

11. Ibid.

12. Cited in Brad Hayward, "Black, Latino Admissions Fall," *The Sacramento Bee*, April 1, 1998, pp. A1, A16.

13. Ibid., p. A16.

14. Bronner, "U. of California Reports Big Drop in Black Admission," p. A1.

15. "Acceptance of Blacks, Latinos to U.C. Plunges," *The Los Angeles Times*, April 1, 1998, p. 1.

16. Ibid., p. A20.

17. Cited in Kollars, "Fewer Blacks, Latinos among Fall Freshman at Cal, UCLA," p. A19.

18. Hayward, "Black, Latino Admissions Fall," p. A16.

19. Weiss and Curtius, "Acceptance of Blacks, Latinos to UC Plunges," p. A20.

20. Ibid., p. A20.

21. Weiss and Curtius, "Acceptance of Blacks, Latinos to UC Plunges," p. A20.

22. Cited in Bronner, "Minority Enrollment at U. of California Will Dip in Fall," p. A20.

23. Ibid.

24. Pamela Burdman, "Regents Doubtful on Admissions Plan," *San Francisco Chronicle*, May 19, 1998, p. A16.

25. Ibid.

26. Ibid.

27. "CCRI Is about 'Preferential Treatment'," letter to the editor in the *San Francisco Chronicle*, July 8, 1996, p. A16.

28. Cited in Paul Berman, "Redefining Fairness," *The New York Times Book Review*, April 14, 1996, p. 16.

29. Cited in Larry Mitchell, "Richter Insists: King Would Back Prop. 209," *Chico Enterprise Record*, September 18, 1996, p. 1A.

30. Cited in Larry Mitchell, " 'Angry White Guy' Says Richter's Wrong, Rev. King Backed Racial Preferences," *Chico Enterprise Record*, September 17, 1996, p. 1A.

31. Ibid., p. A16.

32. "Defeat Prop. 209," *The San Francisco Examiner*, September 15, 1996, p. C14.

33. *The Sacramento Bee*, Forum Section, April 12, 1998, pp. 1, 2.

34. Ibid., p. 2.

35. Steven A. Holmes, "Washington State Is Stage for Fight Over Preferences," *The New York Times*, May 4, 1998, pp. A1, A15.

36. Ibid., p. A15.

37. Ibid., p. A15.

38. See Anthony Lewis, "Turn of the Tide?," *The New York Times*, May 6, 1998; See also: "House Rejects Affirmative Action Ban in Higher Education," *Chico Enterprise Record*, May 7, 1998, p. 5A.

39. Cited in Anthony Lewis, "Turn of The Tide?," p. A23.

40. Cited in Anthony Lewis, "House Rejects Affirmative Action Ban in Higher Education," p. 5A.

41. David E. Rosenbaum, "White House Revises Policy on Contracts for Minorities," *The New York Times*, June 25, 1998, pp. A1, A18.

42. Ibid.

43. Ibid.

44. Frank Bruni, "The California Entrepreneur Who Beat Bilingual Teaching," *The New York Times*, June 14, 1998, pp. A1, A24.

45. Cited in Scott Shepard, "Time Is Winding Down on America's Dialogue on Race," *The Atlanta Journal-Constitution*, June 14, 1998, p. A8.

46. Ibid.

47. Roger Wilkins, "The Case for Affirmative Action," *The Nation*, March 27, 1995, p. 412.

48. Cited in Bronner, "U. of California Reports Big Drop in Black Admission," p. A23.

49. Cited in Jack E. White, "I Have a Scheme," *Time*, February 3, 1997, p. 46.

50. Ibid.

51. "Goodbye to Affirmative Action?," p. 28.

52. Cited in Freedberg, "After 20 Years, Bakke Ruling in the Spotlight," p. A16.

53. Ibid.

54. "Let Affirmative Action Die." In "Affirmative Action: A Dialogue on Race, Gender, Equality and Law in America," *Focus on Law Studies*, Vol. XIII, no. 2 (Spring, 1998), p. 2.

55. Cited in Edward Lempinen, "A Question of Identity," *San Francisco Examiner*, May 12, 1996, p. 3.

3

Organizational Response to Affirmative Action: Substance or Symbolism?

Sharon M. Collins

Prior to the mid-1960s, black employment patterns in major industries reflected the American cultural norm of *de facto* segregation and discrimination against black workers (Wilson 1978; Jaynes and Williams 1989). In Chicago, blacks tended not to be placed in the principal office of multi-establishment firms (U.S. Commission on Civil Rights 1969). Rarely did they fill white-collar jobs, such as sales and clerical jobs, and they were almost exclusively absent in professional and managerial jobs in white-dominated settings (U.S. Commission on Civil Rights 1969). The Urban League, for example, found a pattern in Chicago in 1965 whereby blacks were virtually excluded from policy-making positions (Chicago Urban League 1977). From about the mid-1960s onward, however, major white-owned corporations began to hire blacks into white-collar jobs, in particular, professional and managerial positions (Freeman 1981, 1976a, 1976b; Farley 1984; Landry 1987).

We know that many large- and mid-size U.S. companies during the 1960s and 1970s found ways to incorporate a new echelon of skilled and college-educated African Americans into higher paying occupations. This chapter more precisely describes the jobs and roles filled by some of these people after they entered corporations. Interviews in 1986 and again in 1993 with seventy-six of some of the most successful black managers in Chicago corporations revealed that these managers dispro-portionately filled new affirmative action and related functions that or-ganizations elaborated during the civil rights period. A race-based division of labor evolved in major corporations as African Americans entered them. Here I argue that the allocation of specialized jobs to blacks during the civil rights era helped to maintain occupational ine-quality despite evidence of gains in the black middle class.

Literature on organizations highlights processes by which organiza-tions adopted mechanisms to comply with government antidiscrimination mandates, in particular how public and private employers adapted to affirmative action and equal employment opportunity initiatives (Edel-man 1990, 1992; Dobbin et al. 1993; Abzug and Mezias 1993). Such research has raised important questions about both the symbolic and the substantive consequences of organizational responses to antidiscrimina-tion policies for improving the status of women and minorities.

For example, studies of human resource departments found managers adjusted personnel practices to reduce ambiguity in civil rights legislation by creating and instituting formal hiring, evaluation, and promotion pro-cedures (Dobbin et al. 1993). Although these practices appear to manifest greater fairness in personnel procedures, procedural biases—for instance, pro-male and same-race biases in performance evaluations—are well documented (Foschi, Lai, and Sigerson 1994; Kraiger and Ford 1985, 1990; Nieva and Gutek 1980; Oppler, Campbell, Pulakos, and Borman 1992).

Similarly, human resources managers developed formal mechanisms to handle discrimination complaints and addressed affirmative action mandates by creating new personnel and affirmative action offices (Ed-elman 1990, 1992; Dobbin et al. 1988; Abzug and Mezias 1993). Again, this structural elaboration of departments demonstrated attention to the law but the existence of these offices was found to be equated with compliance, quite apart from any particular substantive result of their efforts (Edelman 1990, 1992). Thus, institutional practices that symbolize efforts to promote greater equity can substantively protect white mana-gerial prerogatives and restrict the opportunities available to women and minorities (Baron et al. 1991; Edelman and Petterson 1994). Put another way, research on organizational behavior suggests that responses to gov-ernment antibias mandates may help to maintain—rather than eradicate—work force inequality.

This chapter is an attempt to meld findings from this literature with theory developed in research in the area of race and class inequality. Research on organizations has focused on the response of organizations to government antidiscrimination legislation by analyzing personnel policies and practices. This chapter extends the images surrounding the repercussions of these personnel practices by analyzing the attributes of black managerial careers. First, I will illustrate that Chicago corporations deployed highly educated black labor out of the mainstream of organizations into a "racialized" structure of jobs. In this structure are jobs that were created or reoriented during the 1960s and 1970s to address governmental antidiscrimination policies and mediate other black-related pressures, for example, boycotts, demonstrations, and elements of black militancy. Affirmative action, urban affairs, community relations, and jobs in purchasing are examples. Next, I show the impact of filling these jobs on executives' upward mobility. Initially, these jobs enhanced the job holders' status in the company, thus attracting black talent. Over time, however, this opportunity structure underdeveloped skills that are valued by corporations. Racialized structures marginalized the job holder's skills and, consequently, marginalized the job holder. Ultimately, occupants' probability of moving into, competing for, and/or performing in, mainstream areas that lead to corporate power and decision-making positions (that is, general management, sales/marketing, production, finance/accounting, and human resources) was greatly diminished because they filled these jobs.

THE STUDY

I considered blacks to be "successful executives" if: (1) they were employed in a banking institution and had a title of comptroller, trust officer, vice president (excluding "assistant" vice president), president or chief officer; or (2) they were employed in a nonfinancial institution with a title of department manager, director, vice president or chief officer. In the mid-1980s, these people held some of the more desirable and prestigious positions in Chicago's major corporations. About two-thirds (52 of 76) had the title of director or above, including three chief officers, thirty vice presidents, and nineteen unit directors. (The total includes three people with the title "manager," whose rank within the organization was equivalent to director.) In addition to being the successful stories in Chicago in 1986, participants in this study were among the highest ranking black executives in the country. Five of the executives interviewed were the highest ranking blacks in corporations nationwide. Almost half (32 of 76) were the highest ranking black in a company's nationwide management structure.

To locate these managers, I identified the fifty-two largest white corporations in Chicago using the *Chicago Reporter* (1983, 1986) listings of industrials, utilities, retail companies, transportation companies, and banks. Second, I asked knowledgeable informants familiar with the white corporate community in Chicago to identify blacks who met the study criteria. These same informants also identified employees of the targeted companies who might be able to provide names of higher level black officers. Snowball sampling from this starting point was then used. Eighty-seven managers were identified. Eleven of these eighty-seven people were not interviewed, either because they declined to participate, because of logistical problems, or because they did not meet my criteria.

The level of education in this group closely paralleled that of white male senior-level executives. For instance, 94 percent of top executives in Fortune 500 companies surveyed in 1986 had bachelor's degrees. Forty-two percent had graduate degrees (Korn/Ferry 1986). Eighty-nine percent of people in the study had at least a bachelor's degree when they entered the private sector. Over one-third (38%) earned advanced degrees. Moreover, the level of education attained by these people was well above the median level of about one year of college for salaried men managers in 1960 and 1970, the decade in which most of them got their jobs (United States Bureau of Census 1960). In addition, slightly more than one half of the black graduates I interviewed had received their college degrees from a predominantly white institution. Using vitae received prior to the interview, I explored the characteristics of each job held by these seventy-six executives, their career development, and their promotional opportunities.

Looking at the substantive characteristics of blacks' jobs in white corporations, I distinguished parallel job structures within organizations: racialized and mainstream. Jobs in the racialized structure are a substantive and/or a symbolic response to black communities, to black issues, or to antidiscrimination laws at any level of government. For example, one respondent was hired by the chief executive officer of a major retailer in 1968 specifically to identify discriminatory employment practices in the personnel department. I coded this function as part of the "racialized" structure of an organization, since it was a response to antidiscrimination legislation, created at a time when the federal government increasingly required it.

In contrast, line and support functions not geared towards race-related and/or antidiscrimination mandates were coded as part of the mainstream corporate structure. In this category, tasks were oriented to total constituencies and neither explicit nor implicit connections to blacks or government legislation could be found in a job description. A vice president and regional sales manager provides an illustration of a career in the organizational mainstream. This manager was hired as a market researcher for a Fortune 500 East Coast oil company in 1961 where his job involved marketing only to the total (predominantly white) consumer market not to "special" (predominantly black) markets. He was not assigned to black territories as a salesman nor as a sales manager although, he said, "those kinds of things even happen now [and once] happened a lot." Neither was he ever responsible for developing an affirmative action plan or program or urban strategies, although this was the case among other respondents who were salesmen.

In this chapter, the mainstream structure of organizations is conceived of as the pipeline of line and support jobs leading to senior executive positions that oversee the strategic planning, human resource/personnel development, or production components of a company. For example, the manager cited above moved up through the mainstream sales hierarchy from salesman to sales manager, from zone manager to district manager, from area manager to division manager and, finally, to his current position as a firm officer. Granted the pipeline narrows as it moves upward, the flow of occupants in this part of the structure fills the executive vice president, senior vice president, group vice president, functional vice president, and corporate specialist slots that comprise company officers. Korn/Ferry (1990) surveyed executives and found the typical track to top jobs in major corporations is through profit-oriented positions such as sales, operations, and finance. To a lesser degree, corporate vice presidents, senior vice presidents, executive vice presidents, and group vice presidents were in personnel or public relations departments (Korn/Ferry 1990). Conversely, as we shall see, the racialized structure in organizations creates a pipeline to nowhere, or to glass ceilings.

A CORPORATE DIVISION OF LABOR

African American managers implemented and administered the jobs and departments elaborated in organizations to address employment legislation and other external pressures to increase blacks' access to social and economic resources. In this study, twelve of seventy-six (16%) had one job and about half (39 of 76) had two or more jobs of this nature. Conversely, African American executives with work histories exclusively in the mainstream structure of private corporations stand out as the exception; they are not the rule. Only one third of the people I interviewed (25 of 76 managers) built entire careers in the organizational mainstream of race-neutral jobs.

Jobs in the racialized structure of management are not necessarily extensions of respondents' port of entry into private corporations. About one half of forty-five people who filled affirmative action and urban affairs roles started in the corporate mainstream in line positions. These twenty-two were explicitly recruited into a system of administrative jobs organizations adopted to meet new legal and social pressures for non-discrimination. Senior-level white management, usually either senior vice presidents or chief executives officers, personally solicited twelve of the twenty-two recruits (55%) from the mainstream. Eleven (50%) were given salary increases, more prestigious job titles, and promises of future rewards. Nine people turned down the first attempt at recruitment because they evaluated the job to be a dead end, despite high pay and elevated titles, but were approached a second time by top management. Occupants of affirmative action and urban affairs jobs who were from mainstream line areas commented that black-oriented jobs appeared to be a route by which talented blacks could advance rapidly in companies.

Over 80 percent of the first affirmative action/community relations jobs that managers filled in their careers did not exist previously, but were established by the respondents. Because these functions were new, top management looked to them for guidance and direction in shaping these areas. One manager—who worked in sales before he took on affirmative action responsibilities—reminisced in a voice filled with irony that "it was supposed to be an honor." The ability to provide guidance gave these managers a unique, if temporary, status in companies. A director moved into affirmative action from sales because, he said, "I remember the CEO saying, 'we want you to take this beautiful job. It's going to pay you all this money. It's going to make you a star.' " Indeed, managers who filled jobs in this structure were on a first-name basis with corporate CEOs, as well as with black nationalists from the streets. Their ability to walk between these conflicting groups made some of them favorite sons in corporations, at least during the turmoil of the civil rights era. However, as I show next, when filling these jobs they also participated in creating an organizational structure that fed their demise.

RACIALIZED ORGANIZATIONAL STRUCTURES AND MOBILITY

To compare the advancement associated with racialized and mainstream organizational structures, I selected respondents employed in the white private sector at least since 1972 to construct a career typology, a total of sixty-two people. (I selected 1972 as the cut-off year based on the proposition that the number of years required to advance in a company is associated with the size of the company, with more time required in larger concerns. The Chicago Urban League [1977] found that, on average, it takes about fifteen to twenty years to reach upper-management positions in the major companies in the nonfinancial sector of Chicago.) Three types of managerial careers—mainstream, mixed, and racialized—emerged based on the jobs that were found in this group of executives. Respondents having no jobs in the racialized structure during their careers were coded as having mainstream careers (24 of 64). Respondents whose careers incorporated at least one, but not a majority, of jobs in the racialized structure were coded as having mixed careers (22 of 64). The careers of respondents having a majority of jobs in the racialized structure were coded as racialized (18 of 64).

LOWERED JOB CEILINGS

Using last job titles as a measure of status, racialized respondents experienced less advancement than mainstream respondents. The top executive titles represented in this study, (i.e., chief officers and senior vice presidents) were held by people who spent a majority of their careers in the mainstream arenas. There is little difference in the executive job titles associated with mixed and mainstream careers, possibly because the vast majority of mixed careers had only one or two racialized jobs in a racialized structure. In distinct contrast, careers evolving in racialized arenas show a more limited pattern of upward mobility, although careers were not necessarily finished. Eighty percent terminated with director or manager titles versus only 38 percent of the mainstream careers and 46 percent of mixed careers. Not one racialized manager progressed above vice-president.

The limitations inherent in this structure of jobs is also reflected in a finding that only four of eighteen (22%) managers with racialized careers were the highest-ranking black executive in a company's Chicago location. In contrast, thirty-one of forty-six (72%) managers who had a majority of mainstream functions in their careers were the highest-ranking black executive in a Chicago company. The racialized respondents acknowledged the advancement limitations associated with this structure of jobs. It alternately was described as "dead-end jobs [that had] no power," "nigger jobs," and "money-using" versus "money-producing" jobs.

It was not surprising, therefore, that a manager's position in the corporate division of labor coincided with the level of optimism expressed by an individual about his or her future in a company. Kanter (1977, p. 135), in particular, comments on the relationship between aspirations and level of opportunity. About three-quarters of (19 of 26) mainstream but less the one quarter of (4 of 20) racialized respondents reported they believed their chances for a promotion or a lateral move leading to promotion in the company was "good" or "very good." Respondents in racialized careers reported that they were at the end of their career ladders in white companies. Sixty-five percent (13 of 20) said there would be no additional moves for them in the company, either lateral or promotional. Moreover, their pessimism extended to their perceptions of their opportunities for upward mobility on the open job market. One director of affirmative action summarized this shared perception of future mobility concisely when he said, "ascension for me is over."

The white executive elite I interviewed informally also expressed the opinion that African American managers in racialized jobs were "out of the mix" (i.e., not in the running for top jobs in a company). Such an assessment is consistent with the fact that racialized functions consist predominantly of staff, or support, positions. In general, most support functions are among the worst routes to top jobs in a company (Korn/ Ferry 1990). They tend to be less desirable than line jobs because they lack influence and have shorter and more limited chains of career opportunities (Kanter 1977). I suggest that the chain of opportunity becomes even shorter in an organizational structure of support jobs linked to racial purposes. This structure of jobs not only imposed relatively lower career ceilings among these managers, they were underdeveloped over time as valuable commodities in corporations and, therefore, marginalized.

LIMITED SKILL DEVELOPMENT

Pressures placed on companies by federal legislation and by protest in urban black communities made racialized functions valuable to companies because they buffered corporations from external turmoil. At the same time, these new functions required little or no investment on a company's part in terms of job preparation and training. They relied, instead, on good interpersonal skills, persuasiveness, and black managers' external relationships.

One man described his urban affairs job as if it were an ambassador-at-large. He said, "I just moved about. Traveled. Everything was coming out of the community and I was there. I'd make 10, sometimes 12, meetings [in the black community] a day." An executive in the food industry described his affirmative action job in a strikingly similar way. He said, "I spent most of my time in the [black] community trying to . . . let people know that there were jobs and positions available in this company. I did a lot of speaking with community groups." An executive in a communications firm said, "Mostly I worked with local community agencies to get the word out that there were opportunities [in the company]." A company director was ombudsman during the 1970s whose task was, he said, to "promote the visibility and good name" of the bank in the black community in Chicago. A vice president spent part of his tenure in an affirmative action/urban affairs job. He said, "after the civil disorders, the riots . . . there was a tremendous movement . . . to have black [representation in the company]. Basically [my] job was to work with the [company] and come up with minority candidates."

A director of urban affairs was recruited to sales and asked to develop a new relationship between his company and civil rights and black social service organizations in Chicago. He succeeded and became skilled at brokering the interest of his company and successfully "absorbing" the tensions between the company and urban black constituencies. He said that in 1971, "[My role was to] make [the company] look good. I did what they needed done to look good in the community. They utilized me in that fashion. For eleven years I was just their spook who sat by the door, and I understood that. Certainly I was, and I charged them well for it."

Jobs associated with administering affirmative action, equal employment opportunity, and other race-conscious functions evolved into routine work. When I asked managers for job descriptions associated with various promotions, one man, who built a career in affirmative action, dismissed the question, indicating that he was "essentially doing the same thing" at each level. Affirmative action and related goals were reduced to a narrow set of administrative tasks extracted from generalist personnel and external relations functions. One respondent noted the job in the 1970s involved recruitment of blacks but not whites into a company. Another mentioned the job was essentially "[black] number counting." A third said the company promoted him, but he nevertheless recognized his experience in personnel was distinctive. He said, "You have a little stepladder . . . a logical progression [of personnel functions] you have to go through if you are to ever become a personnel director. I wasn't doing any of that. As far as I could see, the company wanted black folks to be my only responsibility." His experience distinctly contrasts with reports from managers in mainstream personnel, who mention at least six distinct components of their personnel experience—including employee relations, employment, compensation and benefits, and labor relations. The gulf between mainstream personnel and the racialized version of the job was summarized in the following way: "If you stay in affirmative action, when you go looking for a job you're going to be seen as the affirmative action person. And personnel jobs are bigger than that."

As marginalized job holders, in short, respondents weren't inaugurated into cross-functional training. The trade-off in a racialized structure that relied on personal persuasion and external networks was that managers became cut off from other functions. They lacked the confidence of their peers and the support of internal networks that are important to advancement (Thompson and Di Tomaso 1988; Kanter 1977; Tsui and Gutek 1999). This meant that their job success segregated them and reproduced career segregation, a quandary that created and solidified barriers to the mainstream of an organization by conferring information about respondents' abilities. In short, people who stayed in these jobs became marginalized managers because their value in mainstream corporate functions was called into question.

People in the segregated structure faced two alternatives for enhancing their chances for upward mobility. One was to make a lateral move into the mainstream structure by taking any available job. The second was to move to the mainstream component that mirrored the racialized area (i.e., from community relations to public relations). People who specialized in affirmative action, community relations, and other jobs in the racialized structure were stymied in both routes by real or perceived limits to their utilitarian value in the mainstream structure. When an affirmative action manager (who, originally, was a comptroller) tried to reenter the corporate mainstream, she found she was locked into her racialized niche at each turn. She said, "I tried to negotiate myself out [of affirmative action]. There didn't seem to be a lot of . . . future. I wanted to try to get back into merchandising at that point. Or go back into comptrolling or to go somewhere else in personnel. You know, nothing ever came out of it. I even took a special class to get accreditation in personnel, as a personnel generalist. Which I completed. [It] had absolutely no effect on me going anywhere." Finally, she said, "It got to where the [job] level and the salary level to go and change fields is too high . . . to be able to sell me to someone else. The likelihood of me going outside of [affirmative action] at this point is pretty well zero."

A community relations manager for a major electronics corporation—when noting that his company's commitment to urban affairs programs for blacks began to decrease noticeably in the 1980s—also illustrates this dilemma. Observing, as he put it, the "handwriting on the wall," he made multiple attempts to move out of his dissolving niche in the racialized company structure. He first attempted to get into production and next into general administrative services. Describing these attempts he said, "I was just not able to make that break. I talked to [people] in various divisions that I was interested in, and I got the lip service that they would keep [me] in mind if something opened up. As it happened, that just did not develop. I can never remember being approached by anyone. Nothing [happened]—that I can really hang [onto] as an offer. People would ask, 'have you ever run a profit and loss operation?' " Finally, he describes himself as talking "hat in hand" and approaching senior management in 1982 to request duties he knew to be available in a general administrative area. He said, "Frankly, this was an attempt to seize an opportunity. This time I went and I asked for a [new assignment]. We had some retirement within the company and some reorganization. I saw an opportunity to help myself. The urban affairs was shrinking. A number of jobs we created [in urban affairs] were completely eliminated. It just happened that the opportunity [to pick up administrative services] was there. It had a significant dollar budget and profit and loss opportunity . . . it was concrete and useful. So I asked for it."

Yet he was only temporarily successful in his try to exchange urban affairs for a more stable assignment in administrative services. One year later he was invited to resign from the company, reportedly because of poor performance. The story told by a second urban affairs manager—who tried a move to warehouse distribution in a retail company—reveals similar constraints. This manager was a department director, a job that was targeted to be cut from a company. He also discovered that the trade-off for rising in a company in urban affairs was an inability to shift into any mainstream corporate function. Here is his assessment: "I was too old to do what you had to do to compete. . . . I was competing with 21- and 22-year-olds to get into the system. They couldn't charge [my salary] to a store and have me doing the same thing the others [were] doing [for much less money]. You need the ground-level experience. When I should have gotten it, I was busy running an affirmative action department." Indeed, from a practical standpoint, investing in retraining this individual would not likely reap a long-term benefit because of his age. Consequently, I asked this manager why he didn't move laterally into mainstream public relations, an area (apparently) he was more qualified to pursue. He responded, "I thought about it very seriously. I wondered where I was going with the system. It came up quite often. I talked about it when I first accepted this job. And at the end, they told me, 'We don't know. We'll have to get back to you.' They never did."

That his superiors never got back to him "at the end" may result from the fact that the organization needed him precisely where he was placed. Or, it may result from the fact that he lacked a skill base and/or that his superiors perceived his skills differed from those managers who had moved up the ladder in mainstream public relations. The latter point is highlighted by the comments of a manager who failed in his attempt to transfer into compensation and benefits—precisely because his past concentration in affirmative action made him underqualified for the job. He explained, "I moved over . . . as director. Now, mind you, I'm going from a corporate [affirmative action] job . . . to . . . compensation and benefits. I told the chairman of the company I didn't have any experience in that field. I might not be his man."

DISCUSSION

Although affirmative action and related programs may reflect corporate good-faith compliance efforts, they also constituted race-conscious systems of administering programs and services. Such systems, in turn, have generated corresponding race-conscious processes of job allocation that tracked blacks into what are essentially race-specific organizational niches. This finding reflects a functional segregation of blacks and the production of ghettoized components to their relative gains in management. In other words, internally segregated or segmented systems of occupational allocation were created.

Some view the limited progress of blacks through the organizational hierarchy as a function of time. However, "time" isn't a vacant variable; something happens "in" it. The talents and training that these managers brought initially to their occupations were systematically filtered through a peripheral system of jobs and cumulative work experience. As respondents moved in—and then up in—racialized management assignments, they were locked out of mainstream jobs in management. A devaluation of their abilities occurred that eventually constrained their progress in executive arenas. A race-based system of job allocation created a deficit in on-the-job training and experience. This structurally imposed deficit, in turn, is exposed—and interpreted—as black human capital deficits that create barriers to advancement.

The observations derived from this study have various implications. The first suggests that if black occupational attainment results from organizational responses to special political and legal conditions, these attainments are arguably fragile. Personnel offices and practices are viewed as important boundary-penetrating structures that mediate between the organization and the larger environment. As the environment changes, we expect related changes in organizational behavior and occupational outcomes. Indeed, this argument is born out in this study of black managers and executives, as findings indicate recruitment and allocation of blacks into racialized occupations during periods of social upheaval and in response to governmental demands. Conversely, when political pressures abated, racialized jobs tended to lose their value in organizations, and the occupational status of many of the black executives collapsed.

The 1990s witnessed increased intensity in attacks on antidiscrimination policies and programs. Given this social and political environment, we must ask whether there are substantive characteristics in the jobs attained by blacks that would make them particular targets for occupational instability and erosion. Indeed, the occupational status of black managers is vulnerable to both changes in public policy and shifting economic trends.

The second implication concerns the more abstract problem of how inequality is manufactured. To the extent that blacks occupy jobs cut off from core company goals, they are cut off from core skill development. When viewed through the lens of my analysis, the often-noted—but rarely explored—high concentration of blacks in corporate support jobs implies some process of deskilling highly educated blacks through the absence of on-the-job profit-centered work experiences. How such a concentration occurred is a critical research question surrounding the status of blacks in professional and managerial occupations. In the current study, the black managerial vanguard entering the white private sector was eased out of the running for top executive jobs via racialized careers because of a mix of corporate pressure, career naivete, and blacks' perceptions of race-related corporate barriers that skewed decision making and personal preference (Collins 1997). This has broad implications for organizations and occupational outcomes, especially in light of current debates on discrimination and workplace inequality.

My interpretation of the findings in this study are nested in a broader paradigm of inequality. Using the conceptual framework of a conflict perspective, the career construction witnessed here can be viewed as part of a process of social closure to defend the existing advantage of white managers. The corporate role in the allocation of jobs—and the assessment of their value—was not a function of objective or impersonal supply characteristics but of race-conscious employment discrimination. It is not clear that the subsequent deskilling of a cohort of blacks depressed their wages, as Braverman (1974) might have suggested. Rather, this apparent deskilling can be viewed as serving a more pressing purpose. The problem for white corporate elites was to incorporate protected groups of minorities while protecting managerial prerogatives. Racialized structures were an efficient way of meeting both goals. They were both mechanisms to appease governmental legislation and black demands for more economic resources, and a system of assignments that reduced the threat of increased competition for organizational power along racial lines. The peculiar evolution during the 1960s and 1970s of careers documented in this study diminished the black executive pool in Chicago corporations who could compete to manage mainstream units in organizations in the 1980s and beyond. Consequently, gains respondents made over the last three decades did not—and could not—blossom into meaningful numbers of black executives in powerful decision-making roles.

REFERENCES

Abzug, R. and S.J. Mezias. 1993. "The Fragmented State and Due Process Protections in Organizations: The Case of Comparable Worth." *Organization Science* 4:443–453.

Baron, J., B.S. Mittman, and A.E. Newman. 1991. "Targets of Opportunity: Organizational and Gender Integration with the California Civil Service, 1979–1985." *American Journal of Sociology* 96:1362–1401.

Bielby, W.T. and J.N. Baron. 1984. "A Woman's Place Is with Other Women: Sex Segregation with Organizations." Pp. 27–55 in *Sex Segregation in the Workplace: Trends, Explanations, Remedies*, edited by B.F. Reskin. Washington, DC: National Academy Press.

———. 1986. "Men and Women at Work: Sex Segregation and Statistical Discrimination." *American Journal of Sociology* 91:759–99.

Braverman, Harry. 1974. *Labor and Monopoly Capital: The Degradation of Work in the Twentieth Century.* New York: Monthly Review Press, 1974.

Chicago Reporter. 1983. "Annual Corporate Survey." December: 2–6.

———. 1986. "Annual Corporate Survey." January: 7–10.

Chicago Urban League. 1977. *Blacks in Policy-Making Position in Chicago.* Chicago: Chicago Urban League.

Collins, S.M. 1997. *Black Corporate Executives: The Making and Breaking of a Black Middle Class.* Philadelphia: Temple University Press.

Dobbin, F.R., J.R. Sutton, J.W. Meyer, and W.R. Scott. 1993. "Equal Employment Opportunity Law and the Construction of Internal Labor Markets." *American Journal of Sociology* 99:396–427.

Edelman, L.B. 1990. "Legal Environments and Organizational Governance: The Expansion of Due Process in the Workplace." *American Journal of Sociology* 95:1401–1440.

————. 1992. "Legal Ambiguity and Symbolic Structures: Organizational Mediation of Civil Right Law." *American Journal of Sociology* 97:1531.

Edelman, L.B. and S. Petterson. 1994. "Symbols and Substance in Organizational Response to Civil Rights Law." Manuscript, Department of Sociology, University of Wisconsin, Madison.

Farley, R. 1984. *Blacks and Whites: Narrowing the Gap?* Cambridge, MA: Harvard University Press.

Foschi, M., L. Lai, and K. Sigerson. 1994. "Gender and Double Standards in the Assessment of Job Applicants." *Social Psychology Quarterly* 57: 326–339.

Freeman, R. 1976a. *The Black Elite*. New York: McGraw Hill.

————. 1976b. *The Over-Educated American*. New York: Academic Press.

————. 1981. "Black Economic Progress after 1964: Who Has Gained and Why." Pp. 247–295 in *Studies in Labor Markets*, edited by S. Rosen. Chicago: University of Chicago Press.

Jaynes, G.D. and R.M. Williams, Jr. 1989. *A Common Destiny: Blacks and American Society*. Washington, DC: National Academy Press.

Kanter, R.M. 1977. *Men and Women of the Corporation*. New York: Basic Books.

Korn/Ferry. 1986. *Korn/Ferry Internationals' Executive Profile: A Survey of Corporate Leaders in the Eighties*. New York: Korn/Ferry International.

————. 1990. *Korn/Ferry Internationals' Executive Profile: A Decade of Change in Corporate Leadership*. New York: Korn/Ferry International.

Kraiger, K. and J.K. Ford. 1985. "A Meta-Analysis of Ratee Race Effects in Performance Ratings." *Journal of Applied Psychology* 70:56–65.

————. 1990. "The Relation of Job Knowledge, Job Performance, and Supervisory Ratings as a Function of Ratee Race." *Human Performance* 3: 269–279.

Landry, B. 1987. *The Black Middle Class*. Berkeley: University of California Press.

Nieva, V.F. and B.A. Gutek. 1980 "Sex Effects on Evaluation." *Academy of Management Review* 5:267–276.

Oppler, S.H., J.P. Campbell, E.D. Pulakos, and W.C. Borman. 1992. "Three Approaches to the Investigation of Subgroups Bias in Performance Measurement: Review, Results and Conclusions." *Journal of Applied Psychology Monograph* 77:201–217.

Tompson, D. and N. Di Tomaso. 1988. *Ensuring Minority Success in Corporate Management*. New York: Plenum Press.

Tsui, A.S. and B. Gutek. 1999. *Demographic Differences in Organizations: Current Research and Future Directions*. Latham, MD: Lexington Books.

United States Bureau of Census. 1960. *Characteristics of the Population. Detailed Occupations. PC-60*. Washington, DC: Department of Commerce.

U.S. Commission on Civil Rights. 1969. Staff Memorandum Feburary 4. Washington, DC: U.S. Government Printing office.

Wilson, W.J. 1978. *The Declining Significance of Race*. Chicago: University of Chicago Press.

4

Social Networks and Occupational Mobility: African Americans' Promotion in the Public Sector

Marlese Durr

Social scientists have suggested that affirmative action policies move racial minorities and women from historical work-social positions into racially and ethnically diverse employment settings, dislodging the minority-white boundary and theoretically building relationships among all levels of employees. Others imply that these policies recast the labor market to include newly created regulatory and supplemental occupations within organizational management structures (e.g., Director of Affirmative Action, Affirmative Action Officer I & II) that act as ports of entry for employees once outside of the traditional lines of managerial selection and advancement. Still others perceive these policies as an avenue for bringing affirmative hires in contact with administrators and officials, presenting an opening for idea exchange and evaluation of skills.

Abbott and Smith (1984) advise that this activity within the labor market represents governmental control over the labor supply as a result of its focus on equity in the workplace. Di Prete (1987) argues that these modifications by government have penetrated the administrative and professional model of personnel organization, and that the beneficiaries of the program are primarily women and minorities employed in lower-level managerial positions, who have been hired and promoted due to pressure from civil rights groups during the 1960s and 1970s.

Whichever supposition is supported, it highlights that the inclusion of these posts has enlarged the labor market to include formally excluded employees within organizational managerial structures, spawning a new managerial class in the public sector and leading to the creation of new career ladders. However, many of these hires are not part of a series of occupations that workers must pass through to reach the highest rank within a work structure before moving to the next set of occupations (Spilerman 1977). Moreover, the mobility chains created by these occupations do not mandate a sequence of jobs in which individuals may be employed and shape their careers (Piore 1975).

Therefore, for African Americans whose organizational port of entry was secured through affirmative hiring, the conditions and ladders of career advancement may differ, because the positions in which they are employed do not originate from within the organization and are not linked to the organizational mission and objectives. In most instances, these occupations divide the upper tier of the primary market into racially defined submarkets, minority and mainstream (Durr and Logan 1996), or what Collins (1983) refers to as "racialized" labor markets. These positions are the outcome of societal action and are dependent on public sentiment (to amend customs and policies that have historically created structural inequalities). This is unusual, since internal labor markets are typically created to satisfy a need for skills and services and to provide job opportunities that emphasize promotion and advancement within an organizational framework, thereby determining which employees and jobs have possibilities for mobility (Broom and Smith 1963), which are associated with related skills or work experience, job content, a common functional or departmental organization, and a single work focus (Doeringer and Piore 1971; Loveridge and Mok 1979). However, occupations created through employers' enforcement of affirmative action policies are a direct result of federal regulations to guide employers in their efforts to hire affirmatively.

Thus, the minority submarket is comprised of occupations whose incumbents are largely racial minorities employed in regulatory and supplemental positions (e.g., Equal Employment Opportunity Specialists, Human Relations Specialist, although personnel officers exist). Mainstream submarket positions are established occupations that possess linkages to upper-level management posts within organizations and provide incumbents with opportunities for job mobility and career advancement.

But for employees wishing to make a job change from posts in the minority submarket to the mainstream submarket (via promotions), career mobility may be difficult, especially since in many cases these personnel act as buffers between organizations and federal penalties, ensuring compliance with federal regulations. Because of these key functions, few opportunities exist for advancement, even though these occupations do not fall within the peripheral market in which women and minorities have traditionally been employed. Consequently, employees wishing to move into the mainstream submarket must use personal contacts that are cross-ethnic (black to white). This chapter investigates job changes through the use of personal contacts that may assist African Americans in moving from the minority submarket to the mainstream submarket.

WEAK TIES AND EMPLOYMENT OPPORTUNITIES

In a empirical study of recent job changers, Granovetter (1974) found that professional, technical, and managerial workers were more likely to hear about a new job through weak ties. In a similar study, Ericksen and Yancey (1984) noted that most acquaintances were work-related and 31 percent of these respondents who were managers had used weak ties. Lin, Ensel and Vaughn (1981), in an empirical study examining the relationship between the strength of ties and occupational status, found a strong association between the use of weak ties and occupational attainment. This association was found to exist only when weak ties connected respondents with individuals who were well placed (upper-level managerial positions) within the occupational structure.

Granovetter's (1974, 1982) strength-of-social-ties argument describes weak ties as a relationship between actors who are less likely to be socially involved and are likely to move in different social circles, providing them access to sources of new information. Such relationships are forged between individuals through occupations and are rooted in successive features of their interaction guided by: (1) the amount of time the individual spends with the resource or contact; (2) the degree of emotional intensity within the relationships; (3) the degree of reciprocity in exchange activities; and (4) the degree of intimacy within their relationship (Granovetter 1973, 1974). These properties emphasize the importance of weak ties to social integration and highlight the salience of proximity and communication between individuals as vital to the job-change process. Through these types of associations Granovetter (1974) contends that weak ties integrate individuals into society and expose them to a wider spectrum of viewpoints, activities, and exchange of ideas. Thus, job information that is shared is likely to be more current than would be the case when strong ties are involved.

What Granovetter (1974) fails to consider is that for African Americans the development of weak ties requires frequent work-social interaction and communication with whites. Fraternization between these groups historically occurred in a context of subordination, segregation, and limited social interaction, except for tasks associated with prescribed social positions. This stratified context and frequency of interaction is addressed in an empirical study by Lin, Dayton, and Greenwald (1977), who examined the effects of social stratification on the communication process through the use of weak ties. By tracing a specific activity, the search for a stranger by race, sex, and occupational prestige in each chain, volunteers were asked to send a packet to: (1) a stranger; (2) a person who may know the stranger; or (3) a friend of the stranger. Targets varied by race and gender. A key finding of this study was that volunteers experienced great difficulty in moving the packet from white participant networks to African American networks (to reach black targets). Even when targets were identified racially, it had no effect on the likelihood of the packet reaching an African American target.[1] But the identification of a white target increased the likelihood of the packet reaching its destination. Lin et al. (1977) conclude that racial identity is a major stratifying factor in American urban communities that establishes communication barriers; while arguing that communication that does not cross racial boundaries is essentially ineffective. Also, successful instrumental action is associated positively with the social resources provided by the personal contact. According to Lin et al., the race variable in their study displayed the segmentation of society in terms of communication flow. It defines the structural boundary for two segments of the population. Within racially defined networks, communication flows downward more effectively in a hierarchy from males to females than from females to males or from persons of higher occupational status to persons below.

The Albany Study (Lin et al. 1981) examined social and personal resources of job seekers aged 21–64 seeking their first and current job in the Albany–Schenectady–Troy area. Lin's analysis of the socioeconomic status of a contact (social resources) used by the individual to obtain a job showed that personal resources (father's occupation and job seeker's education) had an effect on the contact reached, as well as on the prestige of the first job. When examining job seekers' current jobs, the status of the first job had a stronger direct effect on the strength of the tie between the job seeker and the contact and on the contact's status than did personal resources. The contact's status, his/her tie to the firm, coupled with the job seeker's education and first job status, directly assisted the seeker in obtaining a prestigious current job even after personal resources had been taken into account.

When examining the social resources used by individuals seeking their first job, Lin and his colleagues (1981) found that the role of social resources in moving the individuals from initial status (family environment) to achieved work status (work environment) persisted throughout their socioeconomic life. For respondents who were weakly tied, their mean current income was $2,500 more than respondents who used strong ties. Thus, a strong relationship between social resources (indexed by contact status) and attained job status was found. In the second phase of this study, Ensel (1979) found differences in the use of contacts by males and females for first and current jobs. For the majority of males aged 20–64, contacts used were males (nearly 90%) for first and current jobs. On the other hand, females used women contacts 57 percent for the first job and 45 percent for their second job. Moreover, women relied on family background to locate weak ties, which tended to be males who led them to higher-status contacts. Therefore, gender presented an additional barrier in their job seeking.

In an extension of this work, Lin (1982) examined the use of a personal contact to achieve a goal corresponding to obtaining wealth, status, power, which he labeled as resources (e.g., promotions). Within this study, he assumed that the social structure is pyramid-shaped, consisting of a network of persons. Positions at or near the top of the structure have greater access to positions at lower rankings. Actors in lower positions must reach upward to contacts who have the requisite information and influence for instrumental purposes. Therefore, actors must move outside of their intimate social circles, using weak ties to obtain information and influence otherwise not available (Lin et al. 1981).

Neither of these models incorporates the race of the actor and personal contact in measuring the success of instrumental action within organizational hierarchies. Rather, they provide general theoretical and empirical explanations for the use of contacts through weak ties. From these findings it could be argued that mobility opportunities through the use of personal contacts should operate similarly for racial minorities; however, this is not the case. Kluegel (1978) points out that job changes via promotions within organizational hierarchies are not only subject to socioeconomic achievement and ambiguity, but also to informal interaction (casual gatherings within and outside of the workplace influence that assist employers in identifying employees for promotion). Thus, the

Table 4.1
Conceptual Model of Movement from Minority to Mainstream Submarket

		Types of Tie Used for Current Occupational Position	
		Ethnic Tie	Cross-Ethnic Tie
Current Occupational Position	Minority Submarket	A	C
	Mainstream Submarket	B	D

omission of race as a variable in the work of Lin and his colleagues (1981, 1982) and Granovetter (1974, 1982) raises three important questions:

1. Do African Americans use personal contacts in the job-change process?
2. Are these personal contacts ethnic (black to black) or cross-ethnic ties (from black to white)?
3. Do these contacts represent better social resources (e.g., better positions, job authority) than ethnic ties (from black to black)?

Given these observations, and the expectation that African Americans wish to move from minority submarkets to mainstream submarkets, I hypothesize that for African Americans employed in the minority submarket:

H1. African Americans using ethnic ties are more likely to end up in the minority submarket than in the mainstream submarket.
H2. African American using cross-ethnic ties are more likely to end up in the mainstream submarket than in the minority submarket.
H3. African Americans using cross-ethnic ties are more likely than those using ethnic ties to end up in the mainstream submarket.
H4. African Americans using male ties are more likely than those using female ties to end up in the mainstream submarket.
H5. African Americans who use ties whose salary grades are at higher levels are more likely to end up in the mainstream submarket than those who use ties within lower salary grades.

DATA, METHOD, AND MEASURES

Data for this study were collected during the spring and summer of 1991 using a snowball sampling technique to identify African Americans employed full time within New York state government managerial salary grades SG 23 through SG 38. Constructing a probability sample presented several problems. First, the New York State Department of Civil Service does maintain these data by race and ethnic identification codes. Second, when I contacted Civil Service to obtain percentages of African Americans promoted to salary grade 23 or above, either across the state or by county, for 1989–1997, I was informed that these data were not available (according to our respondents, such information is considered to be too sensitive for public release). Third, the state does not provide information (data) on the racial composition of specific job titles, mobility between job titles by race, or on the civil service status of job incumbents by race. Therefore, the most systematic basis for evaluating the existence of a minority submarket in state government was unavailable. While this technique did not produce a random sample of respondents, it was the best approach given the characteristics of the population. Because of these missing pieces of information, probability sampling was deemed unlikely to yield a sufficient number of cases. Thus, data were collected through intensive personal and telephone interviews. The interviews were short (an average length of 25 minutes by phone or personal interview in respondents' offices) using a sixteen-item questionnaire that was administered to all respondents. In instances where respondents were less reserved about discussing promotions, interviews lasted an average of forty minutes.

Sampling began by contacting an African American employed within New York state government in salary grade SG 18 (not included in the sample) and requesting the names of five persons employed in salary grade SG 23 or above within her agency or others. Each of these persons was interviewed. At the end of each interview, each respondent was asked for the names of five persons they knew who were employed in salary grade SG 23 and above. Many potential respondents canceled their interviews, some of them explicitly due to concern over their supervisors' possible reaction to learning of their participation. A total of seventy-nine respondents were interviewed, all of whom resided in the Albany and New York City areas.

This nonrandom sample reflects a wide range of respondent occupation titles and functions across 19 state agencies. Nearly half of the sample, 46 percent, came from the New York State Education Department where the first informant was employed (and where the agency's director formally approved of the study). Of these respondents, 30 percent are males and 70 percent are female, reflecting the overrepresentation of women among black professionals. Their education level is high: 74 percent have advanced degrees (MA or Ph.D.), although a small number (8%) have only a high school diploma. Respondents' length of employment in their current position was 5.8 years, while in their previous positions their length of employment was 10.8 years. Sixty-four percent of these respondents had been employed in their current positions for less than or about five years.

The mean income reported was $50,000 a year, with salaries ranging from $25,000 to $99,000 a year. Over half, 64.3 percent of the respondents were employed in lower-level managerial grades 23–28, 20 percent in mid-level managerial grades 29–33, and about 16 percent (15.7%) in upper-level managerial grades 34–38. Seventy-four percent ($N = 52$) of the sample had used personal contacts employed within salary grades SG 23 and above to obtain their current occupational positions. These cases are the primary focus of analysis.

CHARACTERISTICS OF JOB SOURCE CONTACTS

Most respondents (65% used personal contacts, of which 96% obtained the information from contacts within the agencies) reported the use of job source contacts to obtain their current positions from four job source categories: friends, current supervisor, former supervisor, and someone in the agency. Only 4 percent obtained job information outside of their agencies (e.g., from university professors, relatives, and friends of friends). Over half, 58 percent, of respondents' personal contacts were administrators, 24 percent were managers, 13 percent were politicians, and 4 percent were nonspecific about the occupational category of their job source contact. Sixty-nine percent of these contacts were male and 31 percent were female. Fifty-eight percent were cross-ethnic ties (White) and 36 percent were ethnic ties (African American), and 6 percent of these were others.[2] Sixty-seven percent of these ties were employed within salary grades SG 34–38, 19 percent were employed within salary grades SG 29–31 and 14 percent were in salary grades 19–22. These data reveal that ties within the respondents' employing agency within the highest occupational positions are especially important in assisting African Americans in acquiring promotions from the minority submarket to the mainstream submarket. To examine the movement of employees from the minority submarket to the mainstream submarket,

Table 4.2
Occupational Mobility by Submarket Location

		Previous Occupational Position	
		Minority Submarket	Mainstream Submarket
Current Occupational Position	Minority Submarket	6 (60%)	5 (20%)
	Mainstream Submarket	4 (40%)	20 (80%)
		100% ($N = 10$)	100% ($N = 25$)

$p > .05$
Chi Square $= 3.60938$
Significance $= .0575$
Degrees of Freedom $= 1$

respondents' previous occupational positions were controlled for and examined.

EFFECTS OF THE TYPE OF TIE USED

In examining respondents' previous positions, Table 4.2[3] shows that 60 percent of the employees employed in the minority submarket remained there, while 40 percent moved to the mainstream submarket. This table also reveals that 20 percent of the respondents whose previous occupations were in the mainstream submarket moved to the minority submarket, while 80 percent who were employed within the mainstream submarket remained there. Such a large percentage of respondents located within mainstream submarket suggests that they are an elite group of employees whose employment within this submarket represents implementation of a variety of employment and promotion decisions (i.e., new entrants to state service, promotion from management feeder grades SG 14–18 through competitive examination, administrative transfers, and nonlist appointments) within state government.

Respondents who moved from the mainstream submarket to the minority submarket implies mobility through political appointment and affirmative action decisions in response to social issues. In such instances, employees are placed within specially created one-of-a-kind positions

Table 4.3
Relationship Between Current Occupational Position and Type of Tie
Used for Persons Previously Employed in the Minority Submarket

		Type of Tie Used	
		Ethnic	Cross-Ethnic
Current Occupational Position	Minority Submarket	4 (80%)	2 (40%)
	Mainstream Submarket	1 (20%)	3 (60%)
		100% ($N = 5$)	100% ($N = 5$)

Fisher's Exact Test	**One-Tail**	**Two-Tail**
	.26190	.52381

Note: Fisher's Exact Test provided the exact probability value for 2×2 tables when there are fewer than 21 cases and the expected value in each cell is less than 5.

through upgrading lines from their departments and others. The job titles of these posts generally reflect the specialized tasks incumbents have been charged to accomplish. Respondents acknowledge that whole or- ganizational units within the New York State Education Department have evolved in this fashion; for example, the Division of School Improve- ment.

Table 4.3 shows that 80 percent of the respondents who used ethnic ties remained within the minority submarket, while 20 percent moved to the mainstream submarket. However, 40 percent of the respondents who used cross-ethnic ties remained in the minority submarket and 60 percent moved to the mainstream submarket. These findings are consistent with the relationship hypothesized for the use of cross-ethnic and ethnic ties (Hypothesis 1 and 2). In addition to these findings, this table shows that respondents using cross-ethnic ties were more likely to move into the mainstream submarket (60%) than those using ethnic ties (20%). This confirms the third hypothesis of this study, which states that African Americans using cross-ethnic ties are more likely than those using ethnic ties to end up in the mainstream submarket. It is important to note, however, that these findings are based on very small numbers, so the reader should remain aware that these results are suggestive.

Table 4.4
Current Occupational Position by Job Source Contact's Gender for Persons Previously Employed in the Minority Submarket

		Gender of Resource	
		Male	Female
Current Occupational Position	Minority Submarket	3 (50%)	3 (50%)
	Mainstream Submarket	3 (50%)	2 (25%)
		100% ($N = 6$)	100% ($N = 4$)
Fisher's Exact Test		**One-Tail** .45238	**Two-Tail** .57143

Note: Fisher's Exact Test provided the exact probability value for 2×2 tables when there are fewer than 21 cases and the expected value in each cell is less than 5.

GENDER, RACE, AND STATUS OF SOCIAL TIES

Table 4.4 shows the gender of social ties without regard for ethnicity. Fifty percent of the respondents who used male ties remained within the minority submarket and 50 percent moved into the minority submarket. Among the respondents who used female ties, 75 percent remained in the minority submarket. This pattern of relationships between gender and occupational position suggests that male ties are more instrumental in assisting African Americans in moving out of the minority submarket and into the mainstream submarket than female ties. Previous research conducted by Lin, Dayton, and Greenwald (1977) supports this finding. They found that information flowing from males was more successful in helping women to achieve employment. But it should be noted that in most cases men already hold most upper-level positions within organizations. Although the numbers are small, Hypothesis 4, which states that male ties will be more effective than female ties in facilitating movement from the minority submarket to the mainstream submarket, has been supported.

This finding led to a closer examination of female respondents who used personal contacts, given that a large proportion of the sample was female and the increased presence of women in upper-level managerial

positions in the labor market. Respondents were cross-classified according to current and previous market location controlling for gender. Five
women (63%) who were previously employed within the minority submarket remained there, while three (37%) moved to the mainstream submarket. However, four (22%) women previously employed within the
mainstream submarket moved to the minority submarket and fourteen
(78%) remained within mainstream submarket.

Of the male respondents previously employed within the minority submarket, one (50%) remained within the minority submarket, and one
(50%) moved to the mainstream submarket. For males within the mainstream submarket, one (14%) moved to the minority submarket, while
six (85%) moved to the mainstream submarket. On the basis of this
analysis it can be assumed that the majority of respondents who remained
within the minority submarket were women, while men moved to the
mainstream submarket; however, their numbers are small. This is an
important finding since popular opinion credits African American women
with moving into upper-level prestigious positions within the public and
private sector.

When examining current occupational position by job contacts' ethnicity and gender, one (50%) moved to the mainstream submarket,
while three (75%) of the respondents who used female ethnic ties remained within the minority submarket. Of the respondents who used
cross-ethnic ties, two (50%) moved to the mainstream submarket, while
of the respondents using cross-ethnic female ties, one moved to the
mainstream submarket. Male cross-ethnic ties had the same effect as
male ethnic ties in facilitating the movement from the minority submarket to the mainstream submarket. However, female cross-ethnic ties
were more instrumental in facilitating movement in the mainstream
market only.

Of the two respondents using contacts employed within lower-level
managerial salary grades SG 23–27, one remained employed within the
minority submarket, and one moved into a position within the mainstream submarket. The three respondents who used personal contacts in
middle-level management salary grades SG 28–33 all remained within
the minority submarket. However, five respondents who used personal
contacts in high-level managerial salary grades 28–33 all remained
within the minority submarket. However, of the five who used personal
contacts in high-level managerial salary grades SG 34–38, two, or 40
percent, remained within the minority submarket and three, or 60 percent,
moved to the mainstream submarket. This pattern of relationships suggests that respondents who move from the minority submarket to the

mainstream submarket rarely become employed in upper-level managerial posts.

DISCUSSION

This work confronts the problems facing African Americans in minority submarkets composed of lower- and middle-level managerial posts developed as corollaries of affirmative action policies, which have had a limiting effect on their chances for mobility or promotion to upper levels of management. Promotion from a minority submarket to a mainstream submarket was more likely to be achieved through the use of cross-ethnic ties; males ties were more successful in facilitating movement from the minority submarket to the mainstream submarket; female ethnic ties were more likely to facilitate promotions within the minority submarket, while female cross-ethnic were likely to facilitate promotions into the mainstream submarket; and the use of ties employed in low- and middle-management positions was more likely to facilitate promotions in the minority submarket, while ties with higher grade contacts facilitated the acquisition of posts in the mainstream submarket.

An unanticipated finding of this study was that 80 percent of the respondents whose previous positions were in the mainstream submarket remained in their current job, while 20 percent of these respondents moved from the mainstream to the minority submarket. This result suggests that these mainstream respondents were an elite group of employees whose positions signify a combination of employment and promotion strategies, while those who moved to the minority submarket generally represented newly created posts focusing on minority issues. Conversations with respondents should be interpreted with caution. That is, respondents often reported that administrative and managerial personnel are appointed to posts within the mainstream submarket based on political decisions. These frequently include affirmative action considerations and current social issues (e.g., domestic violence, high school dropouts in high-needs communities).

The findings in this research demonstrate the diversification of the labor market (e.g., a division of its upper tier to include women and minorities) as a result of government intervention. Of key importance is the formation of a new managerial class whose positions evolved as a result of societal response to social issues (discriminatory hiring practices), unlike organizationally designed positions. As society's attitude changes regarding particular social issues, especially race/ethnic issues, the future of this class becomes questionable.

NOTES

1. There were too few African American participants to allow assessment of the flow of the packets from blacks to whites, but it was evident that communication flowed mainly within ethnic groups.

2. "Others" refers to Asians (2%) and Latinos (4%), whose relationships were not the focus of this study.

3. The number of cases within this analysis has decreased from fifty-two to thirty-five because of the missing information on the variable previous occupational position.

REFERENCES

Abbott, A. and Smith, D.R. 1984. "Governmental Constraints and Labor Market Mobility: Turnover Among College Athletic Personnel." *Work and Occupations* 11: 29–53.

Broom, L. and Smith, J.H. 1963. "Bridging Occupations." *British Journal of Sociology*, December 1963.

Collins, S. 1983. "The Making of the Black Middle Class." *Social Problems* 30: 369–382.

———. 1989. "The Marginalization of Black Executives." *Social Problems* 36: 317–331.

———. 1993. "Blacks on the Bubble: The Vulnerability of Black Executives in White Corporations." *Sociological Quarterly* 34: 429–447.

DiPrete, T. 1987. "The Professionalization of Administration and Equal Employment Opportunity in the U.S. Federal Government." *American Journal of Sociology* 3: 119–140.

Di Tomaso, N. and Thompson, D.E. 1988. "The Advancement of Minorities into Corporate Management: An Overview." *Research in the Sociology of Organizations* 6: 281–312.

Doeringer, P.B. 1967. "Determinants of the Structure of Industrial Type Internal Labor Markets." *Industrial Labor Relations Review* (January): 206–220.

Doeringer, P.B. and M. Piore. 1971. *Internal Labor Markets and Manpower Analysis*. Lexington, MA: Heath Books.

Durr, M. and Logan, J.R. 1996. "Racial Submarkets in Government Employment: African American Managers in New York State Government." *Sociological Forum* (1997).

Ensel, W.M. 1979. "Sex, Social Ties and Status Attainment." Ph.D. Dissertation, Department of Sociology, State University of New York at Albany.

Ericksen, E. and Yancey, W. 1984. "Class, Sector, and Income Determination." Unpublished paper, Department of Sociology, Temple University.

Granovetter, M. 1973. "The Strength of Weak Ties." *American Journal of Sociology* 78: 1360–1380.

———. 1974. *Getting a Job: A Study of Contacts and Careers.* Cambridge, MA: Harvard University Press.

———. 1982. "A Theory of Weak Ties: A Network Theory Revisited." In Peter V. Marsden (ed.), *Social Structure and Network Analysis.* Thousand Oaks, CA: Sage, p. 105–130.

Kluegel, J.M. 1978. "The Causes and Costs of Racial Exclusion from Job Authority." *American Sociological Review* 43: 85–301.

LaSalle, R. and Baskt, L. 1987. "Statistics on Women and Minorities in Public Employment." Working Paper No. 6B. Albany, NY: Center for Women in Government.

Lin, N. 1982. "Social Resources and Instrumental Action." In Peter V. Marsden (ed.), *Social Structure and Network Analysis.* Thousand Oaks, CA: Sage, p. 131–145.

Lin, N., Dayton, P. and Greenwald, P. 1977. "Analyzing the Instrumental Use of Relations in the Context of the Social Structure." *Sociological Methods and Research* 7: 149–166.

Lin, N., Ensel, W. and Vaughn, J.C. 1981. "Social Resources and the Strength of Ties: Structural Factors in Occupational Status Attainment." *American Sociological Review* 46: 393–405.

Loveridge, R. and A.K. Mok. 1979. *Theories of Labor Market Segmentation.* London: The Hague.

Piore, M.J. 1975. "Notes for a Theory of Labor Market Segmentation." In Richard C. Edwards, Michael Reich, and David M. Gordon (eds.), *Labor Market Segmentation.* Lexington, MA: Heath.

Spilerman, S. 1977. "Careers, Labor Markets, and the Process of Wage Attainment." *American Sociological Review* 40: 645–665.

5

Does Race Matter Less for the Truly Advantaged? Residential Patterns in the New York Metropolis

John R. Logan and Richard D. Alba

Civil rights have been replaced with affirmative action in policy discussion and have been understood by both advocates and opponents as providing minorities with tangible special advantages to compensate for *past* discrimination. Our research on the residential patterns of racial and ethnic groups over the past several years has yielded findings that conflict with two key assumptions of the current debate, at least as it applies to housing issues.

The first is that housing discrimination is by and large a historical relic, that a substantial share of the minority population now benefits from essentially equal access to the neighborhoods they seek and can afford. This is a critical assumption, because federal and state law clearly establishes the right of equal access and assesses penalties for those who transgress this right. If it were widely recognized that the law has been ineffective, that civil rights are guaranteed only for a few, the policy debate might shift in another direction. Our research indicates that a high level of housing segregation remains that cannot be attributed to economics or preferences. If this is correct, it is a considerable achievement for those who are less concerned with racial equality to have diverted public attention from the issue of discrimination. And it may be a strategic error for advocates to have allowed the policy debate to become focused on affirmative action.

The second assumption is about who requires protection in order to have equal access. This question is controversial among civil rights advocates. Should the lines be drawn by race and, if so, who should be classified as a minority? Or should policies be targeted more specifically to the poor and working class, the "truly disadvantaged" (to use Wilson's [1987] term)? The predominant view seems to be that the issue of equal access arises consistently for the whole range of racial and ethnic groups that have been defined as "protected classes"—African Americans, Hispanics, and Asians, regardless of economic background or nativity. This definition of who is a "minority" is tied to the view that all nonwhite groups have experienced a special handicap in this country (Takaki 1993). It is also, of course, related to political strategy. Minority status is typically a goal for which groups lobby hard, and advocates of minority rights may prefer a broad definition as a means of expanding their political base. The present definition is consistent with a rhetoric that dichotomizes society as white versus minority, a strategy of polarization that potentially strengthens both minority advocates and their opponents (who is more strengthened probably varies over time and across regions of the country).

It is not our intention to take sides on this political question, but we have found that the evidence of unequal access as it applies specifically to the housing market varies significantly among racial and ethnic groups. The clearest evidence is for African Americans and for nonwhite Hispanics; the weakest is for Asians and white Hispanics. Our findings also point to variations by class and nativity, in a pattern that differentiates among minorities in complex ways: Rising socioeconomic standing allows Asians and Hispanics, but not African Americans, to live in neighborhoods more similar to those of comparable whites. Hispanic immigrants experience a special "newcomer" disadvantage, but immigrant blacks experience less discrimination than native African Americans. So class and nativity do make a difference, but not in the same way for every group. These variations reinforce our misgivings about understanding discrimination in the traditional terms of whites vs. minorities.

RACIAL AND ETHNIC COMPOSITION AND SEGREGATION IN NEW YORK, 1990

We will illustrate our findings with data from the New York–New Jersey metropolitan area in 1990. This region encompasses more than

17 million persons, including New York City and surrounding cities and suburbs. Some background information on the racial and ethnic diversity of the region will help place the discussion in perspective. What is most relevant about New York is its continuing influx of people from around the world. A largely white ethnic domain earlier this century, New York became the home of substantial African American and Hispanic populations after World War II. Now, like many other major urban centers, the region has been reshaped by massive immigration from Latin America, the Caribbean, and Asia. Table 5.1 provides population data for 1990.

Note first of all that the region still has a white majority (more than 10 million of the 17 million total). A few large ancestry groups comprise a large share of the white population. The classification of whites in ethnic groups is based on the 1990 census report of "ancestry" (more precisely, by the first ancestry named on census survey forms). Ethnicity defined this way is not limited to immigrants or children of immigrants. Indeed, less than a fourth of any European ancestry group are first- or second-generation immigrants. The largest ancestry group is Italians, with two and a half million, followed by Germans and Irish, and then Russians.

As recently as 1960, almost all minority residents were from two specific sources: They were either African Americans of Southern origin or Puerto Ricans. Only about 100,000 West Indian immigrants were included in the black population, and about the same number of non-Puerto Ricans among the Hispanic population. The Asian population was under 100,000. Since then, as Table 5.1 demonstrates, much of the growth in the black population has been comprised of immigrants from the Caribbean, who now make up about a sixth of non-Hispanic blacks. Similarly, although the biggest single Hispanic group is Puerto Ricans, the greatest increase has come from immigrants from other areas, especially Dominicans. (Other large categories, not shown in the table, are Salvadorans, Ecuadorans, and Colombians.) The biggest single Asian group, as has long been true, is Chinese, but Indians, Koreans, and Filipinos are now also present in large numbers.

Thus, New York represents both the old lines of cleavage in American society—those that divided white ethnic groups from African Americans and Puerto Ricans (or, in other parts of the country, Mexicans)—and the impacts of post-1965 immigration. More important, this is a region where the distinctions among all these diverse groups are socially salient. This can be seen, for example, in the levels of segregation among them, measured by the standard Index of Dissimilarity. These values for 1990, for

Table 5.1

Composition of the New York Metropolitan Region (CMSA), 1990

	Number (in thousands)	Proportion of total
Total population	**17087**	**1.000**
Non-Hispanic white total	**10647**	**.623**
Italian	2517	.147
German	1437	.084
Irish	1620	.094
Russian	534	.031
Other white	4539	.265
Black	**2886**	**.168**
African American	2396	.140
Afro-Caribbean	490	.029
Hispanic	**2704**	**.158**
Puerto Rican	1196	.069
Dominican	403	.023
Cuban	156	.009
Mexican	95	.005
Other	854	.049
Asian	**850**	**.049**
Chinese	317	.018
Indian	187	.010
Korean	117	.006
Filipino	104	.006
Japanese	40	.002
Other	85	.005

Note: White ethnic groups are defined by the "first ancestry" indicated on census questionnaires. Asians are classified on the basis of racial categories; African Americans and Afro-Caribbeans on the basis of race and national origin; and Hispanic groups on the basis of Hispanic identity and national origin questions.

the metropolis as a whole, are presented in Table 5.2. The key findings here are:

1. There are very low levels of segregation among the older white ancestry groups (English, German, and Irish)—.30 or less. But Russians demonstrate an surprising durability of residential separation with levels of segregation of about .50 from other white groups. This may be partly due to the continuing immigration of Russians into the region, but probably primarily due to the religious distinctiveness of this population, which is (and historically has been) predominantly Jewish.

2. There is significant segregation within the other three major racial/ethnic categories: among blacks (.43 between African Americans and Afro-Caribbeans), Hispanics (.50 between Puerto Ricans and Dominicans), and Asians (above .60 for the three groups listed). The unique identities of these national origin ethnic groups are clearly preserved and reflected in urban space.

3. There are generally even higher levels of segregation between white ethnics and the non-European groups: typically above .75 with blacks and Hispanics, and above .65 with Asians. But a similar degree of segregation is found between blacks and Asians, Hispanics and Asians, and even (despite the fact that black and mixed-race persons are included among Puerto Ricans and Dominicans) between blacks and Hispanics.

These simple results in themselves raise doubts about progress against housing discrimination and about how much the several "minority groups" have in common. They are not convincing, however, because they are subject to at least two interpretations: Segregation could merely reflect the socioeconomic and other differences between these groups, or it could signal racial and ethnic divisions within the housing market. Probably both are true, and our purpose in the following sections is to distinguish between them.

OUR APPROACH TO STUDYING SEGREGATION

Our approach here differs significantly from the usual method of calculating indices of segregation and comparing them between different groups (as we did above) or between different cities or regions. The most systematic application of that method in the past decade has been the program of research conducted by Massey and Denton (1995). They have demonstrated that white-black segregation remains extraordinarily high in most of the country compared to white-Hispanic or white-Asian segregation. This finding supports their characterization of the African

Table 5.2
Segregation Among Selected Racial and Ethnic Groups, New York Metropolitan Region (CMSA), 1990

	1	2	3	4	5	6	7	8	9	10	11
1. German	—	.19	.27	.49	.83	.85	.75	.87	.67	.62	.69
2. Irish		—	.26	.51	.83	.84	.73	.86	.66	.62	.68
3. Italian			—	.52	.83	.84	.73	.86	.64	.61	.68
4. Russian				—	.84	.83	.78	.88	.62	.65	.66
5. African American					—	.43	.57	.71	.85	.79	.89
6. Afro-Caribbean						—	.67	.75	.84	.76	.89
7. Puerto Rican							—	.50	.73	.71	.82
8. Dominican								—	.80	.77	.88
9. Chinese									—	.61	.63
10. Indian										—	.66
11. Korean											—

American experience as the "American" apartheid, quite distinct from the Hispanic or Asian case.

The principal defect of this method is that traditional segregation indices do not adjust for the very different socioeconomic composition of white, African American, Hispanic, and Asian populations. Critical to a conclusion of unequal access to housing is a clear answer to the question of whether differences are attributable to race or ethnicity, or to other market-relevant traits such as income, family composition, or immigration status. Massey and Denton have taken such factors into account only at the aggregate level. For example, they have investigated whether black segregation from whites is lower in regions where the average African American has a higher income, or whether Hispanic segregation from whites is lower in regions where a smaller proportion of Hispanics are immigrants. But analyses at the aggregate level can lead to false conclusions about what happens to individuals. A case in point is the finding that African Americans are not more suburbanized in metropolitan regions where they have a higher average income level (Massey and Denton 1988). This may be true at the aggregate level, but it masks the fact that individual African Americans with higher incomes within any region are more likely to live in the suburbs (Alba and Logan 1991).

Our procedure is to estimate multivariate models for individuals that predict the racial composition of their neighborhood, taking directly into account their own personal or household characteristics other than race or ethnicity. Having controlled for these other characteristics, we ask whether net differences remain—and how large these differences are— where people of different groups reside. These net differences are analogous to a segregation score that has been standardized by income, education, and all the other characteristics entered into the model.

Our technique differs in another significant way. We are interested not only in the racial composition of people's neighborhoods but also in neighborhood quality. In other words, we investigate not only whether whites, African Americans, Hispanics, and Asians live in different neighborhoods, but whether their neighborhoods are equal. This is an important step for two reasons: First, limiting attention solely to racial composition implies—whether intended or not—that integration per se is valued. Indeed, integration has been valued throughout much of this century, but always partly because residential integration was perceived to be an indirect indicator of groups' full social incorporation. To that extent, it makes sense to study more directly the quality of people's residential environment. Second, and related to the first point, a prefer-

ence for living with members of one's own group is one source of segregated neighborhoods. Some observers contend that it is the principal
source, and that what appears to be evidence of unequal access is really
an expression of choice. Up to now, nobody has maintained that living
in a poorer community, or a community with a higher crime rate or worse
public schools, is a preference of any group. Thus, to the degree that we
find group differences not only in the racial composition of their neighborhoods but also in neighborhood quality, we can be more certain that
what is operating is unequal access.

DISPARITIES IN RESIDENTIAL LOCATION

Let us turn now to models of locational attainment: the analysis of
characteristics of the neighborhoods where people live. As discussed
above, we study two aspects of neighborhoods. The first is the percentage
of residents who are non-Hispanic whites, which serves as an indicator
of integration with the majority group. Second, as a general-purpose
indicator of neighborhood quality we use the median household income
of the tract. Information on data sources, other variables introduced into
the models, and estimation methods are provided in detail elsewhere (see
especially Alba and Logan 1992).

Table 5.3 summarizes the overall averages for persons of various racial
and ethnic backgrounds, and also provides predicted values for a specific
type of person based on the locational attainment equations. Let us consider first the results for racial composition. Note that the "white percentage in the tract of the average group member" is itself a common
measure of segregation—the P* or exposure index (see Lieberson and
Carter 1982)—though it has somewhat different properties than the index
of dissimilarity. The predicted values for racial composition are in effect
"standardized" exposure indices.

As would be expected from a review of the dissimilarity indices above,
the groups differ greatly in the racial composition of their neighborhoods.
The average white lives in a tract that is 82 percent white, compared to
57 percent for the average Asian, 40 percent for the average Hispanic,
and only 18 percent for the average African American. Differences
among white ethnic groups are insignificant: Whites of all ancestries live
in predominantly white neighborhoods. Larger differences are found
within the Hispanic and Asian national origin groups. Among Hispanics,
Dominicans and Puerto Ricans have much lower exposure to whites than
do Cubans, Mexicans, or other Latin Americans. Among Asians, the
Japanese stand out as living in communities nearly equivalent to the

average white, while Chinese live in areas where whites comprise barely half the population.

Again, the main question that arises from these differences in neighborhood racial composition is whether they represent strictly racial and ethnic effects or whether they are no more than a reflection of the socioeconomic standing of each group. In other words, are more Asians in "whiter" neighborhoods than are Hispanics or African Americans because of their higher personal income, or do these group differences persist even for people with comparable personal characteristics? What, by contrast to the experience of the "truly disadvantaged" inner-city poor discussed by Wilson (1987), is the experience of the "truly advantaged" members of each racial and ethnic group?

The effects of characteristics other than race and ethnicity can be partialled out and held constant through the use of multivariate equations in which the dependent variable is the racial composition or income level of one's tract. These equations include a person's income, education, and a range of other relevant traits (such as age, gender, family composition, homeownership, nativity, and English language ability). Such equations have been estimated for 1990 for the New York region (see also Logan, Alba, McNulty and Fisher 1996, for analyses based on the 1980 census). Table 5.3 summarizes the results by calculating the predicted value of neighborhood median income for group members with a distinct array of personal traits that represent an "affluent urban native" American. Disparities in these predicted values are differences that can be attributed to group membership, not to other aspects of one's personal background. The predicted values are for a male, aged 25–64, living in a married-couple household in the central city. Affluent means that he is a home-owner, with a college education and over $100,000 income. Native means that he was born in the United States and speaks only English at home. (The estimation equation for Hispanics also included the person's race, and figures in this column refer specifically to white Hispanics.) Such "truly advantaged" people are theoretically strategic because they appear to have overcome whatever obstacles to mobility they may have encountered. The pattern of group differences would be similar but not exactly the same for other background profiles.

Remarkably, the disparity between African Americans and whites is almost unaffected by these standardization techniques. The predicted value for whites (78%) is slightly below the unadjusted average mainly because it refers to the situation of whites in central cities of the region rather than the suburbs. The predicted value for African Americans (23%) is slightly above the unadjusted average because it refers to the

Table 5.3
Average Values of the Racial Composition and Median Household Income of Tracts Where Group Members Live and Predicted Values for an "Affluent Urban Native" of Each Group

	% White		Median Income	
	Average value	Predicted value	Average value	Predicted value
Non-Hispanic White	**82.2%**	**77.8%**	**$47,700**	**$54,500**
British	83.4	77.0	51,800	55,400
German	83.6	78.5	49,200	55,700
Irish	82.3	77.1	47,600	53,400
Italian	82.0	78.2	45,700	53,700
Polish	80.6	77.1	44,800	52,500
African American	**18.1%**	**23.4%**	**28,500**	**37,900**

	39.5%	63.6%	30,100	44,500
Hispanic				
Puerto Rican	29.0	60.6	24,800	43,800
Dominican	19.1	59.7	22,800	44,600
Cuban	45.3	65.6	33,000	46,000
Mexican	41.6	66.6	29,900	45,300
Central/South American	43.3	68.6	32,500	47,700
Asian	**57.4%**	**61.7%**	**39,500**	**48,100**
Chinese	53.6	62.3	35,900	47,400
Indian	57.2	58.2	41,600	45,400
Korean	61.6	58.3	42,000	45,200
Filipino	59.6	57.7	40,800	47,200
Japanese	76.3	72.8	53,200	55,890

Note: The predicted values for Hispanics and Hispanic subgroups refer specifically to white Hispanics. These values are 17.7% (for racial composition) and $3,700 (for median tract income) higher than the predicted values for black Hispanics.

case of very affluent African Americans. But a 54 percent gap remains even after we introduce these controls. This finding demonstrates that race has a substantial impact on the residential choices of even wealthy, college-educated African Americans. Ghettoization, in terms of living in a largely minority community, is not experienced only by the black underclass.

The Hispanic case is quite different. For the particular profile considered in the table—white Hispanics, who suffer the disadvantages of neither low socioeconomic status nor recent immigration—Hispanics come much closer to the racial composition predicted for comparable non-Hispanic whites. Assimilation in these respects offers greater residential integration with the white majority. Yet, this same case also illustrates limits to assimilation. First, there remains a 14% gap between whites and Hispanics, even for this profile. Second, the gap is more than twice as great for otherwise comparable Hispanics of black race. Third, significant differences remain between Puerto Ricans/Dominicans and other Hispanics, differences that greatly complicate any summary statement about the "Latino" experience in New York.

The predicted value for Asian groups, taken together, is nearly as high as that for white Hispanics. It too remains considerably below the value for whites, reflecting a degree of segregation of urban Asians, even the most affluent, into residential enclaves. And the distinction within the Asian category between Japanese (living in neighborhoods that are 73% white) and other nationality groups (hovering around 60%) is not much reduced by multivariate controls.

Now let us turn to the income level of people's neighborhoods. Not surprisingly, since whites have higher incomes than other groups, they also live in higher-income neighborhoods (an average tract income of $42,100). Asians live in nearly comparable environments ($39,500), but Hispanics' and African Americans' neighborhoods are clearly poorer ($30,100 and $28,500, respectively). There also appears to be a hierarchy within each of these broad racial categories. Persons of British and German ancestry live in neighborhoods that are $5,000 or $6,000 richer than those of Italians and Poles. Cubans' and Central and South Americans' neighborhoods rank about $10,000 above those of Puerto Ricans and Dominicans. And Japanese areas ($53,200) again stand out remarkably above the Asian average ($39,500), with Chinese substantially below this average (at $35,900).

In one respect, the controls for background characteristics (reflected in the predicted values in the last column) simplify the results. Subgroup differences among whites, Hispanics, and Asians continue but are considerably narrower than are the gaps in the overall, unadjusted averages. The main exception is the continued large disparity between Japanese and other Asian ethnicities. This means, for example, that although Puerto Ricans and Dominicans, or Chinese and Koreans, or British and Italians may live in different neighborhoods (as indicated by the segregation scores reviewed above), they live in more or less equal ones—if they have the same income, education, and other personal characteristics.

On the other hand, deep inequalities are once again revealed between the four larger racial/ethnic categories. The widest divide, as before, is between whites and African Americans. The net disparity between these two, a gap of $16,600 in the neighborhood's average income, is only negligibly reduced from the gross difference of $19,200 shown in the first column of Table 5.3. Black-white differences are also revealed in the effect of race among Hispanics: The predicted values for white Hispanics are $3,700 higher than would be predicted for comparable black Hispanics. But even white Hispanics live in substantially worse neighborhoods than comparable non-Hispanic whites.

Predicted values for Asians are closer to whites. Indeed, for a slightly different profile—suburban rather than urban—Asian values would actually be higher than those for whites. This is because Asians in the central city, particularly Chinese, are highly concentrated in relatively low-income enclaves. Their suburban residential settlements, by contrast, are quite affluent.

CONCLUSION

The predicted values in Table 5.3 demonstrate very clearly the racial/ethnic hierarchy of the New York region. They are especially poignant with regard to the continuing handicap of wealthy and highly educated African American residents, which would be difficult to explain except as a manifestation of racial discrimination. Though some analysts interpose in-group preferences by African Americans as a counterexplanation of racial segregation, our results raise difficult problems for that view. Why would in-group preferences be so much more strongly felt by African Americans than by Hispanics or Asians, for whom the literature emphasizes self-segregation into ethnic economic enclaves? And what degree of in-group preference would be required to induce African Americans to choose to live in neighborhoods that are 15 percent poorer than those of comparable Hispanics, 20 percent lower than comparable Asians, and 30 percent poorer than comparable whites?

These results also underscore the heterogeneity of African American,

Hispanic, and Asian minorities in the region. Race has strong effects among Hispanics even after controlling for other background character- istics; Puerto Ricans and Dominicans are disadvantaged in relation to other Hispanics; Japanese live in very different kinds of neighborhoods than do comparable Asians of other origins; and there are great overall differences between African Americans, Hispanics, and Asians.

These findings are relevant both for a sociological understanding of contemporary race relations and for their implications for public policy. We outline a few of these implications here.

Mobility and Incorporation in the City

New racial and colonial issues were introduced by the large-scale movement of Southern African Americans and Puerto Ricans into the city through 1960. Early observers (e.g., Glazer and Moynihan 1963) recognized the marginalization of these minorities, but guessed that they would experience a gradual, if delayed, assimilation into the urban main- stream, eventually replicating the incorporation of white ethnic groups. We have seen that opportunities for mobility, which are present to some extent for members of every group studied here, exist within the frame- work of group boundaries that give some people a special advantage or handicap. On the whole, education, work experience, language ability, and familiarity with the local environment improve residential opportu- nities, as presumed by the assimilation model that continues to be em- braced by mainstream America. But people compete for position both as individuals (or families) and as members of racial and ethnic groups, and their resources at both levels (their individual traits and the collective standing of their groups) both affect the outcomes. Thus, members of every major racial/ethnic category live in better neighborhoods to the extent that they have higher incomes, can arrange to buy their homes, or manage to move to the suburbs. Yet, having taken into account these individual characteristics, there remains a hierarchy of racial and ethnic groups that points strongly to discrimination in the housing market.

The Underclass Neighborhood: Racism after All

The evident failure of incorporation into the mainstream, especially by African Americans, has provoked a variety of explanations. Of these, the one most compatible with the assimilation hypothesis is the theory of the underclass neighborhood (Wilson 1987). In Wilson's view, the very success of minority incorporation—the emergence of a black middle class and its increasing access to better neighborhoods—has narrowed the class basis of traditional ghetto areas. At the same time, new external forces—deindustrialization of the economy and suburbanization of the remaining manufacturing base—have left many remaining ghetto residents jobless. (Deindustrialization of the city began in the 1950s, and neither African Americans nor Puerto Ricans ever participated in large proportions in the relatively high-wage, unionized sector of New York manufacturing. So the argument must be that they never got the chance that they otherwise would have had in this sector, not that they actually lost their niche in the labor market.) Wilson's emphasis on the underclass neighborhood presumes the incorporation of more successful blacks into the mainstream, both socioeconomically and residentially. The black poor have thus become a special case in a new kind of ghetto.

Our results undermine this interpretation. African Americans today—and, to a lesser degree, Puerto Ricans and Dominicans—live in ghettos, in the sense that their neighborhoods are less white and are poorer than those of comparable whites. This is true even when they achieve high socioeconomic status and escape traditional inner-city neighborhoods. The same racially specific residential process operates in underclass neighborhoods in the city and in new black suburban enclaves.

Acknowledging Diversity

The contemporary metropolis is no longer black and white, nor even black, Hispanic, and white. This is especially true of centers of immigration such as New York and Los Angeles, but the same trend toward racial and ethnic diversity is occurring throughout the country. Holding on to the traditional concept of minority groups, as though all nonwhite minorities met the same response in mainstream society, obscures useful distinctions among groups. It also directs attention away from variations in the implications and manifestations of racism, variations among groups and across historical periods, and emerging issues of relationships among minority groups. The tensions among groups are visible manifestations of their different experiences. These are highlighted in several studies of the New York region, including especially Kasinitz's (1992) research on Afro-Caribbean immigrants. Torres (1995) argues that there are strong parallels between the experience of Puerto Ricans and African Americans in New York and that these are the basis for a growing political solidarity; he is less sure, however, of the impact of new immigrant groups. In California, Horton (1995) demonstrates similarly complex interethnic relationships in Monterey Park, the "first Chinese suburb." (For other examples of these issues, see the case studies reported by Lamphere 1992; also see Waldinger 1986–87 for an analysis of their appearance in the labor market.)

Acknowledging the diversity of minority groups robs the white-nonwhite dichotomy of some of its meaning. The heterogeneity of group experiences defies a simple model. The theoretical challenge is to understand the particularities of group identities and experiences, taking into account the background of each group and the conditions and timing of its entry into the metropolis.

Policy Implications

The most important practical implication of these findings is that public policy can and should be focused on persistent discrimination in the housing market. It may be necessary, in light of the evident failure of current civil rights laws in this area, to discuss how to achieve more energetic enforcement of the law—providing more funds and organizational support for proactive investigation, for example, or introducing stronger criminal penalties. Or it may be necessary to consider methods to compensate minorities for the informal mechanisms that limit their access to private housing, such as targeted mortgage funds, support for housing search expenses, or funding for legal counsel. Periodically the federal government's Department of Housing and Urban Development announces its intention to pursue housing discrimination more actively, but action falters in the face of controversy over the more general issues of affirmative action in employment and contracting. To the extent that current discrimination is at the root of minority housing problems, however, it may be effective for advocates to emphasize law enforcement. In terms of political legitimacy, this remains strong ground.

Another advantage of an enforcement strategy is that it could be reinforced by court action. In some cases of school segregation, for example, jurists have concluded that public policy tools are inadequate to remedy segregation, and have established a legal entitlement of minorities that their local schools—if separate—at least should be equal. The legal entitlement, for example, that has directed hundreds of millions in public funds into the Kansas City school system, has proved much more potent than the fragile political claims of inner-city residents for disappearing social service and community development funds. It is surprising that housing advocates have shown so little interest in such approaches, investing heavily in attacks on restrictive zoning ordinances (see, for example, Haar 1996) rather than challenging government to enforce existing civil rights law. One reason, perhaps, is that an influential segment of the academic community has been convinced that discrimination is no longer a factor, a conclusion that is less tenable in light of the evidence presented here.

Another implication is that achieving unity among minority representatives on this question is unlikely. Affirmative action has the advantage that it seeks to increase the share of public resources accrued to all members of the protected class. Antidiscrimination policies, on the other hand, benefit only those members of the class who suffer discrimination. In the field of housing, at least, the strongest interest should be found among African Americans, but neither Asians, nor perhaps some Latino groups (those who represent a more affluent, linguistically assimilated and white constituency), may have more than a theoretical interest in housing discrimination. Thus, acknowledgment of diversity among minorities is potentially controversial and it may not be a politically successful approach. Nevertheless, diversity is a practical if inconvenient reality in the contemporary metropolis.

REFERENCES

Alba, Richard D. and John R. Logan. 1991. "Variations on Two Themes: Racial and Ethnic Patterns in the Attainment of Suburban Residence." *Demography* 28: 431–453.

———. 1992. "Analyzing Locational Attainments: Constructing Individual-Level Regression Models Using Aggregate Data." *Sociological Methods and Research* 20: 367–397.

Glazer, Nathan and Daniel P. Moynihan. 1963. *Beyond the Melting Pot*. Cambridge, MA: MIT Press.

Haar, Charles M. 1996. *Suburbs under Siege: Race, Space, and Audacious Judges*. Princeton, NJ: Princeton University Press.

Horton, John. 1995. *The Politics of Diversity: Immigration, Resistance, and Change in Monterey Park, California*. Philadelphia, PA: Temple University Press.

Kasinitz, Philip. 1992. *Caribbean New York: Black Immigrants and the Politics of Race*. Ithaca, NY: Cornell University Press.

Lamphere, Louise. 1992. *Structuring Diversity: Ethnographic Perspectives on the New Immigration*. Chicago: University of Chicago Press.

Lieberson, Stanley and Donna Carter. 1982. "Temporal Change and Urban Differences in Residential Segregation: A Reconsideration." *American Journal of Sociology* 88: 296–310.

Logan, John R., Richard D. Alba, Thomas McNulty, and Brian Fisher. 1996. "Making a Place in the Metropolis: Locational Attainment in Cities and Suburbs." *Demography* 33: 443–453.

Massey, Douglas and Nancy Denton. 1988. "Suburbanization and Segregation in U.S. Metropolitan Areas." *American Journal of Sociology* 94: 592–626.

Massey, Douglas and Nancy Denton. 1995. *American Apartheid*. Cambridge, MA: Harvard University Press.

Takaki, Ronald T. 1993. *A Different Mirror: The Making of Multicultural America*. Boston: Little, Brown & Company.

Torres, Andres. 1995. *Between Melting Pot and Mosaic: African Americans and Puerto Ricans in the New York Political Economy*. Philadelphia, PA: Temple University Press.

Waldinger, Roger. 1986–1987. "Changing Ladders and Musical Chairs: Ethnicity and Opportunity in Post-Industrial New York." *Politics and Society* 15: 369–401.

Wilson, William Julius. 1987. *The Truly Disadvantaged: The Inner City, the Underclass, and Public Policy*. Chicago: University of Chicago Press.

6

Inner-city Entrepreneurship: Is Self-Employment a Cure for Poverty?

Cedric Herring, Hayward D. Horton, and Melvin E. Thomas

Self-employment has frequently been proposed as a method of adjustment to American society and as a route out of poverty for various racial and ethnic groups (e.g., Wilson and Martin 1982; Cobas 1985, 1986; Light and Sanchez 1987; Horton 1988; Sullivan and McCracken 1988; Bates 1989; and Butler 1991). In addition, entrepreneurship is often promoted by states and the federal government as a way for those dependent on social welfare or on the unemployment rolls to become self-sufficient. For example, the state of Iowa has developed a self-employment loan program targeted at recipients of Aid to Families with Dependent Children to assist in the start-up of businesses and to provide the training necessary for welfare recipients to become self-employed and thereby reduce welfare dependency (Blaine, Theodore, and Zukosky 1993). Similarly, the state of Oregon has entertained legislation whereby unemployed workers would receive lump-sum payments to aid in enterprise start-up in lieu of unemployment compensation payments. In Vermont, the Agency of Human Services designed a job start program to assist low-income individuals interested in starting businesses. And the very existence of agencies such as the federal Small Business Administration is based on the premise that government can and should play a role in spurring the supply of entrepreneurship.

Yet, the literature on urban poverty suggests that there are clear exceptions to the pattern of upward mobility through self-employment (e.g., Sullivan and McCracken 1988; Torres 1988; and Butler and Herring 1991). Despite the idea that business ownership is a means of socioeconomic development for racial and ethnic minority groups, some racial and ethnic groups concentrated in America's inner cities have not "made it" through such routes.

To what degree can entrepreneurship be used to reduce levels of poverty in America's inner cities? Why are members of some ethnic groups in the inner city likely to become self-employed while members of others seldom engage in such activity? In this chapter, we seek to provide answers to these questions. Using data from the 1987 Urban Poverty and Family Structure Survey, we explore the determinants and outcomes of self-employment among inner-city residents from various racial and ethnic backgrounds. We examine the relationship between entrepreneurship and factors derived from the literature on ethnic entrepreneurship as well as the relationship between entrepreneurship and socioeconomic attainment among inner-city residents of Chicago. We then raise questions about assumptions that these literatures make concerning the viability of self-employment as a mode of upward mobility for various ethnic groups. Finally, we examine the policy implications of our findings.

THEORETICAL CONSIDERATIONS

During the past three decades, the U.S. economy has undergone dramatic changes in employment, occupational structure, and industrial location. Sectorial shifts in employment growth and decline undergird the pattern of uneven economic development. And while these sectorial shifts have affected the structure of employment opportunities for residents in different community types, many of these changes have had devastating effects on the neighborhoods in urban areas (Wilson, 1987).

As economic restructuring has reshaped the U.S. economy, inner-city neighborhoods have had a difficult time expanding or even retaining their employment bases. In several instances, government has promoted a more entrepreneurial approach to stimulating economic growth. Such an approach emphasizes the need for more entrepreneurial activity in depressed inner-city neighborhoods. Despite five-year business dissolution rates of 50 percent (and even higher among certain racial and ethnic groups) (U.S. Small Business Administration 1992), many of the strategies that focus on entrepreneurship hold implicit theories about entrepreneurship and assumptions about entrepreneurship as a means of upward mobility for racial and ethnic minorities.

Entrepreneurship has been hailed as a valuable source of innovation, employment, and economic development. It has been estimated that about one out of every two hundred adults in the U.S. labor force is involved in new firm start-ups each year (Reynolds and Miller 1990). While rates of business ownership vary by race and ethnicity, it has been argued that "even a relatively small number of entrepreneurs can offer employment opportunities to a substantial portion of their co-ethnics" (Evans 1989, p. 22). Because of its "multiplier effect," entrepreneurship would account for 24 percent of an ethnic group's work force if only 6 percent of that ethnic group were self-employed and hired as few as three co-ethnics to work along side them (Evans 1989).

The analysis of ethnic variations in entrepreneurship has a long history (Du Bois 1899; and Weber 1904). Several theoretical formulations have been put forth to account for racial and ethnic differences in business ownership. Most formulations call attention to cultural characteristics of ethnic groups and structural elements of American society that tend to facilitate or hinder entrepreneurship among various racial and ethnic groups (e.g., Light 1972; Portes and Bach 1985; and Butler 1991). Still, these works tend to emphasize certain factors over others, and for ex-positional purposes can be classified as "cultural" in their orientation or as pointing to the role that "disadvantage" plays in promoting or hindering entrepreneurship. Below, we review some of the more prominent formulations and use them to inform and guide our analysis.

CULTURAL THEORIES

The linkage between culture and entrepreneurship goes back at least as far as Weber's *Protestant Ethic and the Spirit of Capitalism* (Weber 1904). In this seminal work, Weber sought to account for Protestants' much higher involvement in capitalism than that of other religious groups. He argued that there were cultural elements of Calvinism that promoted distinct patterns of behavior that encouraged success in the material world.

Contemporary work on the linkage between culture and business also tends to make arguments about cultural elements of particular societies that promote or hinder entrepreneurship and business development (Ouchi 1981). This research has documented the process by which ethnic groups move into business enterprise (Bonacich and Modell 1980), how their cultures contribute to the development of enterprises (Light 1972), the types of enterprises in which they engage, and the importance of family members within firms (Bonacich 1973; and Bonacich and Modell 1980). Such formulations also identify cultural and structural patterns of various ethnic groups that facilitate or hinder success in the business world.

Cultural explanations seeking to account for entrepreneurship in the United States tend to stress the development of small business enterprises within ethnic communities (e.g., Frazier 1957; and Bonacich 1973). These formulations also bring out the importance of the relationship between the culture of ethnic groups and entrepreneurship. They suggest that those ethnic groups that originated in societies in which traditions of buying and selling have long been established are more likely to pursue entrepreneurial careers than those that lack such traditions in their cultures (e.g., Frazier 1957; Light 1972; and Sowell 1975).

"Ethnic enclave" variants of this perspective suggest that ethnic enclaves within American cities serve to reinforce cultural forms from the ethnic group's homeland (Portes and Manning 1986; and Wilson and Portes 1980) and make it more possible for group members to mobilize resources collectively and to maintain cooperative social and economic relations in ethnic businesses. For example, Portes and Bach (1985) note that from the start, the economic orientation of the Japanese and Jews stressed the acquisition of property and the search for entrepreneurial opportunities that would give them an edge in America's marketplace. So, such theories focus on how traditional social relations brought from a group's homeland serve to replicate the social and economic order of their native land in the American context. As Portes and Jensen (1992, p. 420) put it, the ethnic enclave formulation presents a picture of "a network of small enterprises that offer employment comparable to those of the mainstream economy to recent immigrants and those who speak little English. This network creates new entrepreneurial opportunities for the newcomers—opportunities that are absent elsewhere."

Another variant of cultural theory is what is commonly known as "middleman minority" theory (Bonacich 1973; Bonacich and Modell 1980; Bonacich, Light, and Wong 1980; and Light and Bonacich 1988). Middleman minorities are entrepreneurial groups that emerge in racially divided societies with rigid stratification systems that need intermediary groups to promote trade and commercial activity between the dominant racial group and subordinate racial groups. The economic role of these middleman groups, for example, is as "rent collectors and shopkeepers to the subordinate population while distributing the products of the elite and extracting tribute for them" (Bonacich and Modell, 1980, p. 14). This perspective suggests that as middleman minority groups adjust to American society by developing enterprise, hostility is generated toward them from both the dominant racial group and the subordinate racial groups. This hostility promotes ethnic solidarity, which in turn promotes further business development and entrepreneurial culture. This entrepreneurial culture prevents such groups from falling to the bottom of the economic system.

Another kind of cultural explanation that seeks to account for differential rates of entrepreneurship among diverse ethnic groups is social learning theory (e.g., Scherer et al. 1989). This perspective proposes that role models act as important environmental factors in forming the career preferences of those who witness the behavior of their parents and significant others. Observing, identifying with, and appreciating the behavior of others makes certain callings more salient. Through a process of vicarious learning, people form cognitive evaluations of the overall attractiveness of specific career options. They are either encouraged or discouraged to enter a particular vocation. People are more likely to enter a particular career or profession if they have seen role models successfully performing the activities associated with that career. By the same token, they are less likely to pursue a path in which significant others have been unsuccessful. Research has established the relationship between social learning and entrepreneurial behavior, as it has been shown that a significantly higher proportion of entrepreneurs come from homes where their parents or close relatives owned a small enterprise (Butler and Herring 1991). Because members of certain ethnic groups are more likely to be exposed to entrepreneurial behavior, we expect that the pursuit of entrepreneurship will vary by ethnicity.

Cultural explanations are important in the sociology of ethnic entrepreneurship literature, and they pose some difficult challenges for analysts who want to understand the effects of cultural elements on ethnic entrepreneurial behavior. Because culture is so expansive, our approach is to allow ethnicity to act as a proxy for cultural elements. In addition, however, we will provide indicators for those structural manifestations of cultural differences to the degree possible.

DISADVANTAGE THEORY

Disadvantage theories also attempt to account for racial and ethnic variations in entrepreneurship. Here, however, the focus is on the disadvantages that various racial and ethnic groups experience in the U.S. labor market rather than their cultural characteristics. While acknowledging the importance of culture in accounting for ethnic variations in entrepreneurship, these explanations generally argue that aspects of American society and labor market conditions contribute to business formation among certain racial and ethnic groups while retarding business development among other groups. Variants of such theories do, however, differ in what they emphasize as being the nature and extent of disadvantage that dissimilar racial and ethnic groups face.

Light (1979), for example, argues that racial and ethnic minorities turn to self-employment in response to labor market discrimination. He maintains that a countercyclical relationship emerges between the rate of small business ownership and economic instability for minority workers: In periods of economic downturn, self-employment is one response to unemployment. Conversely, when employment opportunities are plentiful, particularly in larger industries, the number of minority small-business entrepreneurs significantly declines.

Butler (1991) also puts forth an "economic detour" variant of disadvantage theory that tries to explain Afro-Americans' lower-than-average levels of business ownership. In contrast to cultural arguments, Butler maintains that it is not a lack of entrepreneurial spirit that prevents African Americans from business ownership, as "the initiation rates of self-employment among Afro-American men and women are nearly three times those of white men and women and twice those of white women" (Butler 1991, p. 311). Rather, he maintains that it has been legal obstacles, terrorist activities by racist whites, and discriminatory behavior by lenders and consumers that have truncated the development of Afro-American business in America.

Butler argues that there has always been a portion of the Afro-American community that has attempted to adapt to racism and discrimination in the same way as middleman minority groups. This "truncated Afro-American middleman" group is grounded in the tradition of self-help, education, and entrepreneurship. This group is responsible for the creation of Afro-American businesses, educational institutions, and organizations within the Afro-American community. Because a great deal of institution building took place in segregated environments, this group's aspirations were grounded in their community rather than the white community, and they supported and took pride in Afro-American institutions even when they began to live in integrated communities.

So, while labor market discrimination may be a factor pushing African Americans into self-employment, there is also a great deal of aspiration for business ownership among Afro-Americans. These aspirations, however, are often impeded and thwarted by discrimination in the business world when lending institutions refuse to give credit to would-be Afro-American business owners and in the greater society when consumers refuse to engage in exchange with Afro-American businesses.

HUMAN CAPITAL AND OTHER EXPLANATIONS

"Human capital theory" attributes the disadvantages in business ownership of certain racial and ethnic groups to their lack of skills and education, their lack of fluency in English, or their being unaccustomed to American culture and society (e.g., Mincer 1974; and Chiswick 1978, 1982). This theory would suggest that the inferior economic performance of groups such as Blacks, Puerto Ricans, and Mexican-Americans is a consequence of their limited marketable skills (Portes and Zhou 1993). Thus, while this formulation has implications for group differences in self-employment, it stresses the attributes of individuals. Within this literature, a familiar motif in research on entrepreneurship has been the differentiation of individuals who choose to pursue self-employment from those who take other career paths.

Other explanations that seek to account for entrepreneurial activity are those that focus on the economic and financial resources available to would-be entrepreneurs (e.g., Fratoe 1988; and Torres 1990a); those that explore the business management skills and human capital of business people (e.g., Torres 1988; and Zhou and Logan 1989); those that emphasize the psychological characteristics and personality traits of business owners (e.g., Hornaday and Abound 1971; and Torres 1990b); and those that highlight the sociodemographic and sociological attributes of the self-employed (e.g., Horton 1988; Butler and Herring 1991; and Horton and DeJong 1991). We incorporate insights from these formulations to guide our analysis.

Previous research has also shown that education (Mescon 1980; Diffley 1982; and Butler and Herring 1991); income (Brockhaus 1980); and age (Sullivan and McCracken 1988; Mescon 1980; and Brockhaus 1980) exert a positive influence on entrepreneurship. We also know that coming from a home where parents were self-employed increases the likelihood of entrepreneurship by the offspring (Bonacich and Modell 1980; and Butler and Herring 1991). Further, the literature has shown that for every decennial census taken since 1880, the foreign born evidenced higher rates of self-employment than the native born (Light 1972). Because these kinds of variables have been utilized to predict entrepreneurship, we utilize them as control variables in our analysis.

METHODS

The City of Chicago, the setting for our study, is one of the few major cities in the United States with substantial proportions of all three of the major minority groups in the urban poverty literature (i.e., African Americans, Puerto Ricans, and Mexican Americans) as well as a fair number of impoverished whites. The Urban Poverty and Family Life Survey was the data source for our analysis. The survey consists of 2,490 face-to-face and telephone interviews conducted with a multistage, stratified probability sample of parents aged 18 to 44 years old residing in City of Chicago poverty census tracts in 1986.

The city's high-poverty areas were singled out for treatment in the survey so that representation of the poor could be maximized. Interviewers trained by the National Opinion Research Center conducted virtually all the interviews in face-to-face interview situations. This reduced the threat of such problems as nonrepresentativeness (due to undercoverage of households without telephones), which are particularly problematic in studying low-income populations. Because some respondents moved out of the city and/or state between the time of the screener and interview, and because some respondents were only willing to give a phone interview, a small number of interviews were conducted by phone. Still, we acknowledge that the generalizability of our findings here may vary across issues on the basis of conditional factors beyond the mere technical issues of sample representativeness.

OPERATIONALIZATIONS

Entrepreneurship or self-employment, the dependent variable for most of the analysis, was operationalized by responses to the following question: "Are you self-employed, that is, do you own your own business or do work at which you are your own boss?" Respondents who said yes were coded 1; others were coded 0. Another dependent variable was whether a person had ever been self-employed, and a third dependent variable was whether one was nominally self-employed in such entrepreneurially oriented activities as selling things, providing personal services, repairing appliances, or providing entertainment.

To measure "race," respondents were asked: "What race do you consider yourself to be—white, black, Indian, or some other." In addition, to measure "ethnicity," respondents were asked: "What is your ethnic background?" Combined, these two questions made it possible to distinguish among respondents who were Black (and non-Hispanic), of Mexican descent (and of any racial background), of Puerto Rican descent (and of any racial background), or white (and non-Hispanic), or of some other racial or ethnic background. Respondents were dummy-variable-coded as black, Mexican, Puerto Rican, or white or other racial/ethnic group.

Sex was coded 1 for female and 0 for male. Educational attainment was coded as highest grade or year of regular school completed from 0 (for no education) through 17 (for graduate or professional school education). Immigrant status was ascertained by asking respondents where they were born. Those born outside the United States were coded 1, and others were coded 0. Marital status was dummy-variable-coded 1 to indicate respondents currently married and 0 for others. Job training refers to whether the respondent had ever received any type of job training or placement in a government program. Those who had received such training or placement were coded 1, and others were coded 0. "Other language" is an indicator to determine whether some language other than English was spoken in the respondent's home. Respondents who said that some language other than English was most frequently spoken in their home were coded 1, and others were coded 0. Age was recorded in years, and ranged from 18 through 47.

Parents' self-employment status was measured by the question: "Did your parents or the people who raised you ever own . . . a business?" Respondents who answered yes were coded 1, and others were coded 0. To measure grandparents' self-employment status, respondents were asked: "Did your grandparents on your mother's side ever own . . . a business?" and "Did your grandparents on your father's side ever own . . . a business?" Respondents who answered yes to either of these questions were coded 1, and others were coded 0.

An enclave is "a concentration of ethnic firms in physical space— generally a metropolitan area—that employ a significant proportion of workers from the same minority" (Portes and Jensen 1992, p. 418). To determine whether respondents worked in an ethnic enclave, they were asked: "Of the people where you work who do the same kind of work as you, how many are [of your same ethnic group]? Would you say almost all, most, about half, a few, or almost none?" Nonwhite respondents who responded "most" or "almost all" were coded 1, and others were coded 0.

To determine whether respondents had been denied a job for which they applied, they were asked: "Think back to the last job you applied for . . . Were you offered the job?" Respondents who answered no were coded 1, and others were coded 0. To determine whether respondents worked in "racialized industries," they were asked what kind of business or industry they worked in. Those who worked in industries in which the majority of customers for minority-owned businesses were nonwhite according to estimates from the 1987 Economic Censuses: Survey of Minority-Owned Business Enterprises were coded 1. Others were coded 0. To determine whether respondents had been denied credit, they were asked whether they had ever applied for and received a loan from a bank or credit union. Those who reported that they had applied and not received a loan were coded 1, and others were coded 0.

DATA ANALYSIS AND RESULTS

Do inner-city residents of differing racial and ethnic backgrounds differ in their tendencies to be self-employed? Table 6.1 presents the percentage of African Americans, Mexican Americans, Puerto Ricans, and whites and others currently self-employed, ever self-employed, and nominally self-employed. This figure shows that 4 percent of African Americans, 4 percent of Mexican Americans, 3 percent of Puerto Ricans, and 11 percent of whites and others were currently self-employed. About 7 percent of blacks, 10 percent of Mexican Americans, 5 percent of Puerto Ricans, and 16 percent of whites and others reported that they had ever been self-employed. And 23 percent of blacks, 14 percent of Mexican Americans, 14 percent of Puerto Ricans, and 18 percent of whites and others were nominally self-employed in personal services. In each case, the ethnic differences in entrepreneurship are statistically significant at $p < .001$.

While the proportion of each racial and ethnic group currently self-employed is smaller than is the case for those nominally self-employed, we find some differences in the rank order of the various groups. In particular, while blacks are among the least likely to be currently self-employed, they are the most likely to be nominally self-employed. These findings hint that there may be some differences between being self-employed generally and being self-employed in personal services.

The results presented in Table 6.1 did not take into account other factors that could affect the relationship between self-employment and ethnicity among inner-city residents. Table 6.1 presents evidence from logit analysis that examines these relationships, net of sociodemographic and human capital variables that are potentially related to self-employment.

The logit (logistic probability unit) model—a special case of the general log-linear model—is appropriate when the dependent variable can

Table 6.1

Logit Models Predicting the Log Odds of Self-Employment with Race and Ethnicity, Net of Sociodemographics, and Human Capital Characteristics[a]

Independent Variables	Currently Self-Employed	Ever Self-Employed	Self-Employed in Personal Services
Constant	-3.122***	-2.154	.251
African	-.948***	-.772***	.133
Mexican American	-1.411***	-1.067***	-.829***
Puerto Rican	-1.729***	-1.644***	-.742***
Female	-.853***	-.908***	-.514***
Education	.064**	.032	-.018
Immigrant	.538*	.579**	.162
Married	.055	-.059	-.229**
Job Training	.048	-.221	.011
Other Language	.126	.124	.247
Age	.018	.016	-.034***
R^2 Analog[b]	.067***	.061***	.032***
N	2402	1936	2402

* $p < .1$
** $p < .05$
*** $p < .01$

[a] Coefficients are unstandardized. For the dummy (binary) variable coefficients, significance levels refer to the difference between the omitted dummy variable category and the coefficient for the given category.

[b] The R^2 analog statistics is the proportion of reduction in a baseline model X^2 (a model fitting only the constant term) attributable to the model shown. It is calculated as follows:

R^2 = (Baseline model X^2—Selected model X^2) / Baseline model X^2.

take on only limited values, and thus, violates the Ordinary Least Squares (OLS) regression model assumptions that the variables will be continuous and measured on an interval scale. It assumes that the underlying probabilities are logistic, that is, in the form: $F(p) = 1/(1 + e\text{-}P) = \ln(P/1\text{-}P)$, where p is the probability of the occurrence of an event and e, an irrational number, is the base of natural logarithms such that $\ln(ex) = X$ and the antilog of X is ex.

The logit is the logarithm of the odds of success; that is, the ratio of the probability of the occurrence of an event to the probability of a nonoccurrence of that event. The function confines the value of (p) between 0 and 1. When the odds of success are even (.5), the logit (coefficient) is zero; when they are greater than even, the logit has a positive value; and when they are less than even, its value is negative.

Table 6.1 shows that even when one takes into consideration such factors as sex, education, immigrant status, marital status, experience with job training programs, English language skills, and age, African Americans, Mexican Americans, and Puerto Ricans are significantly less likely than comparable whites to be currently self-employed or ever to have been self-employed ($p < .01$). Mexican Americans and Puerto Ricans are also less likely than whites to be self-employed in personal services ($p < .01$). This is not the case for African Americans, however. African Americans are no less likely to be involved in nominal self-employment than are similarly situated whites. This pattern is consistent with Butler's idea about a segment of the Afro-American community having entrepreneurial aspirations but experiencing impediments in terms of business ownership.

Of the other variables considered, gender, education, immigrant status, marital status, and age also have effects on self-employment. Women are less likely than men to be currently self-employed ($p < .01$), ever self-employed ($p < .01$), and self-employed in personal services ($p < .01$). The higher one's education, the more likely a person is to be currently self-employed ($p < .05$). Immigrants are marginally more likely than nonimmigrants to be currently self-employed ($p < .1$) and significantly more likely ever to have been self-employed ($p < .05$). Married respondents are significantly less likely than others to be self-employed in personal services ($p < .01$). And the older one is, the less likely one is to be self-employed in personal services ($p < .01$).

These results again suggest that there are some systematic differences between being self-employed generally and being self-employed in personal services. These patterns persist even after sociodemographic and human capital factors are taken into consideration. Tables 6.2–4 attempt to show the relative roles that cultural and structural factors play in these patterns.

Table 6.2 presents the relationship between race/ethnicity and self-employment while controlling such factors as parents' self-employment status, grandparents' self-employment status, and whether one works in an ethnic enclave as well as the sociodemographic and human capital factors. This table also shows that African Americans, Mexican Americans, and Puerto Ricans are significantly less likely than whites to be currently self-employed and ever to have been self-employed, net of the other correlates of self-employment ($p < .01$). Again, however, these patterns do not hold true when it comes to nominal self-employment, as African

Table 6.2

Logit Models Predicting the Log Odds of Self-Employment with Race and Ethnicity and Cultural Factors, Net of Sociodemographics, and Human Capital Characteristics[a]

Independent Variables	Currently Self-Employed	Ever Self-Employed	Self-Employed in Personal Services
Constant	-2.362***	-1.682***	.384
African American	-1.656***	-1.097***	.011
Mexican American	-1.629***	-1.184***	-.807***
Puerto Rican	-2.147***	-1.828***	-.826***
Female	-1.103***	-1.002***	-.519***
Education	.059*	.012	-.018
Immigrant	.375	.461*	.170
Married	.080	-.041	-.232**
Job Training	.108	-.168	-.014
Other Language	.134	.145	.241
Age	.017	.016	-.034***
Self-Employed Parents	.217	.411**	-.190
Self-Employed Grandparents	.626***	.366**	.122
Enclave	-3.579***	-.968***	-.343**
R^2 Analog[b]	.150***	.086***	.033***
N	2363	1905	2363

* $p < .1$
** $p < .05$
*** $p < .01$

[a] Coefficients are unstandardized. For the dummy (binary) variable coefficients, significance levels refer to the difference between the omitted dummy variable category and the coefficient for the given category.

[b] The R^2 analog statistics is the proportion of reduction in a baseline model X^2 (a model fitting only the constant term) attributable to the model shown. It is calculated as follows:

R^2 = (Baseline model X^2—Selected model X^2) / Baseline model X^2.

Americans are no less likely than whites to be involved in such activities. Of the "cultural factors" considered in these models, having parents who were self-employed significantly increased the chances that one would ever have been self-employed ($p < .05$). Similarly, having self-employed grandparents significantly increased the likelihood that one would be currently self-employed ($p < .01$) and ever have been self-employed ($p <$

Table 6.3
**Logit Models Predicting the Log Odds of Self-Employment with Race and
Ethnicity and Disadvantage, Net of Sociodemographics and Human
Capital Characteristics**[a]

Independent Variables	Currently Self-Employed	Ever Self-Employed	Self-Employed in Personal Services
Constant	-2.297***	-1.793***	.078
African American	-.946***	-.795***	.134
Mexican American	-1.735***	-1.241***	-.783***
Puerto Rican	-1.689***	-1.637***	-.719***
Female	-.671***	-.799***	-.535***
Education	.028	.014	-.013
Immigrant	.659*	.663**	.161
Married	-.094	-.151	-.208**
Job Training	.036	-.236	.007
Other Language	.046	.075	.223
Age	.014	.016	-.032***
Denied a Job	2.006***	1.534***	.312
Racialized Industry	-1.194***	-.759***	.135
Denied Credit	-1.001***	-.848***	.047
R^2 Analog[b]	.106***	.083***	.032***
N	2391	1926	2391

* $p < .1$
** $p < .05$
*** $p < .01$

[a] Coefficients are unstandardized. For the dummy (binary) variable coefficients, significance levels refer to the difference between the omitted dummy variable category and the coefficient for the given category.

[b] The R^2 analog statistics is the proportion of reduction in a baseline model X^2 (a model fitting only the constant term) attributable to the model shown. It is calculated as follows:

R^2 = (Baseline model X^2—Selected model X^2)/ Baseline model X^2.

.05). But contrary to the expectations of ethnic enclave theory, working in an area with a high concentration of one's own ethnic group is associated with a decrease in the prospects of being currently self-employed ($p < .01$), of ever having been self-employed ($p < .01$), and of being self-employed in personal services ($p < .05$). Other factors retain their same basic relationship to self-employment as reviewed previously.

Table 6.3 presents the relationship between race/ethnicity and self-employment while controlling such factors as reporting experiences with being denied a job, working in a racialized industry, and having experiences with being denied credit. Again, the analysis also includes sociodemographic and human capital factors. The same basic racial and ethnic patterns of self-employment persist, as African Americans, Mexican Americans, and Puerto Ricans are less likely than whites to be currently self-employed or ever self-employed and Mexican Americans and Puerto Ricans are less likely than whites to be self-employed in personal services. Consistent with disadvantage theory, this table also shows that those who report experience with being denied a job were more likely to be currently and ever self-employed ($p < .01$). Those who worked in racialized industries were less likely to be currently and ever self-employed ($p < 01$). And those who report that they had been denied credit were significantly less likely to be currently and ever self-employed ($p < .01$).

Table 6.4 presents logit models predicting the log odds of self-employment with race and ethnicity, cultural factors, and disadvantage, net of sociodemographics and human capital factors. Here we see that blacks, Mexicans, and Puerto Ricans are all less likely than whites and others to be currently self-employed. Other factors do, however, make a substantial difference. In particular, consistent with disadvantage theory, those who report that they had been denied a job were significantly more likely to be involved in self-employment, those who worked in racially segregated industries were significantly less likely to be self-employed, and those who had been denied credit were marginally less likely to be self-employed. Consistent with cultural theories, those whose grandparents had been self-employed were significantly more likely to be self-employed themselves. But contrary to this perspective's expectations, those who worked in ethnic enclaves were significantly less likely to be self-employed. The only other factor that has an effect on being self-employed is being a woman, which significantly decreases one's prospects. Combined, these factors account for more than a fifth of the variance in being self-employed.

The results are very similar when predicting whether one has ever been self-employed. Again, however, there are somewhat different patterns when examining nominal self-employment in personal services. Blacks are not less likely than whites and others to be involved in nominal self-employment, and the disadvantage variables do not help determine who is or is not self-employed.

To what degree can entrepreneurship be used to reduce levels of poverty in America's inner cities? Table 6.5 presents the effects of

Table 6.4

Logit Models Predicting the Log Odds of Self-Employment with Race and Ethnicity, Cultural Factors, and Disadvantage, Net of Sociodemographics, and Human Capital Characteristics[a]

Independent Variables	Currently Self-Employed	Ever Self-Employed	Self-Employed in Personal Services
Constant	-.853	-.969*	.245
African American	-1.981***	-1.287***	.029
Mexican American	-2.073***	-1.412***	-.762***
Puerto Rican	-2.289***	-1.908***	-.784***
Female	-.794***	-.841***	-.527***
Education	.009	-.012	-.015
Immigrant	.384	.494*	.168
Married	-.086	-.144	-.214**
Job Training	.089	-.171	-.018
Other Language	.036	.100	.209
Age	.011	.016	-.033***
Self-Employed Parents	.224	.459**	-.182
Self-Employed Grandparents	.666***	.372**	.136
Enclave	-4.032***	-1.236***	-.314**
Denied a Job	2.247***	1.699***	.336
Racialized Industry	-1.771***	-1.083***	.092
Denied Credit	-.561*	-.673**	.043
R^2 Analog[b]	.215***	.117***	.033***
N	2352	1895	2352

* $p < .1$
** $p < .05$
*** $p < .01$

[a] Coefficients are unstandardized. For the dummy (binary) variable coefficients, significance levels refer to the difference between the omitted dummy variable category and the coefficient for the given category.

[b] The R^2 Analog statistics is the proportion of reduction in a baseline model X^2 (a model fitting only the constant term) attributable to the model shown. It is calculated as follows:

$$R^2 = (\text{Baseline model } X^2 - \text{Selected model } X^2)/ \text{ Baseline model } X^2.$$

self-employment on personal earnings. It shows that when all groups in this sample are combined, self-employment has a negative coefficient, but no significant effect. Among African Americans and Mexican Americans, however, these negative effects are significant. For blacks, self-employment translates into a $2,658.32 drop in personal earnings compared with comparable blacks who are not self-employed. For Mexican Americans, self-employment is associated with a $4,120.71 decline in personal earnings. For whites and others, however, self-employment is associated with a $3,143.03 increase in earnings. These results are presented net of the other sociodemographic, human capital, cultural, and structural factors used in the analysis.

SUMMARY AND CONCLUSIONS

This chapter began with the observation that some states have begun to promote self-employment and entrepreneurship as a means of combatting poverty, unemployment, and welfare dependency, especially in America's inner cities. It then noted that members of some racial and ethnic groups in the inner city are likely to become self-employed while members of other groups seldom pursue such endeavors. Moreover, not all groups have been able to use self-employment as a route toward upward mobility. The discussion then turned to two questions: (1) Why are members of some racial and ethnic groups in the inner city likely to become self-employed while members of other groups rarely engage in such activity? and (2) To what degree can entrepreneurship be used to reduce levels of poverty in America's inner cities?

We used insights from several complementary theoretical formulations to guide quantitative analysis: Ethnic enclave theories argue that ethnic enclaves within American cities serve to reinforce cultural forms from the ethnic group's homeland and make it more possible for group members to mobilize collective resources and to maintain cooperative social and economic relations in ethnic businesses. Middleman minority theories argue that certain groups adjust to American society by acting as commerce agents between the dominant racial group and subordinate racial groups. Social learning theory suggests that because role models act as important environmental factors, many enter into entrepreneurship when they see their parents and significant others successfully performing as entrepreneurs. Labor market disadvantage theory argues that racial and ethnic minorities turn to self-employment in response to labor market discrimination. And the economic detour theory argues that it has been legal obstacles, terrorist activities, and discriminatory behavior by lend-

Table 6.5
Regression Models Predicting Personal Income with Self-Employment and Race/Ethnicity, Net of Other Factors[a]

Independent Variables	All Groups	African Americans	Mexican Americans	Puerto Ricans	Whites Others
Constant	417.38	-5994.42***	9331.01***	5102.06*	12743.00***
Self-Employed	-894.88	-2658.32**	-4120.71***	89.02	3143.03*
African American	-2096.39***				
Mexican American	347.40				
Puerto Rican	-322.16				
Female	-3914.69***	-3644.44***	-5241.07***	-1055.65*	-8173.63***
Education	799.59***	1099.80***	281.90***	209.86**	1894.16***
Immigrant	-636.83	-140.11	-830.90	-745.90	388.30
Married	793.16**	1266.08**	979.87*	1575.03**	-1243.02
Job Training	-784.85*	-352.41	945.63	-65.05	-1953.07
Other Language	-1421.37*	-2419.12	-1416.47	4297.29*	-2515.78*
Age	221.47***	267.24***	53.43	-34.00	293.20***

106

Self-Emloyed Parents	108.11	42.63	452.67	-2049.67**	-523.05
Self-Employed GParents	906.34*	532.82	505.71	645.44	-753.50
Enclave	-907.00*	-6197.27	913.37	-2360.96**	4147.49**
Denied a Job	-2417.38*	-2378.53	-7318.36	-4308.68*	3863.45
Racialized Industry	-8034.39***	-9917.42***	-4413.62***	-4947.95***	-7209.03***
Denied Credit	-578.05	-1042.62	-329.56	6557.13**	-960.96
R^2	.346***	.406***	.360***	.208	.443***
N	2199	1035	437	404	323

* $p < .1$
** $p < .05$
*** $p > .01$

[a] Coefficients are unstandardized. For the dummy (binary) variable coefficients, significance levels refer to the difference between the omitted dummy variable category and the coefficient for the given category.

ers and consumers that have truncated the development of black business in America.

Results from our data analysis suggest that lack of access to jobs in the labor market acts as a push factor for some, while work in racially segregated industries and denial of credit impede self-employment. Having parents and grandparents who were entrepreneurs also facilitates self-employment, but working in ethnic enclaves hinders rather than helps one's prospects of being self-employed.

The results raise serious doubts about whether self-employment can be used to reduce levels of poverty in America's inner cities. Among blacks and Mexican Americans the prospects are slim indeed, given that self-employment among these groups in Chicago's high-poverty areas is associated with lower rather than higher incomes.

The results here also serve to undermine the idea that, after decades of economic neglect and decline, capital disinvestment, and deepening poverty, inner-city neighborhoods can reverse their fortunes by merely embracing a "bootstrap" approach to economic development. The capacity for such communities to reinvigorate themselves is severely diminished as long as periods of decline continue to define them. So, while efforts to aid inner-city entrepreneurship do not harm economic development in such communities, it is clear that self-employment alone probably will not solve the problems of poverty and unemployment in America's inner cities.

REFERENCES

Bates, Timothy. 1989. "The Changing Nature of Minority Business: A Comparative Analysis of Asian, Nonminority, and Black-Owned Business." *The Review of Black Political Economy* 17: 25–42.

Blaine, Peter, Nikolas C. Theodore, and John Zukosky. 1993. *Alternative Strategies for Small and Minority Businesses*. Chicago: Chicago Urban League.

Bonacich, Edna. 1973. "A Theory of Middleman Minorities." *American Sociological Review* 38: 583–594.

———. 1972. "A Theory of Ethnic Antagonism: The Split Labor Market." *American Sociological Review* 37: 547–559.

Bonacich, Edna, Ivan Light, and Charles Choy Wong. 1980. "Korean Immigrant: Small Business in Los Angeles." Pp. 184–165 in *Sourcebook on the New Immigration*, edited by R. Simon and B. La Port. New Brunswick, NJ: Transaction Books.

Bonacich, Edna and John Modell. 1980. *The Economic Basis of Ethnic Solidarity*. Berkeley: University of California Press.

Brockhaus, Robert H. 1980. "Psychological and Environmental Factors Which Distinguish the Successful from the Unsuccessful Entrepreneur: A Longitudinal Study." Paper presented at the annual Academy of Management Conference Proceedings.

Butler, John Sibley. 1991. *Entrepreneurship and Self-Help Among Black Americans: A Reconsideration of Race and Economics.* Albany: State University of New York Press.

Butler, John Sibley and Cedric Herring. 1991. "Ethnicity and Entrepreneurship in America: Toward an Explanation of Racial and Ethnic Group Variations in Self-Employment." *Sociological Perspectives* 34: 79–94.

Chiswick, Barry. 1978. "The Effect of Americanization on the Earnings of Foreign-born Men." *Journal of Political Economy* 86: 897–921.

———. 1982. *The Gateway: U.S. Immigration Issues and Policies.* Washington, DC: American Enterprise Institute.

Cobas, Jose. 1985. "On the Study of Ethnic Enterprise: Unresolved Issues." *Sociological Perspectives* 30: 467–472.

———. 1986. "Paths to Self-Employment among Immigrants: An Analysis of Four Interpretations." *Sociological Perspectives* 29: 101–120.

Diffley, Judy High. 1982. "A Study of Women Business Owners and the Importance of Selected Entrepreneurial Competencies Related to Educational Programs." *Dissertation Abstracts* 43: 6.

Du Bois, W.E.B. 1899. *The Philadelphia Negro.* Philadelphia: University of Pennsylvania Press.

Evans, M.D.R. 1989. "Immigrant Entrepreneurship: Effects of Ethnic Market Size and Isolated Labour Pool." Paper presented at the annual meeting of the American Sociological Association.

Fratoe, Frank A. 1988. "Social Capital of Black Business Owners." *Review of Black Political Economy* 16: 33–50.

Frazier, E. Franklin. 1957. *The Black Bourgeoisie: The Rise of A New Middle Class.* New York: Free Press.

Hornaday, John A. and John Abound. 1971. "Characteristics of Successful Entrepreneurs." *Personnel Psychology* 24: 141–153.

Horton, Hayward. 1988. "Occupational Differentiation and Black Entrepreneurship: A Sociodemographic Analysis of Black Entrepreneurs." *National Journal of Sociology* 2: 187–201.

Horton, Hayward Derrick and Gordon DeJong. 1991. "Black Entrepreneurship: A Demographic Analysis." *Research in Race and Ethnic Relations* 6: 105–120.

Light, Ivan. 1972. *Ethnic Enterprise in America.* Berkeley: University of California Press.

———. 1979. "Disadvantaged Minorities in Self-Employment." *International Journal of Comparative Sociology* 20: 31–45.

Light, Ivan and Edna Bonacich. 1988. *Immigrant Entrepreneurs.* Berkeley: University of California Press.

Light, Ivan and Angel A. Sanchez. 1987. "Immigrant Entrepreneurs in 272 SMSAs." *Sociological Perspectives* 30: 373–399.

Mescon, Timothy S. 1980. "Entrepreneurship in the Real Estate Industry: A Comparative Analysis of Independent and Franchise Brokers." *Dissertation Abstracts International* 40: 11.

Mincer, Jacob. 1974. *Schooling, Experience, and Earnings*. New York: National Bureau of Economic Research.

Ouchi, W. 1981. *Theory Z: How American Businesses Can Meet the Japanese Challenge*. New York: Avon.

Portes, Alejandro and Robert L. Bach. 1985. *Latin Journey*. Berkeley: University of California Press.

Portes, Alejandro and Leif Jensen. 1992. "Disproving the Enclave Hypothesis." *American Sociological Review* 57: 418–420.

Portes, Alejandro and Robert D. Manning. 1986. "The Immigrant Enclave: Theory and Empirical Examples." Pp. 47–68 in *Competitive Ethnic Relations*, edited by J. Nagel and S. Olzark. Orlando, FL: Academic Press.

Portes, Alejandro and Min Zhou. 1993. "Gaining the Upper Hand: Old and New Perspectives in the Study of Ethnic Minorities." Paper presented at the Urban Poverty Workshop at the University of Chicago and Northwestern University.

Reynolds, Paul D. and Brenda Miller. 1990. "Race, Gender, and Entrepreneurship: Participation in New Firm Startups." Paper presented at the annual meeting of the American Sociological Association.

Scherer, Robert F., Janet S. Adams, Susan S. Carley, and Frank A. Wiebe. 1989. "Role Model Performance Effects on Development of Entrepreneurial Career Preference." *Entrepreneurship Theory and Practice* 2: 53–70.

Sowell, Thomas. 1975. *Race and Economics*. New York: McKay, Inc.

Sullivan, Teresa A. and Stephen D. McCracken. 1988. "Black Entrepreneurs: Patterns and Rates of Return to Self-Employment." *National Journal of Sociology* 2: 168–185.

Torres, David. 1988. "Success and the Mexican American Businessperson." *Research in the Sociology of Organizations* 6: 313–334.

———. 1990a. "Dynamics Behind the Formation of a Business Class: Tucson's Hispanic Business Elite." *Hispanic Journal of Behavioral Sciences* 12: 25–49.

———. 1990b. "How Do Firms Grow?: Linear Versus Chaotic Effects of Growth on Performance Ratios of Minority Businesses." *Latino Studies Journal* 1: 3–22.

U.S. Small Business Administration. 1992. "Business Dissolution Rates by Firm Size and Number of Jobs Created." Statistical Table prepared by the U.S. Small Business Administration's Data Base Branch of the Office of Advocacy. Washington, DC: Author.

Weber, Max. 1904 [1930]. *The Protestant Ethic and the Spirit of Capitalism*. New York: Charles Scribner's.

Wilson, Kenneth L. and W. Allen Martin. 1982. "Ethnic Enclaves: A Comparison of the Cuban and Black Economies in Miami." *American Journal of Sociology* 88: 135–60.

Wilson, Kenneth L. and Alejandro Portes. 1980. "Immigrant Enclaves: An Analysis of the Labor Market Experiences of Cubans in Miami." *American Journal of Sociology* 86: 295–319.

Wilson, William Julius. 1987. *The Truly Disadvantaged: The Inner City, the Underclass, and Public Policy*. Chicago: University of Chicago Press.

Zhou, Min and John R. Logan. 1989. "Returns on Human Capital in Ethnic Enclaves: New York City's Chinatown." *American Sociological Review* 54: 809–820.

7

The Tattered Web of Kinship: Black–White Differences in Social Support in a Puerto Rican Community

Anne R. Roschelle

THE SOCIAL ORGANIZATION OF RACIAL-ETHNIC FAMILIES IN HISTORICAL PERSPECTIVE

During the past twenty-five years, there has been much debate over the nature and extent of informal social support networks, especially among racial-ethnic families. As a result, a large body of research has emerged in which scholars representing different theoretical perspectives have argued that minority family organization is characterized by extensive participation in kin and nonkin social support networks (Billingsley 1968, 1992; Romano 1968; Montiel 1970; Young 1970; Hill 1972; Ladner 1972; Staples 1973; Nobles 1974; Stack 1974; Aschbrenner 1978; Mathis 1978; Mirande and Enriquez 1979; McCray 1980; Fitzpatrick 1981; McAdoo 1980; Del Castillo 1984; Dodson 1988), predicated on exchange reciprocity, in which women comprise the core of the extended network (Stack 1974).

The major theoretical perspectives underlying this research can be categorized into a cultural approach, a structural approach, and an integrative approach. Within the cultural perspective there are two schools of thought: the pathological or culture of poverty perspective and the adaptive or strength resiliency perspective. The culture of poverty perspective argues that pathological elements inherent in minority cultures are responsible for deviant family structures. Black families are depicted as matriarchal, disorganized, and ultimately dysfunctional, whereas Latino families are characterized as rigidly patriarchal (see, for example, Bermudez 1955; Heller 1966; Lewis 1965; Moynihan 1965; Rainwater 1965, Murray 1984). Extended kinship networks among minority families are therefore seen as deviations from the norm of the middle-class white nuclear family. Paradoxically, culture of poverty theorists assert that African Americans must achieve a patriarchal family structure as a means of transcending their pathological conditions, while simultaneously arguing that this same patriarchal organization is responsible for the impoverished conditions of Latino families.

The strength resiliency or adaptive perspective arose as a response to the negative stereotypes perpetuated by culture of poverty theorists. Proponents of this perspective (Billingsley 1968, 1992; Romano 1968; Montiel 1970; Young 1970; Hill 1972; Ladner 1972; Staples 1973; Nobles 1974; Aschbrenner 1978; Del Castillo 1984) argue that it is the assumptions implicit in the pathological model that reflect minority family disorganization, not problems intrinsic to the African American, Chicano, or Puerto Rican communities themselves. Consequently, the focus of the strength resiliency perspective is on the positive aspects of minority family life. This perspective attributes positive elements of black families to their African cultural heritage, positive elements of Chicano families to the Mexica-Azteca cultural tradition, and positive elements of Puerto Rican family life to the influence of Spanish culture on Puerto Rican society (Billingsley 1968; Nobles 1974; Mathis 1978; Mirande and Enriquez 1979; McCray 1980; Fitzpatrick 1981; Dodson 1988). Essentially, proponents of the strength resiliency perspective contend that participation in extended kinship networks are manifestations of familism, that is, cultural norms that give overriding importance to the needs of the family, as opposed to individual and personal needs (Bean and Tienda 1987).

The structural approach to informal child care networks argues that minority families are more likely to create alternative family structures because of their limited economic resources and greater susceptibility to economic deprivation. The structural perspective stresses economic exploitation, not differences in cultural values and norms, as the major antecedent to divergent family forms. Essentially, this perspective argues that participation in informal support networks is an adaptive strategy used to ameliorate the deleterious effects of poverty (Hill 1972; Stack 1974).

According to Wilson (1991), simplistic notions of "culture" versus "social structure" have impeded the development of a broader theoretical paradigm from which to examine determinants of participation in extended social support networks. Therefore, a more integrative theoretical approach that examines both culture and structure is necessary. An integrative perspective is premised on the assumption that minority families must be examined within the context of their racial-ethnic heritage because racial stratification influences family resources and subsequent patterns of family organization (Zinn 1990).

Examining racial-ethnic context is particularly important for understanding Puerto Ricans, who have a different racial classification system than those traditionally used by North Americans (Rodriguez 1989; Rodriguez and Cordero-Guzman 1992). The black-white dichotomy that pervades the U.S. discourse on race is problematic for Puerto Ricans, who have a more fluid conception of race. For Puerto Ricans, race is not based solely on physical traits but also on cultural identification. As a result, they envision race as a continuum with no clear borders between categories (Ginorio 1986, as cited in Rodriguez 1989). Subsequently, most Puerto Ricans do not identify themselves as either white or black but are often categorized this way by others (Rodriguez 1991; Rodriguez and Cordero-Guzman 1992). This bifurcated racial classification system has important implications for the future of Puerto Rican families, particularly in the 21st century when intermarriage rates will continue to increase and mixed-race families will become a more common thread in the fabric of U.S. life.

Therefore, when building and testing empirical models of family interaction, race-ethnicity must become the center of the analysis, not simply another variable to be examined. In addition, it is imperative to identify the association between the internal dynamics of women's family lives and economic conditions as they are bound up in broader systems of class and race inequality. Subsequently, the analysis of race, gender, and class as interacting hierarchies of resources and rewards is necessary for an accurate depiction of minority family life (hooks 1981; Andrade 1982; Smith 1983; Glenn 1985, 1987; Collins 1990; Zinn 1990). It is therefore essential to examine the interconnections between cultural norms and structural indicators in order to fully understand racial-ethnic family social organization.

Black and Latina feminist scholars were the first to examine the interlocking nature of race, gender, and class oppression (Beale 1970; Lewis 1977; Davis 1981; Zinn 1982; Dill 1983; hooks 1981; Garcia 1990; Collins 1990). The crux of black and Latina feminist thought is predicated on the simultaneity of oppression. Minimizing one form of oppression, while essential, may still leave women of color subjugated in other equally dehumanizing ways (Collins 1986). Analysis of the interlocking nature of oppression shifts the investigative focus from merely explicating elements of race, gender, or class oppression to determining what the links are among these systems.

A more integrative approach to understanding extended kin networks is especially important because social scientists have recently begun to question whether or not participation in informal social support networks continues to characterize minority family organization (Ladner and Gourdine 1984; Wilson 1987; Jewell 1988; Anderson 1990; Collins 1990). In addition, a new body of research is emerging, which suggests that extended kin and nonkin networks traditionally found in racial-ethnic communities are eroding (Cochran et al. 1990; Eggebeen and Hogan 1990; Facio 1993; Menjivar 1997; Roschelle 1997). Therefore, a primary goal of this research is to determine the nature and extent of participation in child care networks among Puerto Rican women and to develop new theoretical interpretations of the links between gender, race, and class oppression by examining both cultural and structural determinants of participation in social support networks.

By using an integrative theoretical perspective, I will provide a more complete understanding of the dynamics underlying participation in child care networks. My strategy of examining the interconnection between culture and structure in relationship to network participation advances the literature on race, class, and gender theory. Unlike grand theories that attempt to explain all social phenomena, I argue that this perspective is contextual and situated historically. Throughout my field work it became clear that race, class, and gender operate at different theoretical levels. Whereas race may be salient in one context, gender and/or class may be more salient in another. Framed within a culture-structure nexus, my research explores the dynamic relationship between race, class, and gender and demonstrates how that relationship is socially constructed. The strategy of using an inductive approach in which empirical observations are used to construct social theory illustrates that network participation is indeed constrained by race, gender, class.

THE SOCIAL ORGANIZATION OF RACIAL-ETHNIC FAMILIES IN A CONTEMPORARY PERSPECTIVE

The current ethnographic study emerged out of a larger research project that examined informal social support networks among African

American, Puerto Rican, Chicano, and non-Hispanic white families using the National Survey of Families and Households (Roschelle 1997). Before discussing the research design of the current ethnographic research, I will briefly discuss the theoretical underpinnings and some of the relevant findings and shortcomings of the initial project and how they informed this ethnography.

In accordance with the theoretical literature discussed above, the most appropriate way to test the tenets of the cultural perspective is to examine attitudes toward individual responsibility to the extended kinship system. The major focus of the structural perspective is that participation in informal social support networks is a survival strategy to mitigate against the devastating effects of poverty. Therefore, within the parameters of this perspective, structure becomes defined as economic factors that reflect various aspects of a person's social position. The integrative approach is an attempt to identify the effects of both culture and social structure on minority family organization. Subsequently, the link between culture and social structure was examined to determine the process by which these two components affected race, gender, and class differences in the likelihood of participation in social support networks.

The results of the data analysis based on the National Survey of Families and Households (NSFH) indicated that participation in extended kinship networks traditionally found in black and Latino communities (for example, see Stack 1974; Mirande and Enriquez 1979; McAdoo 1980; Del Castillo 1984) no longer persist. In addition, contrary to past research findings, lower-income minority families were not characterized by high involvement in kin and nonkin networks. In fact, the data revealed that although women of all racial-ethnic groups hold primary responsibility for child care, non-Hispanic white respondents were more likely than women of color to both give and receive child care help from family and friends irrespective of socioeconomic status (see Roschelle 1997 for a more detailed description of the research design and findings).

The fact that Puerto Rican women were not more likely than Anglo women to participate in child care networks suggests that the interacting systems of race and class oppression prevent minority families from realizing their familistic identities. Unfortunately, because of inadequate measures of cultural attitudes on the NSFH, I was unable to determine the extent to which Puerto Rican women in the sample valued extended kin and nonkin. It is possible that Puerto Rican women are familistic and want to participate actively in exchange networks but are unable to do so because they lack the necessary resources. Despite their adherence to cultural norms valuing familism, the constraints of a hostile economic system may prevent minority families from participating in exchange networks. In addition, externally imposed racial categories that identify some Puerto Rican women as black and others as white may also impact network participation. Consequently, Puerto Rican women are oppressed both culturally and economically: They are unable to live by the values essential to their cultural survival because of racial discrimination and economic disenfranchisement. In addition, the lack of available social support networks reflects gender discrimination, since Puerto Rican women have traditionally derived prominence from their role as kin keepers.

Further supporting this contention was the relationship found between economic resources and network participation. As black and Latina respondents moved down the socioeconomic ladder, they were less likely to participate in child care networks. These data suggest that contrary to the structural theoretical perspective, respondents in this sample did not engage in giving or receiving child care help out of economic necessity.

Many socioeconomic factors may be responsible for the demise of social support networks traditionally found in minority communities. During the early 1980s there was a tremendous influx of drugs (particularly crack) into minority neighborhoods. Increasing unemployment and subsequent economic hardships occurred as a result of the deindustrialization of the inner city. Consequently, there was a disturbing rise in violent crime. In addition, the migration of the middle class out of the inner cities and persistent residential segregation have resulted in increasing social isolation of these communities. Given the overwhelming conditions of social dislocation that characterize low-income minority communities, it is not surprising that informal social support networks can no longer flourish (Ladner and Gourdine 1984; Wilson 1987; Zinn 1989; Collins 1990; Massey and Denton 1993). Perhaps the interacting systems of class and race oppression have become so severe that they supersede cultural norms and values.

Unfortunately, because of methodological constraints (see Roschelle 1997) I was unable to directly test the effects of cultural norms and values on participation in child care networks. Since familism connotes elevating the needs of the collective above those of the individual, it is vital to assess how emotionally committed respondents are to their friends and families. Therefore, the ethnographic study includes specific interview questions about the importance of family and nonfamily members in an individual's life. Attitudinal questions about the exchange of household goods and services, willingness to raise other people's children, and emotional commitment to the family are also included.

A unique finding of the quantitative study was the importance of respondents' place of birth. Much of the past research on participation in social support networks has failed to examine issues of migration. The data illustrated that women born in the United States were more active participants in extended kin and nonkin social support networks than women born elsewhere. In addition, some of the racial-ethnic differences initially found between Puerto Rican women and Anglo women disappeared when place of origin was considered. It became clear from the quantitative analyses that migration status was especially important in examining Puerto Rican involvement in social support networks. Lack of involvement in extended support networks found in the initial study may be a result of circular migration patterns characteristic of many Puerto Ricans. Back-and-forth migration may inhibit the ability of Puertorriquenas to develop strong network ties. Participation in support networks is predicated on exchange reciprocity. Therefore, Puerto Ricans who frequently travel between the United States and Puerto Rico may be perceived as being unable to fulfill their obligation to the network, and therefore denied membership. Subsequently, the ethnographic study includes an examination of the frequency of circular migration to determine whether or not constant movement is in fact a hindrance to cultivating extended support networks.

Finally, the qualitative study allowed me to examine the role of racial identification among my sample of Puerto Rican women to determine if there were differences in network participation among Puerto Rican women externally perceived as black or white. Socially constructed bifurcated racial categories have had an important impact on the experiences of Puerto Ricans in the United States (see, for example, Mills, Senior, and Goldsen 1950; Thomas 1967; Chenault 1970; Rodriguez 1989; Telles and Murgia 1990; Rodriguez 1991; Rodriguez and Cordero-Guzman 1992), but have not been specifically examined in relationship to extended kinship networks.

The results and limitations of the initial quantitative research constitute the underlying assumptions of this project. By conducting ethnographic research I was able to determine the extent of network participation and to identify the specific factors associated with the loss of informal child care networks in the Puerto Rican community. Supplementing the quantitative analysis with ethnographic research allows me to confirm the findings of the quantitative research and to weave a more richly detailed tapestry of Puerto Rican family life.

Based on the above-stated research findings, the focus of the ethnographic project included the following components: (1) Whether or not extended kinship networks traditionally found in racial-ethnic communities continue to thrive among Puerto Rican women. (2) The effects of circular migration patterns on the ability of Puerto Rican women to actively participate in extended social support networks. (3) The impact of externally defined categories of racial identification on network participation. (4) Whether or not the loss of the local production economy, and subsequent lack of resources, has constrained women's ability to participate in exchange networks. And finally, (5) Whether or not low-income Puerto Rican women are replacing traditional community networks with institutional mechanisms of social support.

DATA AND METHODOLOGY

The ethnography includes both observational data and qualitative interviews with Puerto Rican women residing in upstate New York. I conducted the observational research over a fifteen month period. Throughout the project I attended various social and political events in the community such as rallies in support of Puerto Rico's last vote for independence and community meetings regarding racist allegations made against members of the local school board by Puerto Rican teenagers. I went to beauty pageants (extremely popular in Latino communities), Latin American films, concerts, and various cultural events associated with Hispanic Heritage Week. In addition, I spent several months observing women and their children at a cooperative day-care center, which helped me gain access to the local community. I talked with many of the parents about their need for formal day-care and observed the women's interactions with each other as well as with their children both in the community and in their homes.

Using a snowball sample, I spoke with women from various community and civic organizations, who connected me with other willing participants. Throughout the project many of the Puertorriquenas introduced me to friends and family who were also willing to participate. During the course of my field work I conducted informal interviews with many informants and conducted open-ended taped interviews with twenty women. Obviously, one cannot make generalizations from a nonprobability sample to women outside of this ethnic enclave. However, not only did the ethnography confirm many of the earlier findings of the survey research, it elucidated those findings by providing considerable detail about the lives of contemporary Puerto Rican women.

NO MORE KIN: THE LOSS OF INFORMAL SOCIAL
SUPPORT NETWORKS IN PUERTO RICAN FAMILIES

The results of my ethnographic research indicate that familism is a highly valued cultural norm in this Puerto Rican enclave, albeit an illusive one. Although some women argued that informal social support networks still characterize the Puerto Rican community, most of them lamented their inability to participate in exchange networks. For example, Alicia stated that:

When I was a little girl, I remember my comadre taking care of me whenever my mother was sick. Many of the elderly women in the community provided child care in times of crisis. It seems as if women can no longer rely upon one another to take care of each other's children.

Carmen also mourned the loss of familism in the community. She told me that:

In the past Puertorriquenas could always be counted on to take care of people in the community in need of help. It didn't matter if someone was a member of your family, a neighbor, or a coworker—when people needed help someone was always available. Unfortunately, that is just not possible any more. I feel very sad that I can no longer rely on my community for help because it reflects the loss of our cultural heritage.

Throughout my research it was apparent that many women longed for the child care networks of the past. While some women did discuss the importance of child care networks in their community, positive attitudes toward network participation were rarely reflected in their behavior. The majority of women recognized the loss of these traditional networks and articulated a sincere desire to reclaim them. Juana's aspirations to recreate a more familistic community were evident when she stated:

Sometimes I long for the past when women in our community took care of each other's families. I don't know what's happened, but now we must fend for ourselves. I wish things were different—like they were when I was a child.

Likewise Carmen said:

I feel terrible that we no longer care for one another in the traditional way. I am glad my mother is not alive to see what has happened to our community.

Many of the women expressed shame over the loss of traditional child care networks. In fact, few women in the sample exchanged child care help with family or friends, using institutional means of support where available. Nevertheless, they expressed a desire to recreate these lost networks of care. In addition, many of the women articulated that the erosion of kin and nonkin networks signified the loss of an important cultural trait. These findings suggest that the persistence of cultural norms in favor of extended kinship do exist for many women in the community but are in danger of being eradicated. The importance of reclaiming familism among women in this community represents their desire to identify themselves with traditional Puerto Rican culture and resist the hegemonic constraints of American individualism. Furthermore, these women derive status and a sense of community as a result of their participation in exchange networks and are anxious to reclaim those gendered rewards.

When asked why they thought there was no one in their community to help, the women often discussed the role of migration and the economy in their responses. Angela told me that:

Things are different than when I was a kid. There were always mothers in the neighborhood who took care of the children of friends and relatives. But now it seems that in order to make a decent living, many of the older women have to work and can no longer babysit for their daughters or other family friends.

When I asked Angela if she thought frequent mobility was a factor, she added:

Well, some people in the neighborhood do go back to Puerto Rico a lot and some even go to New York City—although why they go to that hell hole is beyond me—so I guess they wouldn't make very reliable babysitters.

When questioned further, Angela did agree that network participation is predicated on exchange reciprocity. She said:

Well, I don't mind watching my friends' kids but if they never babysit in return, I stop. I mean, my time is as important as theirs—right?

Similarly, Laura articulated her frustration with the need for formal daycare. She told me that:

Most Puerto Rican women prefer to have family or close friends take care of their children; however, it is no longer possible. Years ago, particularly in Puerto

Rico, it would be unthinkable to put your child in day-care—that just was not acceptable to the community. Sometimes my friends and I talk about how sad we are that there are no longer people in the neighborhood willing to take care of our children.

When I asked Laura why she thought traditional extended kin networks no longer thrived in her community, she said:

Well, I think it is a result of a lot of things. First of all, most of the women in the community work, even the grandmothers, so they can't help with child care. You know the economy has gotten so bad around here that people are really struggling. There used to be lots of factory jobs here but in the last 10 to 15 years we have seen a lot of them disappear. Now the only jobs available are state jobs, which are hard to get, and service work, which doesn't pay very well. And, of course, people aren't always reliable; you can't trust your children with just anyone.

When I asked Laura to elaborate on the issue of reliability, she further stated:

Well, people have good intentions but they don't always follow through on them, you know. They tell you one thing and then do another. I had one friend who worked out a child care arrangement with her cousin and it worked pretty well for about three months but then the cousin decided to go back to Puerto Rico to find more stable work and my friend was in a real bind. There was no one else available to help her, not even me, that was one of the reasons we started the day-care center.

Many other women I spoke to expressed similar concerns. There was a general feeling that extended networks were important to the cultural survival of the community but had become unavailable, particularly among the lower-income women. Many of these women expressed sadness that something as important as extended kinship networks were deteriorating because of economic disenfranchisement. Because women traditionally comprise the core of the extended kinship network (Stack 1974), informants were particularly upset that their customary role of culture bearers was unavailable. Many of the women also felt betrayed because they had originally moved to upstate New York to escape the poverty of New York City and cultivate a rich ethnic community. Many of the women in the sample had lived in New York City and returned to Puerto Rico several times before settling in upstate New York. The women's migration patterns reflected their search for employment. Some of the women felt angry about having to move to find work because it disrupted their network participation. Marcia told me:

I moved back and forth between Nueva York and Puerto Rico four times in the last ten years. Every time I moved, it was because I was looking for a decent job. I hated moving but my kids were young and I had to feed my family. Moving so many times prevented me getting help raising my children. How could I ask my friends or family members to watch my kids when I couldn't be relied upon to return the favor? You know everyone here is struggling—all the women work and no one has the time or energy to help each other the way that our mothers and grandmothers did.

I did find class and race differences in the likelihood of participation in extended kin and nonkin networks. Professional women in the community and women who worked for the state in secure pink-collar jobs did participate more fully in exchange networks. These women had more flexibility and autonomy and were more able to provide child care services in emergency situations as well as on weekends. However, most of these women were also able to afford to purchase child care help and were therefore less in need of relying on their social support networks.

Interestingly, these financially secure women also tended to be lighter-skinned than the lower-income women in my sample. When I asked the women in my sample if they saw any relationship between racial identification and class, they recognized that they were more likely to be identified as white by individuals outside of their enclave. They also believed that as a result of being perceived as white, they were less likely to be discriminated in the job market. Morrina said:

Anglos always mistake me for white, but I am not white; I am Puerto Rican. I hate it when people assume things about me based on my skin color. I do have light skin but I am not white. I also know that people are prejudiced, and sometimes if you have very dark skin they think you are African American and won't hire you. Lots of my dark-skinned friends have been discriminated against at work because people think they are black.

Germina expressed a similar awareness of the external constraints of race faced by many Puerto Ricans. She told me:

I have a sister who is very dark, what we call negro, and a brother who is blanco like me. When we were young, my sister got beaten up at school and called nigger. She has the same amount of education as my brother and me but she always has trouble finding work.

When asked if perhaps her sister was unsuccessful in the job market because of individual rather than structural characteristics, Germina responded:

It isn't just my sister. All you have to do is look around town and it's really obvious that the Puerto Ricans who are the most poor are also the most dark-skinned. Most of the Puertorriquenas working in the state offices are light and the ones cleaning them are dark. Everyone knows that if you are a dark Puerto Rican, white people all think you are black.

Unfortunately, in addition to experiencing racism, women in the sample who were single mothers or who were from lower-income families also lacked the resources necessary to participate in exchange networks. Estrella articulated her inability to participate in child care networks because of her financial situation when she stated:

I can't take care of other people's children—I am barely able to take care of my own. I work two jobs and am so exhausted at the end of the day the last thing I want to do is watch someone else's kids. Besides, I have just enough money to pay my bills and feed my own kids. I can't afford to feed all the neighborhood children—I mean, I would love to but I just can't.

Similarly, Theresa said:

Life is so hard! I work long hours at the hospital and barely make enough money to survive. When my children are sick, I have to stay home from work because there is no one else to take care of them. If me and my friends had better jobs and made more money, maybe we could help each other more—but right now we have nothing to share.

Finally, Angelica said:

You know, there used to be lots of factory jobs around here. We used to make collars, gloves, and other products. Sure, it wasn't very glamorous, and it was hard work—but at least the pay was good. Now everyone works for the hospital, as maids, or at fast food restaurants.

In addition to their economic struggles, Estrella, Theresa, and Angelica were all dark-skinned women often mistaken for African American. When I asked them if they saw any relationship between race and class, they all agreed that there was a very strong relationship between the two. All three women expressed great frustration with North American society in which their cultural identity was constantly negated. All three had experienced blatant racism and often felt they were victims of discrimination because they were "black." Theresa summed up their feelings succinctly when she said, "People in America are so stupid about race. They can't see beyond black and white and lets' face it, if you are black people treat you like shit!"

Throughout my field work it was clear that familism is highly valued within this community. The importance of child care as an essential component of traditional social support networks is evident among many of these women. In addition, women derive pride from their role as bearers of Puerto Rican culture. Unfortunately, many of these women are unable to participate in giving and receiving child care help because of their disadvantaged economic position. In addition, other forms of lending behavior traditionally associated with extended networks (e.g., sharing food, clothing, transportation, household labor, etc.) were also valued but inaccessible because of the limited resources these women possessed. Most of the women relied on public transportation and would run out of food stamps before the end of each month. Some women with infants did exchange clothing but the majority of women purchased their children's clothes at second-hand stores and consignment shops. In addition, many women told me they were so exhausted that they completed minimal amounts of housework and were not willing to provide household labor to friends or family. Ultimately, Puerto Rican women in this community were forced to rely on inadequate institutional forms of social support such as day-care centers, food stamps, WIC (Women's Infants Children) and Aid to Families with Dependent Children (AFDC).

Combined with racial and economic disenfranchisement, another factor inhibiting network participation is migration status. Past research examining extended kin and nonkin networks has suggested that Puerto Ricans are uninvolved in these networks because of their lack of cultural values regarding familism (see Fitzpatrick 1981). However, the data indicate that it is the unique back-and-forth migration patterns of Puerto Ricans that inhibit them from establishing strong network ties, not the devaluation of these networks (Roschelle 1997). Because support networks are characterized by exchange reciprocity, migratory Puerto Ricans have difficulty being accepted as members because participants fear they may return to Puerto Rico and be unable to fulfill their obligation to the network. Since most Puerto Ricans migrate between the mainland and Puerto Rico in search of work, migration status is another reflection of economic disenfranchisement.

The practice of giving and receiving help with child care has been identified as common network behavior frequently associated with low-income women. The fact that these Puerto Rican women were consistently unable to exchange child care help is contrary to past research based on both cultural and structural perspectives. However, as Collins (1990) argues, this practice has now become difficult for inner-city and lower-income women of color, who are experiencing the perspective that although familism is a valued norm in Latino communities, it is no longer a viable practice. The theoretical literature from the structural perspective argues that extended social support networks ameliorate the deleterious effects of poverty. According to this perspective, women who are impoverished should participate frequently in exchange networks. However, as the data indicate, women in this community did not participate in social support networks out of economic necessity; rather, they were inhibited from participation because of structural constraints.

These data also indicate that although there is still ethnic pride, extended social support networks traditionally associated with minority families are not readily available in this Puerto Rican enclave. In the last twenty years, this neighborhood has seen a loss of its production economy, a subsequent increase in economic deprivation, and an increase in drug use and violent crime, although not on the same scale as major Northeastern industrial centers. Tragically, the interacting systems of race ethnicity, class, and gender stratification have prevented these Puerto Rican women from participating in child care networks vital to their economic and cultural survival.

THEORETICAL IMPLICATIONS: THE CULTURE-STRUCTURE NEXUS

The purpose of this ethnographic study was to explore the nature and extent of informal child care networks, and to develop new theoretical interpretations of the links between race, gender, and class oppression. In order to examine the relationship between race-ethnicity and class, I examined whether participation in extended support networks is primarily a response to economic need, cultural norms, or a combination of both. The data indicate that neither cultural norms nor economic resources alone sufficiently account for the propensity of individuals to participate in informal social support networks. Therefore, scholars must integrate social structural and cultural perspectives by examining the effects of race, class, and gender on network participation. Focusing on race, gender, and class in the investigation of informal social support networks synthesizes the structural and cultural perspectives by including components of each with the analysis of network behavior. It is clear from the research that Puerto Rican women in this community do value extended kinship networks and believe them to be an important part of their cultural heritage. Positive attitudes toward participation in child care networks were evident throughout my research and substantiate claims by advocates of the strength resiliency perspective that Puerto Rican women do possess cultural norms valuing familism. It was also evident throughout the project that women are still primarily responsible for child care and wish to be valued for their role as cultural kin keepers.

The structural argument that network participation is a survival strategy used to mitigate against the deleterious effects of poverty has not been corroborated by this research. Rather, as individuals move down the socioeconomic ladder, they are less likely to participate in child care networks. Furthermore, the finding that dark-skinned Puerto Rican women were frequently perceived as African American, and were likely to be poor, indicates a salient relationship between class and race that is not addressed by the structural perspective. In addition, an examination of circular migration revealed that constant movement is a hindrance to cultivating extended support networks. The inability of Puerto Rican women to develop networks represents structural constraint since constant movement is a response to fluctuations in employment opportunities. Therefore, using an economic framework to understand the dynamics of network participation is useful if we reverse the direction of the expected relationships. A reconceptualization of the structural perspective in which economic deprivation is associated with a decline in participation in social support networks would be worthwhile.

The structural perspective on minority families evolved as an inductive approach in which empirical observations were used to construct social theory. Because the structural perspective was formulated specifically to explain patterns of minority family organization, it is economically and historically grounded. However, as socioeconomic conditions change within minority communities, the theory may no longer be relevant. In fact, other more recent studies of network participation also found that individuals living in poverty were less likely to be involved in exchange networks than individuals with higher incomes (Cochran et al. 1990; Eggebeen and Hogan 1990; Menjivar 1997; Roschelle 1997). Consequently, an alternative explanation for the current lack of network participation among Puerto Rican women is that economic disenfranchisement is eroding traditional kin networks.

Evidently, as people move down the socioeconomic ladder, they become too overburdened to actively participate in their networks. Participating in exchange networks may have become a luxury afforded to people with time and money. Although network participation is not necessary for survival among affluent families, it may enhance the quality of their lives. Perhaps past researchers found thriving networks among minority communities because economic exploitation was less severe than it is now. In fact, scholars argue that national economic shifts and high rates of social dislocation among black and Hispanics have created distinctive forms of racial ethnic poverty (Wilson 1987; Zinn 1989; Ortiz 1991). These newly emerging patterns of poverty are so overwhelming that individuals have neither the time nor the resources necessary to participate in kin and nonkin networks. In addition, since participation in informal networks is predicated on exchange reciprocity, if women cannot reciprocate help, they are dropped from their networks (Edin and Lein 1997). The interacting systems of class and race oppression have become so severe that they prevent individuals from realizing their familistic identities.

Rates of poverty and female headedness among racial-ethnic families have risen dramatically since the late 1970s and early 1980s when most of the research on extended kin networks was conducted. Although minority families were economically disadvantaged, evidently they had the minimal resources necessary to participate in their exchange networks. Unfortunately, the exchange reciprocity characteristic of past involvement in social support networks is no longer a viable strategy against poverty. This research suggests that current economic conditions have become so harsh that they prevent Puerto Rican women from participating in their social support networks because they have nothing to share. The interacting systems of race, gender, and class oppression have become so entrenched that they prevent Puerto Rican women from participating in behavior essential to their cultural identity. Furthermore, if the sharing of child care is no longer routine in minority communities, the survival of their families may be greatly threatened. Policymakers can no longer assume that poor women can endure infinite hardships because of the strength of their community networks. The severe budget cuts and time limitations contained in current welfare reform legislation will surely lead to further erosion of already fragmented extended social support networks among disenfranchised Puerto Rican women.

POLICY IMPLICATIONS

The results of this research have important policy implications. Many of the past assumptions about racial-ethnic family organization have not been substantiated. Puerto Rican families in this enclave do not participate frequently in child care networks. Proponents of both the cultural and structural perspectives argue that exchange behavior is often predicated on child care obligations. Structural theorists argue that minority women share child care responsibilities as a means of survival in an economically hostile environment. Adherents of the cultural perspective argue that because child rearing has high priority in minority families, it is not unusual for a family member who can provide more help to raise the child of a sibling.

The child care component of the social support network was not found to be prevalent among Puerto Rican women in this community. If the sharing of child care is no longer routine among Latino communities, the survival of their families may be greatly threatened. Furthermore, if black Puerto Rican women are systematically disadvantaged as a result of external racial identification, fractioning within the community could result, causing further erosion of already precarious social support networks. The lack of available child care has led to a crisis among poor women, particularly women of color. Policymakers can no longer assume that poor women can endure infinite hardships because of the strength of their community networks. The recent welfare reform measures that eliminate welfare benefits for unmarried mothers under eighteen and Temporary Aid to Needy Families (TANF—formerly AFDC) after five years of lifetime recipiency assume that poor women will rely on extended kinfolk for their survival. Indeed, this will force more women and children into the depths of poverty. It is therefore critical to the survival of low-income minority families that federal child care programs be implemented immediately, particularly since women are now required to replace welfare recipiency with work after five years. Without adequate child care, women with small children cannot be expected to "get a job."

Educational reform and implementation of employment policies are also desperately needed. The transformation of the urban economy has created a mismatch between educational attainment and available employment, particularly for blacks and Latinos living in inner cities. In addition, the movement of the production economy out of the central cities to corresponding suburbs, third world countries, and the South, has exacerbated unemployment rates among minority communities.

Consequently, policymakers must provide job training to low, un-skilled, and skilled workers that will not ghettoize them in the lowest depths of the secondary labor market. In addition, legislative measures must be taken to ensure that jobs pay a living wage. Many poor women prefer work to welfare but are unable to survive on the meager benefits provided by jobs that do not pay a living wage. These women experience monthly disparities between their income and their expenses (Edin and Lein 1997), often making network participation impossible.

Educational reform that corresponds to the needs of a changing pro-duction economy would better prepare individuals to compete in the labor market. The creation of jobs to help rebuild America's decaying infrastructure might be a first step in implementing employment oppor-tunities for undereducated and/or low-skilled citizens. Imposing regula-tions and eliminating tax incentives for companies that move to "off shore" locations would eliminate the continual deindustrialization of the American economy. Providing transportation for inner-city residents to get to jobs in corresponding suburbs would enable them to compete for jobs currently unavailable to them. Rather than altering "pathological" subcultural traits among minority families, policymakers must focus their attention on creating economic opportunities for disenfranchised racial-ethnic families. In addition to improving the general quality of life, ec-onomic reform might facilitate the return of extended social support networks that once flourished among racial-ethnic communities.

Finally, we must broaden the discourse on race and ethnicity. As the United States becomes increasingly more multiracial, we must move be-yond the boundaries of black and white. As this research indicates, de-spite the fact that most Puerto Ricans in the United States do not identify themselves as either black or white, they are often perceived and treated as such by non-Hispanic whites. The recognition that even within racial and ethnic groups there is tremendous diversity and that these racial-ethnic differences are constrained by class and gender must pervade the new politics of race.

REFERENCES

Anderson, Elijah. 1990. *Streetwise: Race, Class, and Change in an Urban Com-munity*. Chicago: University of Chicago Press.

Andrade, Sally J. 1982. "Family Roles of Hispanic Women: Stereotypes, Em-pirical Findings, and Implications for Research" in *Work, Family, and Health: Latina Women in Transition* (pp. 95–106), edited by Ruth E. Zambrana. New York: Hispanic Research Center, Fordham University.

Aschbrenner, Joyce. 1978. "Continuities and Variations in Black Family Struc-
    ture" in *The Extended Family in Black Societies* (pp. 181–200), edited
    by Demitri B. Shimkin, Edith M. Shimkin, and Dennis A. Frate. Haw-
    thorne, NY: Mouton De Gruyter Publishers.
Beale, Francis. 1970. "Double Jeopardy: To Be Black and Female" in *The Black
    Woman* (pp. 90–110), edited by Tony Cade. New York: Signet.
Bean, Frank and Marta Tienda. 1987. *The Hispanic Population of the United
    States*. New York: Russell Sage Foundation.
Bermudez, Maria Elvira. 1955. *La Vida del Mexicano*. Mexico City: Robredo.
Billingsley, Andrew. 1968. *Black Families in White America*. Englewood Cliffs,
    NJ: Prentice Hall.
————. 1992. *Climbing Jacob's Ladder: The Enduring Legacy of African
    American Families*. New York: Simon and Schuster.
Chenault, L. 1970. *The Puerto Rican Migrant in New York City*. New York:
    Columbia University Press.
Cochran, Moncrieff, et al. 1990. *Extending Families: The Social Networks of
    Parents and Their Children*. Cambridge: Cambridge University Press.
Collins, Patricia Hill. 1986. "Learning From the Outsider Within: The Socio-
    logical Significance of Black Feminist Thought." *Social Problems* 33(6):
    S14–S32.
————. 1990. *Black Feminist Thought: Knowledge, Consciousness and Em-
    powerment*. Boston: Unwin Hyman.
Davis, Angela. 1981. *Women, Race, and Class*. New York: Random House.
Del Castillo, Richard Griswold. 1984. *La Familia: Chicano Families in the
    Urban Southwest, 1848–the Present*. Notre Dame, IN: University of No-
    tre Dame Press.
Dill, Bonnie Thornton. 1983. "Race, Class, and Gender: Prospects for an all
    Inclusive Sisterhood." *Feminist Studies* 9(1): 31–150.
Dodson, Jualynne. 1988. "Conceptualizations of Black Families" in *Black Fam-
    ilies* (pp. 77–90), edited by Harriette Pipes McAdoo. Thousand Oaks,
    CA: Sage Publications Inc.
Edin, Kathryn and Laura Lein. 1997. *Making Ends Meet: How Single Mothers
    Survive Welfare and Low Wage Work*. New York: Russell Sage Foun-
    dation.
Eggebeen, David J. and Dennis P. Hogan. 1990. *Giving Between the Genera-
    tions in American Families*. University Park: The Pennsylvania State
    University, Population Issues Research Center.
Facio, Elisa. 1993. "Gender and the Life Course: A Case Study of Chicana
    Elderly" in *Building With Our Hands: New Directions in Chicana Stud-
    ies* (pp. 217–231), edited by Adela de la Torre and Beatriz M. Pesquera.
    Berkeley: University of California Press.
Fitzpatrick, Joseph P. 1981. "The Puerto Rican Family" in *Ethnic Families in
    America: Patterns and Variations* (pp. 189–214), edited by Charles H.
    Mindel and Robert W. Haberstein. New York: Elsevier.

Garcia, Alma. 1990. "The Development of Chicana Feminist Discourse, 1970–1980" in *Unequal Sisters: A Multicultural Reader in U.S. Women's History* (pp. 418–431), edited by Ellen Carol Dubois and Vicki Ruiz. New York, London: Routledge.

Glenn, Evelyn Nakano. 1985. "Racial and Ethnic Women's Labor: The Intersection of Race, Gender, and Class Oppression." *Review of Radical Political Economics* 17(3): 86–108.

———. 1987. "Gender and the Family" in *Analyzing Gender: A Handbook of Social Science Research* (pp. 348–375), edited by Myra Marx Ferree and Beth B. Hess. Thousand Oaks, CA: Sage Publications Inc.

Heller, Celia. 1966. *Mexican American Youth: Forgotten Youth at the Crossroads.* New York: Random House.

Hill, Robert. 1972. *The Strength of Black Families.* New York: The Urban League.

hooks, bell. 1981. *Ain't I a Woman: Black Women and Feminism.* Boston: South End Press.

Jewell, K. Sue. 1988. *Survival of the Black Family: The Institutional Impact of U.S. Social Policy.* New York: Praeger.

Katzman, M. 1968. "Discrimination, Subculture, and the Economic Performance of Negroes, Puerto Ricans, and Mexican Americans." *American Journal of Economics and Society* 27(4): 371–375.

Ladner, Joyce. 1972. *Tomorrow's Tomorrow: The Black Woman.* New York: Doubleday.

Ladner, Joyce and Ruby Morton Gourdine. 1984. "Intergenerational Teenage Motherhood: Some Preliminary Findings." *Sage: A Scholarly Journal on Black Women* 1(2): 22–24.

Lewis, Diane. 1977. "A Response to Inequality: Black Women, Racism, and Sexism." *Signs* 3: 339–361.

Lewis, Oscar. 1965. *La Vida: A Puerto Rican Family in the Culture of Poverty-San Juan, New York.* New York: Random House.

Massey, Douglas S. and Nancy A. Denton. 1993. *American Apartheid: Segregation and the Making of the Urban Underclass.* Cambridge, MA: Harvard University Press.

Mathis, Arthur. 1978. "Contrasting Approaches to the Study of Black Families." *Journal of Marriage and the Family* 40 (November): 667–676.

McAdoo, Harriet P. 1980. "Black Mothers and the Extended Social Support Network" in *The Black Woman* (pp. 125–144), edited by La Frances Rodgers-Rose. Thousand Oaks, CA: Sage Publications Inc.

McCray, Carrie Allen. 1980. "The Black Woman and Family Roles" in *The Black Woman* (pp. 67–87), edited by La Frances Rodgers-Rose. Thousand Oaks, CA: Sage Publications Inc.

Menjivar, Cecilia. 1997. "Immigrant Kinship Networks and the Impact of the Receiving Context: Salvadorans in San Francisco in the Early 1990's." *Social Problems* 44(1): 104–123.

Mills, C.W., R. Senior, and R. Goldsen. 1950. *The Puerto Rican Journey: New York's Newest Migrants*. New York: Harper.

Mirande, Alfredo and Evangelina Enriquez. 1979. *La Chicana: The Mexican American Woman*. Chicago: The University of Chicago Press.

Montiel, Miguel. 1970. "The Social Science Myth of the Mexican American Family." *El Grito: A Journal of Mexican American Thought* 3(4): 56–63.

Moynihan, Daniel Patrick. 1965. *The Negro Family: A Case for National Action*. Washington, DC: U.S. Government Printing Office.

Murray, Charles. 1984. *Losing Ground: American Social Policy, 1950–1980*. New York: Basic Books.

Nobles, Wade W. 1974. "Africanity: Its Role in Black Families." *The Black Scholar* 5(9): 10–17.

Ortiz, Vilma. 1991. "Latinos and Industrial Change in New York and Los Angeles" in *Hispanics in the Labor Force: Issues and Policies* (pp. 119–132), edited by Edwin Melendez, Clara Rodriguez, Janis Barry Figueroa. New York: Plenum Press.

Rainwater, Lee. 1965. "Crucible of Identity: The Negro Lower-Class Family." *Daedalus* 95: 172–216.

Rodriguez, Clara E. 1989. *Puerto Ricans Born in the U.S.A.* Boston: Unwin Hyman.

———. 1991. "The Effect of Race on Puerto Rican Wages" in *Hispanics in the Labor Force: Issues and Policies* (pp. 77–98), edited by Edwin Melendez, Clara Rodriguez, Janis Barry Figueroa. New York: Plenum Press.

Rodriguez, Clara E. and Hector Cordero-Guzman. 1992. "Placing Race in Context." *Ethnic and Racial Studies* 15(4): 523–542.

Romano, Octavio. 1968. "The Anthropology and Sociology of Mexican Americans: The Distortion of Mexican American History." *El Grito: A Journal of Mexican American Thought* 2: 13–26.

Roschelle, Anne R. 1997. *No More Kin: Exploring Race, Class, and Gender in Family Networks*. Thousand Oaks, CA: Sage Publications Inc.

Sassen, Saskia. 1993. "Urban Transformation and Employment" in *Latinos in a Changing U.S. Economy* (pp. 184–206), edited by Rebecca Morales and Frank Bonilla. Thousand Oaks, CA: Sage Publications Inc.

Smith, Barbara. 1983. "Introduction" in *Home Girls: A Black Feminist Anthology* (pp. xix-xvi), edited by Barbara Smith. New York: Kitchen Table Press.

Stack, Carol. 1974. *All Our Kin: Strategies for Survival in a Black Community*. New York: Harper Press.

Staples, Robert. 1973. *The Black Woman in America*. Chicago: Nelson-Hall.

Telles, E. and E. Murguia. 1990. "Phenotypic Discrimination and Income Differences Among Mexican Americans." *Social Science Quarterly* 71(4).

Thomas, Piri. 1967. *Down These Mean Streets*. New York: Knopf.

Torres, Andres and Frank Bonilla. 1993. "Decline Within Decline: The New

York Perspective" in *Latinos in a Changing U.S. Economy* (pp. 85–108), edited by Rebecca Morales and Frank Bonilla. Thousand Oaks, CA: Sage Publications Inc.

Wilson, William Julius. 1987. *The Truly Disadvantaged: The Inner City, The Underclass, and Public Policy*. Chicago: University of Chicago Press.

———. 1991. "Studying Inner-City Social Dislocations: The Challenge of Public Agenda Research, 1990 Presidential Address." *American Sociological Review* 56: 1–14.

Young, Virginia. 1970. "Family and Childhood in a Southern Negro Community." *American Anthropologist* 72: 269–288.

Zinn, Maxine Baca. 1982. "Review Essay: Mexican American Women in the Social Sciences." *Signs* 8(2): 259–272.

———. 1989. "Family, Race, and Poverty in the Eighties." *Signs* 14: 856–874.

———. 1990. "Family, Feminism, and Race in America." *Gender & Society* 4(1): 68–82.

8

The American Population in the Year 2000

Nancy A. Denton

No words of W.E.B. Du Bois are better known than his 1901 statement: "The problem of the Twentieth Century is the Problem of the color-line" (Du Bois 1978 [1901], p. 281). One hundred years later, they still ring true. Even this long after the major civil rights laws of the 1960s, discussions of issues related to race, such as affirmative action, poverty and segregation, frequently come back to the point that all too often people of African descent still stand apart in this nation. Saying this is not to deny progress, but here, too, Du Bois's words are relevant. Writing in 1950, half-way through the 20th century, he noted:

What have we gained and accomplished? The advance has not been equal on all fronts, nor complete on any. We have not progressed with closed ranks, like a trained army, but rather with serried and broken ranks, with wide gaps and even temporary retreats. But we have advanced. Of that there can be no atom of doubt. (Du Bois 1978 [1901], p. 284)

While the problem of the color line is still with us and more remains to be done despite the progress, there is a major difference between the times in which Du Bois wrote and today, namely, the increasing diversity of the U.S. population. The large numbers of new immigrants arriving at our doors, in numbers and from places not anticipated when the 1965 immigration law was passed, and the demographic effects they are having on the distribution of the U.S. population by race and ethnicity, will affect the problem of the color line and the path of African American "progress." African Americans are now one of many different groups of people of color. Though their history is unique, the presence of other visible groups has profound implications for them.

This chapter will expand on this argument in a number of ways. The first part will explore the changes in the total U.S. population by race and ethnicity. While the primary focus is on African Americans, including all groups reveals the changing context in which African Americans in the United States now live, have lived in the past, and will live in during the first half of the 21st century. Once these basic numbers are established, the second part will delve into the meaning of those numbers. Of foremost importance is the nature of and issues surrounding the race/ethnic categories themselves, for the definitions of the categories determine the numbers of people included in them. A related issue is the relative locations of the various groups in the country as a whole, and within metropolitan regions. The increasing population diversity is experienced differently in different parts of the country, which in turn changes the context in which blacks live. The final section of the chapter takes up the question of what the presence of these other groups means for African American progress. What does it mean to have a constant proportionate share of the population in a context where everyone else's share is changing rapidly? What are the effects of a multiethnic society that appear harmful to African American progress? Which effects are helpful? Finally, in the conclusion, I will share some of my thoughts on current sources of what I think of as "misinformation" that limit clear thinking and fruitful discussion of race issues in the United States today.

CHANGES IN THE U.S. POPULATION BY RACE AND ETHNICITY

Everyone knows that the United States is undergoing dramatic changes in the complexion of its population. This fact is commented on nearly every day in the mass media, with some viewing it as positive and some as negative. As of 1998, the United States was home to just over 270 million people. Of these, 195 million identify as non-Hispanic whites, 32.7 million as non-Hispanic blacks, 9.8 million as non-Hispanic Asian and Pacific Islanders, 2 million as non-Hispanic Native Americans, Eskimos and Aleuts, and 30.5 million as Hispanics. In proportional terms, non-Hispanic whites make up 72.3 percent and non-Hispanic blacks 12.1 percent, with Hispanics and Asians at 11.3 and 3.6 percent, respectively (U.S. Census 1998).

In order to understand how unique the current distribution is, we need to look back in time. In 1790, the year of the founding of the United States, blacks made up about 20 percent of the U.S. population (Du Bois 1978 [1911], p. 86), and they remained at that level until 1840 (Farley and Allen 1989, p. 11). By 1850, whites made up 84.3 percent of the total population, while blacks were 15.7 percent. Due largely to the arrival of thousands of European immigrants, the percent of the population that was white rose in the following decades to a high of 87.6 in 1920, while the percent of the population that was black declined to 10.4 in that year. For the first five decades of the 20th century, whites comprised 87 percent of the U.S. population. By 1960 whites were still about 85 percent of the population, declining to just over 75 percent in 1990. Black population as a percent of the total declined from 11.6 in 1900 to 10.0 in 1930, where it remained until it began a gradual rise in 1960 to reach the current value of just over 12 percent in 1998 (Passell and Edmonston 1994, p. 43).

This brief historical look at the ethnic composition of the United States points to two facts. First, given that they made up nearly 90 percent of the population for the first half of the 20th century, it is little wonder that white discourse about our changing population views the white population decrease with alarm. The current percent white is over 12 percentage points lower than it was for the first half of the 20th century. Second, the current proportion white does not seem as dramatically low if one looks further back in history, to 1850 when whites were just over 84 percent of the population or to 1790, when they were about 80 percent of the population. Compared to 1790, the current percent of the population that is white is less than 5 percentage points lower than it was two hundred years ago. In the long-term view, the proportionate share held by the black population has decreased by almost half, from 20 to 12 percent, but in the shorter term, the white population has seen an even larger decrease in percentage points, from 90 to 75 percent. It is also clear that 90 percent represents nearly complete hegemony, whereas both 20 and 12 percent are at best minority shares.

Clearly, a part of these changes in the relative sizes of groups in the population is the effect of immigration, a population process that also plays an important role in defining our current and future population distribution. Throughout the late 19th and early 20th century, the arrival of European immigrants served to *increase* the relative size of the white population and *decrease* the relative size of the black population. Demographic techniques permit us to estimate the racial composition of the population in 1990, had immigration been cut off in each of the preceding decades beginning in 1900. These show that the proportion of the population that was white would have risen to a high of 82.6 if immigration ceased in 1920, 5 percentage points lower than its actual peak as noted above. Thus, the major effect of immigration, pre-1965, was to increase the relative share of the population held by whites (Passell and Edmonston 1994, p. 50). Of course, many of these South, Central and Eastern European immigrants had a long struggle to be accepted as whites, and historical writings about them rival anything written about blacks in terms of racism and bigotry (cf. Lieberson 1980 for examples and references). Put another way, as of 1990 whites owed only 75.5 percent of their population to those who were here in 1900 (Passell and Edmonston 1994, p. 69) while blacks owed 88.2 percent (Passell and Edmonston 1994, p. 68).

Despite the fact that the Hispanic, and to a much more limited extent the Asian, population has been growing for decades, the change in the immigration law in 1965 (which removed the European bias from the law) means that the current population composition of both of these groups is heavily weighted toward post-1965 immigrants. For Hispanics, 42.7 percent of their total population in 1990 was attributable to immigration since 1970 (Passell and Edmonston 1994, p. 66), while for Asians the corresponding percentage was 70.5 (Passell and Edmonston 1994, p. 64). Though the change in the immigration law also meant that more blacks could enter the country, from both Africa and the Caribbean, a mere 5.4 percent of the 1990 black population was composed of post-1970 immigrants (Passell and Edmonston 1994, p. 68). Small as this percentage is compared to those for Asians and Hispanics, it is still more than double the corresponding percentage for whites, among whom only 2.1 percent are post-1965 immigrants (Passell and Edmonston 1994, p. 70). As a result, the effects of immigration vary dramatically across the major race/ethnic groups. Though there are many reasons for the current anti-immigrant sentiment in this country, the stark historical contrast between how immigration in the first half of the 20th century enabled whites to achieve a population dominance of nearly 90 percent, compared to the current effect, which speeds up the decline of the white population share, plays an important role.

If we look at how these immigration effects will play out in the first half of this century, the white relative share of the population decreases further. If current immigration trends continue, by 2050 non-Hispanic whites will comprise just over half of the U.S. population. Edmonston and Passell calculate the exact figure in 2050 as 56.6, with a decline to 48.8 in 2090 (1994, p. 334). Statistics like this attract a lot of attention but it is important to recognize that they are projections, and are driven by the underlying assumptions used to make them (Edmonston and Passell 1994, pp. 328–333). Specifically, assumptions must be made about the trends in fertility and mortality for each group, as well as trends in immigration. Unanticipated changes in any of these assumptions will make the projected population sizes wrong. Though this is not the place to get into the technical details of projections, the current Hispanic and Asian populations are relatively young compared to the white and black populations. As a result, they are more likely to be having children and less likely to be dying than the white or black populations, both of which include higher proportions of elderly (Edmonston and Passell, 1994, pp. 339–340), and thus their populations will increase faster than whites or blacks.

Public discussions of population diversity frequently focus on immigration as the driving force behind the increasing diversity of the U.S. population, ignoring the fact that the immigrants who are already here will contribute to future population growth through the birth of native-born children, regardless of whether or not new immigrants come. The increasing diversity of the U.S. population would be slowed a bit but it would by no means end even if all immigration were to cease immediately. In 1990, 33.7 percent of the Asian population and 59.1 percent of the Hispanic population was native-born, and thus increased our population diversity through births of U.S. born children. If current immigration trends remain the same, in 2040 the Hispanic population will be 67.4 percent native-born and the Asian population 50.6 percent native-born, while the white and black populations will be 96.1 and 90.6 percent native-born, respectively (Edmonston and Passell 1994, pp. 341–342). Children born to more than half of Asian and Hispanic populations will be native-born themselves in 2040, thus contributing to increasing population diversity with native-born Americans of Asian or Hispanic descent. The fact that so much of the future increase in the Hispanic and Asian populations will be increasingly native-born makes the growing diversity of the U.S. population so unavoidable and unchangeable.

What about the future size of the black population? Projections show that the black population will increase substantially in number over the next sixty years, from 30 million to 45.2 million in 2050, and to 66.0 million in 2090 (Edmonston and Passell 1994, p. 334). However, during this time, the black proportion of the total population will hardly change at all, going from 12.1 percent to 12.2 percent in 2050 and dropping to 11.3 percent by 2090. Thus, blacks will feel effects of the changing diversity of the population from a context of increasing numbers but an unchanging proportional share. This experience will be in distinct contrast to whites, who will experience increasing numbers but a dramatically decreasing share, and Hispanics and Asians whose numbers and proportionate shares will both increase. It is to exploring the implications of this flat proportionate share that the rest of this chapter is devoted.

DEFINING RACIAL CATEGORIES

All these projections of the relative shares of the population also assume that the race/ethnic categories will remain fixed. However, the definition and meaning of the race and ethnic categories currently in use are hardly without critics, and definitely not stable. To the extent that the categories themselves change, the numerical values of the predictions reported above will change. The current categories used are what Hollinger calls the "ethno-racial pentagon:" black, white, Native American, Asian and Latino. He goes on to remark that "whatever their shifting labels, have come to replicate the popular color-consciousness of the past: black, white, red, yellow and brown" (Hollinger 1995, p. 32).

These categories are currently subject to much debate (McDaniel 1996), particularly from mixed-race persons, who do not see themselves as part of any category (Zack 1993), as well as from scientists, who protest the lack of any biological significance to the concept of race as defined in the Census (Hollinger 1995, pp. 33–38). Furthermore, scholars increasingly point out that the ethnic categories are "optional" for whites, to be invoked when they are advantageous but not invoked when they are not, an option not available to blacks, Asians, and to a lesser extent Hispanics (Alba 1990; Waters 1990).

The seldom acknowledged but clear politicism of the current categories is clearly explained by Hollinger, who argues that:

When it is said that race affects one's destiny more than ethnicity does, the reference usually turns out to be to different degrees of mistreatment within a social system, not to different degrees of cultural particularity and group enforcement of norms. Some of the various ethnic groups within the Euro-American bloc have had their share of suffering, but it is dwarfed, according to our common if not always stated understanding, by the suffering inflicted on races. Moreover, the Chinese American suffers less as a Chinese than as an Asian, just as the Crow suffers not as a Crow but as an Indian. Although Japanese Americans were interned during World War II as Japanese rather than as Asians, that Asianness made the difference is proven by the less harsh treatment afforded Americans of highly visible German or Italian affiliations. This distinction between degrees of victimization is the key to the place of Latinos in the ethno-racial pentagon and to the assertion of a racial status on their behalf. (Hollinger 1995, p. 37)

In a previous article I have strongly urged the continued use of these incorrect categories for one reason, namely, that they give us data with which to measure inequalities among different groups of people (Denton 1997). To make this argument I have contrasted the concept of individual identity with that of social identity, in short, "how I see myself" versus "how others see me." Individual identity is the search for meaning in one's own life, hence the term "identity politics." Invaluable as this is for personal development, in many cases racism, discrimination, and general ill-treatment in contemporary society are based on "how one looks." It is how you are perceived by outsiders who know very little about you that will determine whether you will be the victim of a hate crime, more likely to be turned down for a job, or denied the information and access necessary to obtain decent housing in a decent neighborhood. To paraphrase Hollinger, it will do little good to have a system whereby a discrimination remedy is denied someone because she does not identify with the group of which the rest of the society treats her as a member (Hollinger 1995, p. 47).

This is not to say that the categories themselves are accurate, have not changed over time, and are even more likely to change in the future. Particularly with regard to individual identity, there is the possibility of enormous change because of the increasing rates of intergroup marriage, as well as from discussions about the nature of race and ethnicity themselves. While cross-racial black-white marriage rates remain low, they have shown a tremendous increase in recent years. As of 1990 there were about one million interracial couples, a substantial change from the 150,000 in 1960 (Harrison and Bennett 1995, p. 165). The children of these marriages have no particular claim to being either white or black on the census forms (Alba 1990, pp. 12–13). Similar problems exist for children of marriages across other categories of the ethno-racial pentagon. As a result, the 2000 census allowed people to choose more than one racial category, in addition to the choice of an Hispanic origin, as in the 1980 and 1990 censuses (U.S. Bureau of the Census 1997).

Nor is it to deny the negative effects of the current categories on self-definition and identity. As Zack points out, the current categories result in some people, particularly those of mixed race, being "racially designated" (1993, p. 172), a not very comfortable position. But giving people a more accurate choice on the census or any other form will do nothing to change the prejudice or discrimination against them if the effects of contemporary racism all too frequently operate on the level of appearance, not identity. Based on my own work on residential segregation (Massey and Denton 1993), and my reading of the social science literature on race, I am convinced that the imperfect current categories, particularly those for African Americans and Hispanic Americans, correlate with and to some extent cause serious social consequences that we need to be concerned about as a society. If we truly want to do away with these inequalities, I fear we need to put up with the categories, imperfect as they may be for defining people as individuals.

REGIONAL VARIATION IN CURRENT POPULATION DIVERSITY

The national figures of the increasing diversity of the U.S. population hide large variations across regions, states, or metropolitan areas, and within the metropolitan areas. To the extent that the increasing diversity is unevenly distributed, African Americans and others will have different experiences of the increasing diversity. Historically, the United States could be quite correctly divided into a black-white world, especially given the decimation of the Native American population. Much of the civil rights movement was based on this premise and many of the legal changes enacted during it reflect a two-group concept. Despite all the talk of increasing diversity of the U.S. population, the elements that really make it different from what it was two hundred years ago, namely, Hispanics and Asians, are not evenly distributed across the U.S. landscape. To the extent that these newer groups are not present, the more appropriate the older ways of thinking about race might be.

The geographical variation in the diversity of the U.S. population has been the focus of a series of papers by William Frey, based largely on the 1990 census. His work clearly shows the racial and ethnic diversity of the population to be greatest in the coastal states, and much less pronounced inland (cf. Frey 1993, 1995a, 1995b, among others). Regionally, the West is clearly the most diverse, with 18.8 percent of its population Hispanic, 7.7 percent Asian, in addition to the 5.1 percent black (Harrison and Bennett 1995, p. 150). In the other three regions, blacks are the largest group by far, though in the Northeast the sum of the percent Hispanic (7.2) and Asian (2.6) comes close to the black percent of 10.3 (Harrison and Bennett 1995, p. 150). Further analyses by Frey also reveal a trend of greater white population migration to the states that are already largely white (Frey 1995b). Thus, in some areas, blacks are competing in a truly multiethnic world, and in others they are in the more familiar black-white landscape, though with varying proportions of whites as well. Depending on where they live in the United States, African Americans will not only have different experiences of the multiethnic nature of U.S. society themselves, but more importantly, given the white power in so many institutions, they will be dealing with whites who have very different experiences of the increasing population diversity as well.

There is well-known overall geographical variation in the distribution of the black population as well. In 1860 nearly 92 percent of the black population lived in the South, and this percent remained about the same until the great migration began in 1910 (Farley and Allen, 1989, p. 109). However, just over half of the black population lived in the South as of the 1990 census (Harrison and Bennett 1995, p. 151). As of the 1990 census, blacks comprised 10.3 percent of the population in the Northeast, 9.5 percent in the Midwest, 18.3 percent in the South, but only 5.1 percent in the West regions of the United States (Harrison and Bennett 1995, p. 150). Thus, the relative size of the black population varies significantly by region, with implications for black experience of diversity and their role in the multiethnic world. Research by Massey and Hajnal (1995) has measured the large-scale segregation of the black population from 1900 to the present, revealing that in the early part of the century African Americans were highly segregated at the state and county level, though the segregation declined at the state level until 1970. Starting in about 1950, however, segregation at the municipal level began to increase. This increase, in combination with the increase in segregation at the neighborhood level, means that over time African Americans have segregated at smaller and smaller geographical units at the same time as they increased their distribution across more and more states.

A more familiar arena for geographical variations in both the size of groups and their distribution across space is the metropolitan area. Specific metropolitan areas are more or less multiethnic in character, and in 1990 the most multiethnic metropolitan areas were located in California, the South, or in Chicago or the New York area (Frey and Farley 1996). Within metropolitan areas there is a strong tendency for blacks to be in the central city rather than the suburbs (Phelan and Schneider 1996), while Asians, and to some extent Hispanics, are found in the suburbs in larger numbers (Logan, Alba, and Leung 1996).

These multiethnic metropolitan areas have implications not only for the context of diversity in which blacks live, but for the spatial distribution of the black population within the metropolitan areas as well. Despite a sixty year history of extreme segregation from non-Hispanic whites, particularly in metropolitan areas in the Northeast and Midwest (Massey and Denton 1993), research from the 1990 census shows that black segregation is both lower and has declined more in the more multiethnic metropolitan areas than the less multiethnic ones (Frey and Farley 1996). However, African American residential segregation, usually about double that of Asians and one and one-half times that of Hispanics, remains at very high absolute levels and will take a long time to decline (Massey and Denton 1993; Farley and Frey 1994). The structure of segregation has been so strongly entrenched in our metropolitan areas for so long, and has led to such disastrous consequences for poor blacks who are forced to live in areas of concentrated poverty (Massey and Denton 1993; Wilson 1987, 1996), that any factor associated with alleviating it is important.

In some places the nature of black segregation is so extreme that it poses an almost independent factor, limiting African American experience of the new multiethnic world. Thirteen metropolitan areas, Baltimore, Buffalo, Chicago, Cleveland, Detroit, Gary, Indianapolis, Kansas City, Los Angeles, Milwaukee, Newark, New York and Philadelphia, were so highly segregated on multiple dimensions of segregation that they were termed "hypersegregated" (Denton 1994). Declines in segregation in the two most recent decades tended to be larger in newer, smaller metropolitan areas in the South and the West, and in those with small proportionate black populations (Massey and Denton 1993; Farley and Frey 1994).

A complete inventory of the causes of residential segregation and discrimination, and the historical documentation to back it up, is beyond the scope of this discussion but has been documented elsewhere (cf. Farley et al. 1993; Massey and Denton 1993; Jackson 1985; Turner and Wienk 1993; Yinger 1995, among others). While there is considerable discussion and debate about the amount of the segregation accounted for by each factor, there is considerable agreement among researchers that the contemporary segregation is the result of the following four factors: differences in suburbanization, differences in income, differences in attitudes, and differences in discrimination. None of these factors alone is sufficient to explain current segregation, especially for the black population. The increases in the Hispanic and Asian populations via immigration are thought to maintain or increase their segregation as the dispersion of longer-term residents is offset by the concentration on the part of the new immigrants (Harrison and Bennett 1995), but for blacks, segregation seems much more rooted in the longstanding racial structure of the United States.

From this analysis of the different distributions of the black population across space, it is clear that the local context, as well as the past history of discrimination in housing, will both play a role in how African Americans seek to solve the problem of the "color line" and further progress in the 21st century. Given the greater variety of conditions in which they find themselves, in itself a sign of progress, there will be a need for different strategies for action and change. As their experiences become increasingly heterogeneous, it will be harder to define "the black position" on issues (if this ever were possible), as even those who share similar goals will be operating in different contexts, depending not only on the size of their own group but on the specifics of the multiethnic context in which they live.

THE MEANING OF DIVERSITY FOR AFRICAN AMERICANS

Thus far, I have shown that while the U.S. population is increasing in diversity dramatically, the proportionate share of the population that is black is not changing much. We have also examined definitional and spatial issues associated with the increasing diversity from the point of view of African Americans. This section rounds out the analysis by focusing on the implications of these changes for African Americans, particularly the stable population share. As shown, African Americans will remain at about 11–12 percent of the U.S. population for the foreseeable future, during a time when non-Hispanic whites will decline to roughly half of the population and Hispanics and Asians will increase to almost 20 and just over 11 percent, respectively. What will this mean for African Americans? Will the effects of living in this multiethnic world be positive or negative?

Taking the negative effects first, any advantage that has accrued to African Americans in the national consciousness as a result of being the largest, the "main," the historically oldest (as a result of the decimation of the Native American population) minority group will cease. As Hispanics come to outnumber blacks by two to one, and as the Asian population grows to almost equal the black population in size, it will be harder to make the case for the uniqueness of the black situation, no matter how historically correct that case may be.

Second, these demographic changes in relative shares of the population will have direct implications for blacks' achievement of greater political power. In a representative democracy, one way to increase political power is by coming to represent a larger share of the population, the situation that Hispanics and Asians will be in. Blacks, with their constant share, will have to gain representation by attracting the votes of non-blacks or through coalitions. However, both of these options are severely limited by the residential segregation and isolation of blacks. To the extent that politicians continue to represent a certain geographical area, the fact that in many center-city areas blacks comprise nearly 90 percent of the population will imply that they continue to waste votes on candidates that could win with only a simple majority. In addition, there is increasingly a rejection of the ideal of integration among certain segments of the black community (Patterson 1997). While understandable, it, too, will limit access to political power.

Third, as a result of the new immigration, it will become increasingly common to compare the status of blacks to both the older Southern, Central, and Eastern Europeans and the new Hispanic and Asian immigrants. These comparisons, based on data showing the relative status differences among the population by race/ethnicity from the 1990 census (Harrison and Bennett 1995), as well as the inequality between whites and blacks in status (Oliver and Shapiro 1995), could easily result in blacks being seen as "failures" twice, once at the beginning and once at the end of the 21st century. From the black perspective, the sting of these negative comparisons, unfair because they ignore structural context, will be compounded by the feeling of having been "passed over" twice in their struggle for full participation in U.S. society, once by the European immigrants and now by the non-European immigrant groups.

Fourth, it is undeniable that the civil rights movement began as a black movement and that its programs and processes have been used as a model for other groups as they sought inclusion in U.S. society. However, to the extent that these other groups are successful, and to the extent that identity politics continues to be important, blacks will find it harder and harder to make their claims for special or unique treatment. Their best allies in this cause would be whites, but whites are precisely the group that has organized the social structure to be what it is, with the corresponding results for blacks. Also, white-black interaction and cooperation is limited by the fact that, as a group, whites have so little individual and personal experience with blacks, though this situation is slowly changing.

These first four implications that I see resulting from the changing

U.S. population diversity for blacks are all negative. I point them out to encourage thought and discussion about how we might best work for change, should they prove true. Ignoring them, and relying on old forms of rhetoric, argument, and action will not suffice. However, increasing diversity also has positive implications for blacks.

The first of these is that a constant share of the population implies that to the extent that the level of black disadvantage can be kept the same, or lowered, there will not be a rapid increase in the number of disadvantaged black citizens for the U.S. population to deal with. Care must be taken to repeatedly emphasize just how few in total number, relative to the total U.S. population, the most disadvantaged blacks are (Jargowsky 1997; Patterson 1997).

A second positive impact of the increasing diversity is that white hegemony might have been easier to maintain when it could be focused on only one "other" group, namely, blacks. The presence of so many different groups may lead whites to see the need to share power, though this will not come easily. However, in studying the dramatic increase in multiethnic neighborhoods in the metropolitan areas of the United States, I am struck by the fact that even though whites still are unlikely to have blacks as neighbors, if they have nonwhite neighbors, then they are likely to have a variety of nonwhite neighbors, including blacks (Denton and Anderson 1995; Denton and Alba 1998). The meaning of this trend and whether or not it will continue in the future are as yet unanswered questions, but the trend is unmistakable. In 1990 nearly half of Houston and Los Angeles neighborhoods contained at least one hundred of each of the four population groups, as did one fourth of the neighborhoods in New York. These multiethnic neighborhoods contained substantial white population, were located in both center cities and suburbs, and arose in a context of dramatic decline in all-white neighborhoods (Denton and Anderson 1995). Using a slightly different standard of either 98 or 95 percent non-Hispanic white to define "all-white," Denton and Alba (1998) found that these all-white neighborhoods had declined almost to the point of nonexistence in center cities, and in suburbs they represented only half of the suburban neighborhoods in the Midwest and Northeast in 1990, and far fewer in the other regions. To the extent that proximity encourages understanding and coalition building, there is progress to report.

A third positive impact that may come from the increasing diversity is that as white proportionate dominance decreases whites, too, will have to look to outside groups for support in the political arena. Black Americans, despite the long history of racism in this country, have the distinct advantage of being American, speaking English, and believing in the American Dream. Research by Hochschild shows this latter point to be especially true for the poorest blacks, while middle-class blacks focus on concerns about the lack of progress of the group as a whole (Hochschild 1995). While whites may seem like the most unlikely of possible allies for blacks, common citizenship and language do provide advantages in this direction compared to new immigrants.

How these positive and negative effects of increasing population diversity will play out for African Americans remains to be seen. No doubt, different effects will be recognized by others and all the effects will operate differently in different places because of the varying contexts described above. It is also likely to be difficult to assess the effects of population diversity for African Americans because some of the positive and negative effects could offset each other by working in opposite directions.

HOW WE DISCUSS RACE

While no doubt others will draw different implications from the effect of the increasing population diversity on blacks, it remains the reality we all face and in which further black progress must be made. Because further black progress will entail new strategies and initiatives, it is important to reflect on how we carry out our discussions regarding race and ethnicity and the problems linked to them in U.S. society. Three distinct areas of "misinformation" are present in many discussions that do nothing to aid our understanding of the problems themselves, or of racial and ethnic groups different from our own. Furthermore, they prevent effective communication and agreement on plans, policies, and programs of action that might help to alleviate the current situation in which too many people of color, as well as poor people in general, find themselves. These areas of misinformation may be summarized as: (1) denial of racism and discrimination as a contemporary force in society; (2) misuse, bordering on abuse, of statistical information to the point where correct information becomes a source of ignorance rather than information; and (3) the inability of groups participating in the discussion of race/ethnic issues to correctly identify their enemies.

The denial of the force of current racism and current discrimination is in part a function of the contemporary nature of both of these phenomena. Racism and discrimination in the 1990s had two primary characteristics that distinguished them from their counterparts in earlier eras: They were increasingly subtle, and thus hard to detect and their decrease over the course of the past thirty, fifty or one hundred years was in itself a mark of the progress we have made in race relations. The subtlety of current racism and discrimination means that they are almost invisible to many, if not most, whites, and to many blacks and other people of color (Yinger 1993). Whites witness few examples of overt racism or discrimination, and thus conclude that there isn't much around. Blacks and other people of color find themselves in situations where they are treated well but denied opportunities they think they should have gotten, which forces them to ask themselves if it was really racism or discrimination (Feagin and Sikes 1994).

Since I am white, people of color sometimes argue with me on this point, saying that a black always can tell if someone is a racist. It is probably true that a black can tell more often than a white can, but if a black goes to a realtor in search of a house or an apartment and is shown three, there is no possible way for her to know that a similarly positioned white was shown six, was quoted more favorable terms and conditions, was called back several times as new units entered the market, and so forth and so on. Housing audit programs routinely find these types of discriminatory treatment that is undetectable by the victim (Yinger 1995).

But it is not only the fact that racism and discrimination are hard to detect that causes people to deny their existence. Another source for this denial on the part of whites, especially, but also blacks, results from a desire to stop discussing issues of race, to move beyond race to a "color-blind" society. Some cite the indicators of absolute progress on the part of blacks as evidence for this point (Patterson 1997; Thernstrom and Thernstrom 1997), ignoring the fact that the remaining gaps between blacks and whites have structural and not just individual causes. Though many would welcome a true color-blind society, an article by legal scholar John Powell in the *San Francisco Law Review* offers a clear, well-documented critique of the use of the concept in the society we live in. He points out that the color-blind position assumes that the law recognizes only individuals and not groups, that race is irrelevant, and that the world is fair (Powell 1995, pp. 892–893), despite the fact that none of these points is true. He goes on to argue that we must strive to end the structure of racial domination and to do that we must know the race of the people being harmed by it.

The second area of concern is how conversations about race misuse and abuse statistics, particularly rates. Rates express the number of events as a function of the population at risk for experiencing such events. They clearly establish the relative risk of events in a group, and can easily be compared across groups of very different sizes. Thus, we can compare the death rate for Rhode Island to the death rate for California without being concerned that California is so much bigger than Rhode Island, and therefore has more people dying each year. However, when these types of comparisons are done across racial groups, particularly on sensitive issues like poverty, joblessness, crime, out-of-wedlock births, drug use, and so on, too often factually correct comparisons are used in ways that are substantively misleading. Taking poverty as an example, if the black poverty rate is triple the white poverty rate, then the probability that an individual black approaching you on the street is poor is three times the probability that an individual white approaching you is poor. That statement is true, but it is completely context-less as a basis for behavior because it ignores the absolute value of the rate itself. According to the 1990 census, the white family poverty rate was 7.0 and the black was 23.9, so 93 percent of the whites approaching you would be nonpoor as would over 75 percent of the blacks. If the goal is to avoid contact with poor people, race makes a poor marker for identifying them.

The example works the same if one is comparing employment, crime, drug abuse, teen pregnancy, or any of the other comparisons regularly focused on in the media. Thus, people form the impression that most blacks (1) do not work, (2) have illegitimate children, or (3) deal drugs based only on the knowledge that they are twice (or three times or four times) as likely to do so as whites, rather than looking at the actual rates of the behavior. An analogous problem occurs with issues relating to the so-called "underclass," those living in high-poverty areas in cities. Even if the rates of "negative" behavior surpass 50 percent, which they seldom do, there is still a substantial proportion of the population in these areas *not* engaging in them. By focusing only on the comparisons between the two racial groups, the larger groups of people who are not poor, not unwed mothers, not on welfare, and so on, are left out of the public's consciousness.

The final aspect of what I am calling misinformation occurs when groups with different proposed solutions to a problem try to decide which solution is correct, will work best, or be funded. As a result of a number of factors, including competition for scarce resources and the tendency to define problems too narrowly, opponents with different means to the same larger goal get turned into enemies, and the fact that both sides have the same larger goal, namely, African American progress, gets lost. For example, concerned people strenuously argue the importance of in-place strategies versus dispersal strategies as solutions to the problems of poor blacks in disadvantaged innercity neighborhoods. These are different solutions to a serious problem. By failing to focus on the larger goal of black progress, concerned groups are left open to manipulation and exploitation by those who do not share the goal of black progress at all.

To get beyond the situation we are in today regarding the unequal status of black Americans in U.S. society, remembering these points will facilitate open discussion. Nothing is helped by denying the existence of discrimination, focusing only on comparisons of rates and not their overall level, and mistaking opponents for enemies. In a complex world, divergent views of a situation are not necessarily contradictory.

What needs to be done now is to focus more on the process of change and how it works. The changes in the status of the black population in the last fifty years have been monumental but so have the changes in society. It is of great concern that so many are still left behind, but it was equally unrealistic to think that all would move ahead at the same rate. The arrival of a multiethnic future poses new challenges and raises old ones in new ways. The task ahead is to maintain the upward momentum of the black middle-class, at the same time reaching back to bring along those left behind. These goals will require that people of all races see that it is in their interest to work together. Nothing will be gained by focusing on any of these goals or groups in isolation. That is the meaning of a multiethnic world.

REFERENCES

Alba, Richard D. 1990. *Ethnic Identity: The Transformation of White America.* New Haven, CT: Yale University Press.

Denton, Nancy A. 1994. "Are African Americans Still Hypersegregated?" in *Residential Apartheid: The American Legacy* (pp. 49–81), edited by Robert D. Bullard, J. Eugene Grigsby, and Charles Lee. Los Angeles: CAAS Publications.

———. 1997. "Racial Identity and Census Categories: Can Incorrect Categories Yield Correct Information?" *Law and Inequality: A Journal of Theory and Practice* XV: 83–97.

Denton, Nancy A. and Richard D. Alba. 1998. "The Decline of the All-White Neighborhood and the Growth of Suburban Diversity." Paper prepared for the Suburban Racial Change Conference, Harvard University, March 28, 1998.

Denton, Nancy A. and Bridget J. Anderson. 1995. "A Tale of Five Cities: Neighborhood Change in Philadelphia, Chicago, Miami, Houston and Los Angeles, 1970–1990." Paper presented at the annual meetings of the Population Association of America, San Francisco, CA, April 6–8.

Du Bois, W.E.B. 1978. *On Sociology and the Black Community*. Edited by Dan
    S. Green and Edwin D. Driver. Chicago: University of Chicago Press.
Edmonston, Barry and Jeffrey S. Passell. 1994. "Ethnic Demography: U.S. Im-
    migration and Ethnic Variations" in *Immigration and Ethnicity: The In-
    tegration of America's Newest Arrivals* (pp. 1–30), edited by Barry
    Edmonston and Jeffrey S. Passell. Washington, DC: Urban Institute
    Press.
Farley, Reynolds and Walter R. Allen. 1989. *The Color Line and the Quality
    of Life in America*. New York: Oxford University Press.
Farley, Reynolds and William H. Frey. 1994. "Changes in the Segregation of
    Whites from Blacks during the 1980s: Small Steps toward a More Ra-
    cially Integrated Society." *American Sociological Review* 59: 23–45.
Farley, Reynolds, Charlotte Steeh, Tara Jackson, Maria Krysan, and Keith
    Reeves. 1993. "Continued Racial Residential Segregation in Detroit:
    'Chocolate City, Vanilla Suburbs' Revisited." *Journal of Housing Re-
    search* 4: 1–38.
Feagin, Joe R. and Melvin P. Sikes. 1994. *Living with Racism: The Black
    Middle-Class Experience*. Boston: Beacon Press.
Frey, William H. 1995a. "Immigration Impacts on Internal Migration of the
    Poor: 1990 Census Evidence for US States." *International Journal of
    Population Geography* 1: 51–67.
————. 1995b. "The New Geography of Population Shifts: Trends Toward
    Balkanization" in *State of the Union: America in the 1990s, Volume Two,
    Social Trends* (pp. 271–334), edited by Reynolds Farley. New York:
    Russell Sage.
————. 1993. "The New Urban Revival in the United States." *Urban Studies*
    30: 741–774.
Frey, William H. and Reynolds Farley. 1996. "Latino, Asian and Black Segre-
    gation in U.S. Metropolitan Areas: Are Multiethnic Metros Different?"
    Demography 33: 35–50.
Harrison, Roderick J. and Claudette E. Bennett. 1995. "Racial and Ethnic Di-
    versity" in *State of the Union: America in the 1990s, Volume Two, Social
    Trends* (pp. 141–210), edited by Reynolds Farley. New York: Russell
    Sage.
Hollinger, David A. 1995. *Postethnic America: Beyond Multiculturalism*. New
    York: Basic Books.
Hochschild, Jennifer L. 1995. *Facing Up to the Dream: Race, Class, and the
    Soul of the Nation*. Princeton, NJ: Princeton University Press.
Jackson, Kenneth T. 1985. *Crabgrass Frontier: The Suburbanization of the
    United States*. New York: Oxford University Press.
Jargowsky, Paul A. 1997. *Poverty and Place: Ghettos, Barrios and the Ameri-
    can City*. New York: Russell Sage Foundation.
Lieberson, Stanley. 1980. *A Piece of the Pie: Blacks and White Immigrants
    Since 1880*. Berkeley: University of California Press.
Logan, John R., Richard D. Alba, and Shu-Yin Leung. 1996. "Minority Access

to White Suburbs: A Multiregional Comparison." *Social Forces* 74: 851–881.

Massey, Douglas S. and Nancy A. Denton. 1993. *American Apartheid: Segregation and the Making of the Underclass.* Boston: Harvard University Press.

Massey, Douglas S. and Zoltan L. Hajnal. 1995. "The Changing Geographic Structure of Black-White Segregation in the United States." *Social Science Quarterly* 76: 527–542.

McDaniel, Antonio. 1996. "The Dynamic Racial Composition of the United States" in *An American Dilemma Revisited: Race Relations in a Changing World* (pp. 269–287), edited by Obie Clayton, Jr. New York: Russell Sage Foundation.

Oliver, Melvin L. and Thomas M. Shapiro. 1995. *Black Wealth/White Wealth: A New Perspective on Racial Inequality.* New York: Routledge.

Passell, Jeffrey S. and Barry Edmonston. 1994. "Immigration and Race: Recent Trends in Immigration to the United States" in *Immigration and Ethnicity: The Integration of America's Newest Arrivals* (pp. 31–71), edited by Barry Edmonston and Jeffrey S. Passel. Washington, DC: The Urban Institute Press.

Patterson, Orlando. 1997. *The Ordeal of Integration: Progress and Resentment in America's "Racial" Crisis.* Washington, DC: Civitas.

Phelan, Thomas J. and Mark Schneider. 1996. "Race, Ethnicity, and Class in American Suburbs." *Urban Affairs Review* 31: 659–680.

Powell, John A. 1995. "An Agenda for the Post-Civil Rights Era." *University of San Francisco Law Review* 29: 889–910.

Rosenbaum, James E. 1995. "Changing the Geography of Opportunity by Expanding Residential Choice: Lessons from the Gautreaux Program." *Housing Policy Debate* 6: 231–269.

Thernstrom, Stephan and Abigail Thernstrom. 1997. *America in Black and White: One Nation, Indivisible.* New York: Simon and Schuster.

Turner, Margery Austin and Ron Wienk. 1993. "The Persistence of Segregation in Urban Areas: Contributing Causes" in *Housing Markets and Residential Mobility* (pp. 193–216), edited by G. Thomas Kingsley and Margery Austin Turner. Washington, DC: Urban Institute Press.

U.S. Bureau of the Census. 1997. "Census 2000 Questionnaire to Allow Multiple Race Responses; No Multiracial Category." *Census and You* 32(11): 1.

———. 1998. "United States Population Estimates, by Age, Sex, Race, and Hispanic Origin, 1990 to 1997." Release PPL-91, updated tables at http://www.census.gov/population/estimates/nation/intfile3–1.txt.

Waters, Mary C. 1990. *Ethnic Options: Choosing Identities in America.* Berkeley: University of California Press.

Wilson, William J. 1987. *The Truly Disadvantaged: The Inner City, the Underclass, and Public Policy.* Chicago: University of Chicago Press.

Wilson, William Julius. 1996. *When Work Disappears.* New York: Knopf.

Yinger, John. 1993. *The 1989 Housing Study: Results and Implications in Clear and Convincing Evidence of Discrimination in America*. Edited by Michael Fix and Raymond I. Steuyk. Washington, DC: Urban Institute Press.

Zack, Naomi. 1993. *American Mixed Race: The Culture of Microdiversity*. Lanthan, MD: Rowman and Littlefield.

9

Old Wine in New Bottles: The Reality of Modern Racism

Joe R. Feagin and Hernan M. Vera

After the O. J. Simpson trial President Bill Clinton made an interesting comment: "I think what has struck all Americans in the aftermath of the trial is the apparent differences of perception of the same set of facts based on the race of American citizens."[1] He added that "I have been surprised by the depth of the divergence in so many areas, and I do think we need to work on it."[2] This is an oddly naive statement, coming as it did not long after the 1992 Los Angeles riot, the open racism of a Los Angeles detective testifying in the Simpson trial, the revelations about police brutality in cities from Philadelphia and New Orleans to Los Angeles, and the openly racist ideologies of militia groups. White leaders' timidity on matters of racial justice and equality is a sign of our political times.

The ideal of equality and justice was proclaimed during the struggle for American independence. The ideal was gradually expanded to include racial equality during the Civil War period and again during the civil rights movement of the 1960s. Yet, from the beginning, this bold ideal has been attacked by conservatives, white supremacists, and other antiequality advocates. The advocates of reaction are growing in number. One might even say that they seem to be plotting a coup against the ideal of equality. Leading white politicians, business leaders, and influential intellectuals are openly questioning the ideals of racial equality and social justice. In order to do this, they are also denying the persisting reality of white racism.

The line dividing the overt ideology of white supremacy and current white-mainstream political and intellectual discourse is blurred. In the area of race, most contemporary supporters of white privilege have abandoned the language of blatant racism for such thinly disguised code words as "quotas," "reverse discrimination," "welfare queens," "street crime," and "undesirable immigrants." The claim that African Americans, Latinos, and other people of color are unintelligent, lazy, welfare-preferring, and criminal, which marked an era in U.S. history said (by whites) to have passed decades ago, is aggressively resurfacing in the speeches, media soundbites, books, articles, and political programs of prominent politicians, media pundits, and academics. For example, since the 1980s many speeches of politicians and many books from major U.S. publishers have targeted the character and cultures of people of color as inferior, openly defended racial elitism, and questioned the fundamental ideals of equality, pluralism, and democracy.

This attack on racial and ethnic equality is not just a matter of passing rhetoric or media fads. The ideas so aggressively disseminated underlie California's Proposition 187, a law that denies immigrants of color basic health care and educational access. These ideas are central to the thinking of members of Congress who are pushing legislation that would keep welfare benefits from legal immigrants, who make up a major portion of Latino Americans. Notions of racial favoritism inspire the defunding of many social programs benefitting poor Americans and Americans of color. Across the nation private and public agencies are dismantling affirmative action and other social justice programs on the claim they create "unfair privileges" for people of color. Criminal justice systems often target people of color while ignoring many white perpetrators of white-collar crimes, and many prisons are becoming warehouses for young black and Latino men.

Today, the main enemies of equality and democracy are not poor Americans, new immigrant workers, allegedly "defective-in-IQ" black and Latino Americans, or African American leaders like the much discussed Louis Farrakhan. The *real* enemies are at, or close to, the centers of power in our society. They are for the most part well-educated white Americans, mostly white men. They include many of the white business and political leaders of this nation. Their understandings of current and future changes in the economy, in politics, and in society are dramatically different from those across the racial divide—the growing numbers of

African Americans, Latino Americans, Asian Americans, and other Americans of color.

Perhaps one reason for current attacks on racial equality and people of color is the cynical exploitation by leading white politicians and opinion makers of the fear among many whites of the demographic transition that is well underway. Whites are a small and decreasing proportion of the world's population. They are currently a statistical minority of the population in four of the five largest U.S. cities, including New York, Los Angeles, Chicago, and Houston. They are a minority in large areas of south Florida and south Texas. Indeed, by the year 2005 whites will constitute less than half the population of California, and by the year 2055 whites will likely be a minority in the United States as a whole. Little can be done to stop these large-scale changes, but many white leaders seem to want to take harsh action.

CRAFTING ANTIEGALITARIANISM

"We need to decide if we want all that equality in America." This comment was made in the mid-1990s when National Public Radio conducted a focus group on the federal budget. Such sharp words make one wonder just how many white Americans hold such a view of the nation's thematic ideal of social and racial equality.

For centuries the systematic propagation of racist ideas has been centered among those at the top of the society, among political and economic leaders and intellectuals. Today, one sees evidence of elite involvement in antiegalitarian efforts everywhere. Take, for example, the strong arguments against racial and social equality in *The Bell Curve*, which has sold at least a half million copies.[3] In this lengthy best-seller the late Richard Herrnstein and Charles Murray use highly suspect data to argue that black and Latino Americans are inferior in intelligence to whites. Interestingly, the openly antiegalitarian arguments in the book have received little attention. After making their "IQ" arguments in great detail, Herrnstein and Murray openly attack the ideals of racial equality and social justice. They see the United States as a divided society where inequality is a *necessary and permanent* feature. Herrnstein and Murray imply that the ideal of equality has "done only some good, but most of its effects are bad."

Other influential analysts go further in rejecting the ideals of democracy and equality. Pulitzer-prize-winning journalist William Henry III argues that the myth of egalitarianism is responsible for what he perceives to be the "dumbing down" of America. He vigorously attacks the

view that everyone has something significant to contribute to society and
the argument that most cultures offer something worth knowing. He re-
pudiates the idea that a just society could provide equal success across
various racial and ethnic groups, arguing that many democratic notions
are hopelessly wrong. Multiculturalism is said to be "deeply harmful,"
and such programs miss the point that European "conquest and coloni-
zation" were successful "in dispersing administratively and technologi-
cally superior cultures and compelling inferior ones to adapt." White
colonizers, from this old myth-creating perspective, brought liberating
civilization to peoples around the globe.[4]

Who is fostering and funding this outburst of rhetoric against citizens
of color in this country? Arch-conservative think-tanks—including the
American Enterprise Institute, the Manhattan Institute, the Political Club
for Growth, and the Heritage Foundation—and the powerful right-wing
interests controlling major magazines and newspapers have conducted an
aggressive indoctrination campaign aimed at shaping public views on
equality and inequality issues. Working alongside these right-wing think-
tanks is a large group of conservative intellectuals, media experts, political activists, and political advisers. The right-wing propaganda is not
just a matter of isolated intellectuals talking to each other. Their elitist
theories create an intellectual atmosphere breathed deeply by business
and political leaders who act on the ideas. Right-wing intellectuals and
pundits advise major politicians and write legislative programs and
speeches.[5]

Talk show commentators like Rush Limbaugh are critical to this right-
wing defense of inequality and the general attack on people of color.
Heard and watched by millions of white Americans, Limbaugh articu-
lates a philosophy celebrating white men and spices his shows with
antigay, antihomeless, and antifemale comments. During the 1992 campaign for the U.S. presidency, George Bush invited Limbaugh to the
White House, and subsequently Limbaugh aggressively campaigned for
Bush. Later, Bush's campaign adviser Roger Ailes became the producer
for Limbaugh's television program.[6] Ronald Reagan called Limbaugh
"the number one voice for conservatism in our country," and former
cabinet official William Bennett described him as "possibly our greatest
living American."[7] Many analysts suggested that the 1994 Republican
congressional victories came in part because of Limbaugh, who is heard
by twenty million Americans on hundreds of radio stations, and other
right-wing talk show hosts.

The assault on equality no longer emanates just from segregationists
and Klan-type groups, which once dominated much racist discourse, but

now comes directly from important groups in the business and political establishments. The defense of inherited privilege and of the cultural superiority of European Americans reflects the interests of many in the dominant white elites. The American Enterprise Institute (AEI) is a major source of new right-wing perspectives on social and racial matters. Charles Murray, Dinesh D'Souza, Milton Friedman, Michael Novak, Lynn Cheney, and Herb Stein, among others, have been linked to this influential think-tank. Sunbelt millionaires and antidemocratic organizations like the Olin Foundation are important sources of funding for AEI and other conservative think-tanks. The AEI is not marginalized on the far right but is linked closely by money and personal ties to the corporate elite and major political figures. One aggressive fund-raising drive for AEI involved no less than the heads of General Motors, General Electric, and Citicorp. Moreover, many in the Reagan and Bush administrations, as well as later Republican leaders, have maintained close ties to the AEI and other right-wing organizations.[8]

The right-wing attack against equality since the 1970s has been rather successful. The dominant white perspective has moved from the moderate liberalism of the 1960s and 1970s toward antidemocratic and more explicitly racist and antiegalitarian perspectives. The intent is to gain white assent for the growing social inequalities in U.S. society.

Why has there been a concerted attack on equality? Aside from the decline in white demographic dominance and the need to reassure the privileged of the legitimacy of their privileges and good fortune, another reason for fostering an antiequality perspective is to deflect the attention of rank-and-file whites from wrenching changes now occurring in the U.S. economy. It is difficult for political, economic, and media elites to explain to these Americans why they must accept lower-wage jobs and reduced life conditions compared to previous generations. As white workers struggle to adjust their lives to less, their anger grows. In recent years many companies have terminated large numbers of employees and many average Americans have had to endure hardship. At the same time, the wealthy have been getting wealthier. For example, the ratio between the earnings of the average corporate CEO and the average U.S. production worker was 120 to 1 in the mid-1990s, up from about 35 to 1 two decades earlier.[9]

The redistribution of income upward has triggered a major legitimacy crisis, with many ordinary citizens questioning the economic or political systems. Significant sectors of the white establishment have responded to this legitimacy crisis with a conservative ideology. Rather than openly discuss the real reasons for political and economic crisis—such as the redistribution of wealth and corporate investment outside the United States—the elites and their minions prefer to focus blame on long-standing white scapegoats for social and economic problems: people of color, new immigrants, and, in certain circles, the Jews. Those in power use scapegoating to reassure white society at large, and themselves, that exploitation of the rest of the population is legitimate.

DENYING RACISM

Recently, a black college instructor, Winona, told us about an encounter she had with a white administrator at a college where she worked. The administrator was helping a white student group raise money for religious work by holding a mock "slave auction," complete with posters showing an African slave. When the black professional objected to this racist activity, the white administrator at first stared blankly into her face, as if to say "What's your problem?," and then retorted that "Slavery has been over for hundreds of years; no one thinks of it in terms of black and white any more, so why make a big deal of it?"[10]

For a short period in the late 1960s and early 1970s there was a more liberal discourse on matters of racial and social equality, discussions influenced by civil rights and other populist protests of the time. Among many white politicians and media commentators, the older perspectives on white racial superiority were abandoned for the ideal of racial equality, and concepts like "white racism," "racial discrimination," and "institutional racism" were used in academic, popular, and media analyses. The 1968 National Advisory Commission's description of "two societies, one black, one white—separate and unequal"—was taken seriously as a national problem in need of speedy redress.[11]

By the late 1970s these egalitarian perspectives were being countered and replaced by a reactionary discourse among prominent white (and a few conservative non-European) intellectuals, media commentators, and politicians. Since that time certain concepts and code words—such as "underclass," "reverse discrimination," "cultural pathology," "culture of poverty," "dangerous immigrants," and "low IQs" among people of color—have been aggressively marketed by commentators as influential and diverse as Nathan Glazer, Thomas Edsall, Nicholas Lemann, Ken Auletta, Daniel Patrick Moynihan, Thomas Sowell, William J. Wilson, Jim Sleeper, Dinesh D'Souza, Peter Brimelow, Charles Murray, and Richard Herrnstein.

One central device of the conservative critics of equality efforts is a firm denial of significant social inequalities rooted in the actions of the dominant white group. In 1975 Harvard professor Nathan Glazer was one of the first American intellectuals to argue, in an influential book, that the United States is winning the battle against discrimination, indeed, that "no one is now excluded from the broadest access" to the economy and society. Glazer attributed continuing black inequality to pathologies internal to black communities and argued that affirmative action was wrong-headed, reverse discrimination.[12] Since the mid-1970s white intellectuals in a variety of fields have embellished these arguments. For example, in his *Wealth and Poverty*, once called the "Bible of the Reagan-Bush administrations," economist and presidential advisor George Gilder declared there was no need for government action to assist black Americans because it was impossible to find a white racist in any position of power and because discrimination had been all but abolished. Whatever inequalities remained were the fault of black Americans and their subculture.[13]

Today, a large majority of white Americans at all levels, including politicians, scholars, and talk show commentators, believe that discrimination is no longer a serious problem in the United States. According to recent opinion polls, most whites believe black Americans have made great civil rights and economic progress and should now be content. In a *New Republic* article, neoliberal intellectual Leon Wieseltier argues that black leaders have exaggerated racism as a cause of problems and that black insistence on widespread discrimination is "madness," that "in the memory of racial oppression, oppression outlives itself. The scar does the work of the wound."[14] Like many white commentators, Wieseltier regards the scars of past discrimination as far more serious than present discrimination.

One editor for *Business Week*, Elizabeth Ehrlich, has praised arguments of conservative commentators about the "declining significance of racism" and suggested that the emphasis of black leaders on racial discrimination and redress is unconstructive.[15] Moreover, in *The End of Racism* the journalist Dinesh D'Souza, whose career has been greatly fostered by the AEI and the Heritage Foundation, argues not only that racism has now come to an end but also that the historical background of racial inequalities has been wrongly perceived. Slavery had some good features, such as bringing Africans into contact with Western "civilization." Citing arguments of the conservative black leader Booker T. Washington, D'Souza concludes that "slavery proved to the transmission belt that nevertheless brought Africans into the orbit of modern civilization and Western freedom."[16] D'Souza further argues that legal segregation was developed by well-meaning Southern elites to protect black

Americans from poor whites angry over losing the Civil War. In spite
of the often preposterous character of his racial claims, D'Souza's book
has been widely reviewed and seriously discussed by white leaders and
intellectuals.

THE REALITY OF MODERN RACISM

The evidence strongly contradicts widespread denials of racism. Today
the overwhelming majority of white Americans still admit to pollsters
that they hold negative attitudes about and stereotypes of African Americans. When asked, most whites show some racist understandings or
inclinations. For example, in a 1992 Anti-Defamation League survey
most whites said they agreed with one or more antiblack stereotypes.
Evaluating a list of eight black stereotypes, including "prefer to accept
welfare" and have "less native intelligence," three-quarters of the whites
agreed with one or more, and just over half agreed with two or more.[17]
In a 1994 National Opinion Research Center (NORC) national survey
whites were asked to evaluate on a scale (1–7) how work-oriented blacks
are. A small percentage, 16 percent, ranked blacks at the hard-working
end; just under half chose the lazy end of the spectrum. In surveys, the
majority of whites also refuse to view racial discrimination as a major
barrier for people of color. In a 1994 NORC survey, when whites were
asked the question, "On the average blacks have worse jobs, income,
and housing than white people. Do you think these differences are mainly
due to discrimination?," more than six in ten said no. When asked if the
differences were mainly due to the fact that most blacks "just don't have
the motivation or will power to pull themselves up out of poverty?," the
majority said yes.[18]

Indeed, many whites defend racial discrimination in some cases. For
example, a 1994 NORC survey found 35 percent of whites saying that
white homeowners should have the legal right to refuse to sell their home
to a black person, which is of course contrary to existing federal law.[19]

There are contradictions in white views and actions on racial matters.
Public opinion polls make it clear that, in the abstract, a majority of
white Americans say they believe in equal opportunity for all Americans.
Moreover, most whites believe that racial equality has already been attained. In a survey for the National Conference a large majority of whites
agreed that black Americans currently have equal opportunities with
whites in regard to a quality education and skilled jobs.[20]

Nonetheless, many whites—sometimes the majority of whites in the
position to act—persist in overt racial discrimination in employment,

housing, and other sectors of U.S. society. A 1990 study of hiring discrimination in Washington, D.C., and Chicago used matched pairs of
black and white (male) testers to apply for entry-level jobs. Twenty percent of the black men received unfavorable and differential treatment.[21]
And a Los Angeles survey of more than 1,000 African Americans found
that within the past year six in ten reported having faced workplace
discrimination, such as being refused a job because of their race or suffering racial slurs. The study also found that a majority of highly educated Asian and Latino workers reported workplace discrimination.[22]
Most strikingly, in a federal survey involving 3,800 test audits in twenty-
five metropolitan areas black testers acting as renters faced some type of
discriminatory treatment *about half the time*, while black homeseekers
faced discriminatory treatment *59 percent* of the time in their initial-
stage encounters with whites. Latino testers encountered discrimination
at a similar rate.[23] In this case it appears that the *majority* of whites with
housing to rent or sell were inclined to discriminate against black and
Latino Americans.

One obvious, if little cited, result of this widespread discrimination is
that *white men still rule most institutional areas of the society*. One 1980s
analysis of top positions in the major economic, political, and educational
organizations in the United States found only twenty black people and
318 nonblack women in the 7,314 most powerful positions.[24] Recent
evidence suggests little change. The clearest evidence of the corporate
world's failure to promote meritorious black employees is the fact that
in 1994 not a single one of the Fortune 1000 companies had a black
executive as its head. According to a report of the federal Glass Ceiling
Commission, about 95 percent of the holders of top corporate positions
(vice president and above) are white men. Yet, white men make up only
about 39 percent of the adult population in the United States.[25]

ATTACKING IMMIGRANT "BARBARIANS" AND MULTICULTURALISM

Over the course of U.S. history, native-born Americans have viewed
wave after wave of new immigrants as a threat to the established society
and its values. Now, antiimmigrant nativism has come back with a ven-
geance, largely because most immigrants are not white or European.[26]
Forbes editor Peter Brimelow, a business leader and immigrant from
Britain, has articulated an antiimmigrant perspective. In a Random House
book, *Alien Nation*, he argues (inaccurately) that the United States is
currently "engulfed by what seems likely to be the greatest wave of

immigration it has ever faced."[27] Brimelow demonizes immigrants and is concerned to preserve the cultural dominance of north-European Americans: "The American nation has always had a specific ethnic core. And that core has been white."[28] As late as 1950, most Americans "looked like me. That is, they were of European stock. And in those days, they had another name for this thing dismissed so contemptuously as 'the racial hegemony of white Americans.' They called it 'America.' "[29]

Brimelow unabashedly opens his book with the claim that "current immigration policy is Adolph Hitler's posthumous revenge on America." Liberals are to blame because, in reaction to Hitler's horrors, they saw to it that the United States "emerged from the war passionately concerned to cleanse itself from all taints of racism or xenophobia." Brimelow's call to restore xenophobia is echoed, though usually less explicitly, in media commentaries, congressional speeches, and political campaigns across the nation.[30]

Xenophobic nativists view English-only language policies as one way to promote white-European values. In 1986 California passed a ballot proposition declaring English to be the official language, and by the mid-1990s such legislation had passed in seventeen states. From the early 1980s to the 1990s an English Language Amendment to the U.S. Constitution has regularly been introduced in the U.S. Congress. Leaders of nativist organizations, such as the California English Campaign and the national group U.S. English, favor outright language discrimination such as prohibiting Spanish as a language in government agencies and cutting off bilingual programs in schools.[31] Prominent politicians have taken up these ideas.

In speeches, articles, and interviews since the early 1990s Buchanan, a leading candidate for the Republican nomination in 1992 and 1996, has strongly articulated the nativists' concern with excluding supposedly unassimilable immigrants of color from the United States. In his announcement for the 1992 presidential race Buchanan openly worried about the racial mix of the U.S. population: "Our Judeo-Christian values are going to be preserved and our Western heritage is going to be handed down to future generations and not dumped on some landfill called multiculturalism."[32] This caustic "landfill" comment targeted immigrants of color. Commenting in a similar vein, Buchanan told an ABC interviewer that "if we had to take a million immigrants in, say, Zulus next year or Englishmen, and put them in Virginia, what group would be easier to assimilate and would cause less problems for the people of Virginia? There is nothing wrong with us sitting down and arguing that issue that we are a European country, English-speaking country."[33] Open expression of racist views has again become acceptable at the highest levels of the United States.

CONTROLLING IMAGES OF U.S. SOCIETY

Images of People of Color

Those who fear increased racial and ethnic equality in this society often allege that the inferiority in intelligence or culture of African Americans and other Americans of color accounts for serious societal problems. In *The Bell Curve* Herrnstein and Murray question the ideal of racial equality because they view blacks and Latinos as inferior in intelligence to whites. This supposed "IQ" inferiority, they claim, results substantially from genetic differences and accounts for social inequalities. Their policy suggestions are seen as following from their data and are in line with the Republican "Contract with America": Do away with strong antidiscrimination laws, eliminate social welfare programs, and reduce democratic participation in politics and society.

Other heralded analysts blame the cultures and values of people of color for the latter's personal and community problems. For example, in higher education white colleges and universities are alleged to be under siege from undeserving students of color. Widely read analysts like Allan Bloom, Dinesh D'Souza, Arthur Schlesinger, Jr., and Richard Bernstein claim that black students and faculty have taken over the curriculum and campuses of historically white universities. These campuses have allegedly experienced a not-white, radical "revolution," setting aside concerns for excellence and replacing them with the corrupting concerns of African Americans and other people of color, who are alleged to have inferior values or cultures.

In a best-selling book, the late Allan Bloom argued vigorously that there is "a large black presence in major universities, frequently equivalent to the black proportion in the general population" and that this black presence is "indigestible" because of black student desires for self-segregation and irresponsible power.[34] In Dinesh D'Souza's view, multiculturalists, who allegedly dominate college campuses, teach students to be cultural relativists hostile to the traditional European values. The core curriculum is "diluted or displaced" by massive celebrations of non-Western cultures. The "current revolution of minority victims" (described as "barbarians") is destroying higher education.[35] Similarly, *New York Times* journalist Richard Bernstein attacks multiculturalism on campuses by comparing it with the oppressive Committee of Public Safety during the French Revolution. He claims that there is "a predominating antiracist ethos on campuses" and that college and university administrations are "eager to assuage the anger of minority students." These multiculturalists have brought "an astonishing repudiation" of the idea of "a unifying American identity."[36]

For these right-wing apologists and ideologues, who are out of touch with realities on campuses, racial-ethnic discrimination is no longer significant at U.S. colleges and universities. The problems faced by students of color, like problems of people of color generally, are located in "these people" themselves, their families, and their cultures. Education analyst George Keller has attributed the lack of black advancement in education to causes primarily within the black community and deemphasized the impact of societal or organizational (college) racism on students of color. He argues that "Petulant and accusatory black spokespersons will need to climb off their soap boxes and walk through the unpleasant brambles of their young people's new preferences and look at their young honestly. . . . Critics will need to stop the fashionable practice of lambasting the colleges as if they were the central problem."[37]

The white public shares these views. The white view that any black person who works hard enough can succeed is reflected not only in the aforementioned surveys but also in such things as white reactions to African Americans in the media. For example, researchers Sut Jhally and Justin Lewis studied whites who felt that the Bill Cosby comedy show, which portrayed a successful black upper-middle-class family, showed a true picture of a country where race no longer matters. For whites in the researchers' focus groups the Cosby Show proves that if blacks are hardworking, they will succeed—and that most blacks, who do not do as well as most whites, are lazy and inferior.[38]

Images of Whiteness

Many people hailed the Oscar-winning movie *Dances with Wolves* (1990) as an example of a sensitive presentation of the history of Native Americans. Numerous white critics said that the age of Hollywood representing "Indians" as evil, blood-thirsty savages was over. Yet, few commentators focused on the key fact that the central character of the movie was a white soldier, not a Native American. This "liberal" movie ends with the idealistic white soldier and a white woman escaping the massacre by whites of a Native American tribe that had adopted them. According to the movie's presentation, the culture of the massacred tribe was preserved by the two whites. This fantasy is significant because it is used to offset the fact that historically whites killed large numbers of Native Americans and attempted to destroy their societies and cultures. The white self is rescued by a heroic white soldier, in fact a historical rarity, who adopts the Native American view of the world.

The movie *White Man's Burden* (1995) reverses the roles of black and white Americans. In this film blacks are the dominant managers and supervisors, the brutal police officers, and the mothers objecting to interracial dating. It is whites who are the abused workers, the poor living in rundown neighborhoods, and those suffering from racial inequality. In this fantasy world the central white character kidnaps the insensitive black manager he blames for his suffering, and more than half the movie is about this white man holding a black man at gunpoint. Apparently, in their less-guarded moments some whites who produce movies fantasize about the ways whites can use to defend themselves from the coming not-white dominance of the nation. It is significant too that the movie is built on the assumption that blacks in power would behave as cruelly and violently as whites in power have long behaved. In effect, this assumption reinforces the legitimacy of white dominance in the everyday world.

Whites in many positions are constructing themselves as actual or potential victims. Even though they remain fully in control of the United States, many influential white men feel threatened by the pressures for equality. In a recent interview, a college-educated business entrepreneur put it this way:

As a white male, I feel like I'm the only subsection of the population that hasn't jumped on the victim bandwagon. And I feel from a racial perspective, as the white man, I have been targeted as the oppressor, and frankly I'm getting a little tired of it, because I haven't done a whole lot of oppressing in my life. I feel like I'm branded with this bad guy label. There was a time when I enjoyed what might be called white man's privilege. . . . Supposedly, as we study gender and race, as white men, we run the world; I never knew that. I think, had I known it, I would have taken greater advantage of it because I'm paying for it now.[39]

One defense many white men use is to assert, however unrealistically, that they are now victims of discrimination too.

Most whites argue that they and their friends are not racist or against racial equality. They say they believe in equality of opportunity for people of color. They do this even as they defend the right of whites not to sell their homes to black homeseekers or as they argue for white superiority and black or Latino inferiority in intelligence or culture. Indeed, they wish their antiminority arguments to be seen in a positive light. In public interviews and in his book, *Forbes* editor Peter Brimelow aggressively argues he's not prejudiced, and other conservative ideologues assert that there are no racists in positions of power in the United States.[40] In *The Closing of the American Mind*, Allan Bloom portrays modern universities as peopled by white students, who "just do not have prejudices anymore." He even criticizes these white students and their faculty for being too egalitarian; they are "egalitarian meritocrats who believe each individual should be allowed to develop his special—and unequal— talents without reference to race."[41]

One example of how these views play out in everyday life can be seen in the case of the president of Rutgers University, Francis L. Lawrence. In fall 1994 Lawrence spoke to a faculty assembly on the admission of black students and commented on low black scores on Scholastic Aptitude Tests: "Do we set standards in the future so that we don't admit anybody with the national test? Or do we deal with a disadvantaged population that doesn't have that genetic hereditary background to have a higher average?" When these comments became public, Rutgers students organized major protests against what they saw as racist views of black inferiority. Yet, the national press did mostly positive reports on Lawrence, noting that, as the *New York Times* put it, his career showed a lifetime effort to open campuses to more students and faculty of color.[42] The *Times* article contained little criticism of Lawrence's remarks. Similarly, *U.S. News & World Report* framed its sympathetic discussion of Lawrence with the sentence "uppity Francis Lawrence . . . his career is in tatters because of a careless phrase." They emphasized that Lawrence had an "impeccable" racial relations record and characterized as venal and misled the many black students who protested Lawrence's harsh comment.[43]

WHITHER THE STRUGGLE FOR RACIAL JUSTICE?

In a 1995 *Newsweek* column Jonathan Alter spoke of whites' irritation at the positive black responses to the not-guilty verdict in the O. J. Simpson trial:

We assumed, unthinkingly, that we occupied some kind of demilitarized zone with moderate blacks. If it wasn't color-blind, it was at least color-farsighted, with certain common values allowed to share the foreground. Suddenly that zone was gone, at least as far as O. J. Simpson was concerned. Black moderates are familiar with the pressure to fall in line with a 'black' position. They feel it again in this case. But for many white moderates, it's jarring to find ourselves identifying not with a set of racially idealistic principles but with the so-called 'white' position. We expected more blacks to look beyond race to facts, as thousands of whites had during the Rodney King trial. When so many blacks didn't, it shocked us—and hardened us in ways that shocked us even more.[44]

As a white man, Alter reflects the racial divide mentioned earlier by then President Bill Clinton.

Before and after the Simpson verdict, many white Americans have felt that they "know" how African Americans feel about the world. They are angered and scared when most "moderate" blacks are militant and, allegedly, unable to "look beyond race to facts" as most whites supposedly can do. This white perspective remains commonplace among white Americans today, yet it is reminiscent of white views during slavery and segregation when fugitive slaves or black protestors, who were supposed to be "happy," revealed a side not previously seen by whites.

The racial and ethnic divisions in our society go very deep. Most whites refuse to see the racist world they and their ancestors have created for what it is. The attack on racial and other social equality is today led by powerful whites in the media, corporations, and political institutions. The increasing inequalities in the nation are currently enforced with little overt repression of the citizenry. Instead, it is imposed with the "velvet glove" of legitimating ideologies. The recent discourse against democracy and equality is an effort to create an ideology supporting ruling elites in their firm belief that they deserve a growing proportion of the national wealth. This ideology encourages the public, especially the white public, to view inequality as just and proper.

Just before his death, Dr. Martin Luther King, Jr. argued that most white Americans are not committed to real equality, that at most whites are only committed to some improvement in the conditions of African Americans and other Americans of color. After some modest improvements for people of color in the 1960s, King noted, most whites "settled easily into well-padded pockets of complacency. Justice at the deepest level had but few stalwart champions."[45] As we have seen, white observers have suggested that equality will come quicker if black Americans worked harder to make themselves worthy. However, King counters this view by noting that African Americans are trying hard, but whites "are not putting a similar mass effort to re-educate themselves out of their racial ignorance. It is an aspect of their sense of superiority that the white people of America believe they have so little to learn. . . . The great majority . . . are uneasy with injustice but unwilling yet to pay a significant price to eradicate it."[46]

The United States has slipped into growing inequality with few large-scale protests and social upheavals. A few demonstrations and large-scale riots have occurred, but nothing yet on the magnitude of the upheavals of the 1960s. In our view this relatively peaceful condition has already begun to change. Witness the 1992 Los Angeles riot, which cost more than four dozen lives and a billion dollars in damage. U.S. and world history books document the dangers faced by a society divided sharply between many hungry have-nots and some overfed haves. There is an increasing tension between the reality of inequality and the ideal of equality that is the cornerstone of liberal democracy.

It is likely that between now and the middle of the 21st century, the United States will be racked by much upheaval and turmoil as the "haves" try to turn back the pressure for change on the part of the "have-nots." In the near future white Americans will need to adjust their perspectives dramatically to fit the new multiracial world in which they increasingly will have to live. Currently white Americans are a statistical minority of the population in major U.S. cities such as Los Angeles and Miami, and over the next five decades they will become a minority in the nation. These impending changes threaten white dominance of national economic, political, and juridical systems. The change from majority to minority status means that democratic institutions, including universal suffrage and the peer-jury system, will no longer be trustworthy tools for maintaining political, cultural, and economic dominance.

The march of the demographic transition cannot be stopped, and the United States will sooner or later have to significantly desegregate its social, economic, and political institutions and redistribute its resources— or go the way of the old South Africa, with its highly repressive, and ultimately unstable, white minority rule.

NOTES

1. Martin Kasindorf, "A Great Divide," *Newsday*, October 1, 1994, p. A3.
2. Ibid.
3. Richard J. Herrnstein and Charles Murray, *The Bell Curve: Intelligence and Class Structure in American Life* (New York: Free Press, 1994).
4. William Henry III, *In Defense of Elitism* (New York: Doubleday, 1994).
5. See Sidney Blumenthal, *The Rise of the Counter-Establishment* (New York: Times Books, 1986), pp. 4–11, 133–170; Peter Steinfels, *The Neoconservatives: The Men Who Are Changing America's Politics* (New York: Touchstone, 1979), pp. 214–277.

6. PBS, "Is He the Most Dangerous Man in America?" *Frontline*, February 28, 1995.

7. Rush Limbaugh, "Voice of America; Why Liberals Fear Me," *Policy Review*, No. 70 (Fall 1994), p. 4; Bennett is quoted in Clarence Page, "It's Time to Clear the Air of the Radical Right's Toxic Fumes," *Chicago Tribune*, August 26, 1992, p. C17.

8. See Blumenthal, *The Rise of the Counter-Establishment*, pp. 32–34.

9. Joe R. Feagin and Clairece B. Feagin, *Social Problems: A Critical Power Conflict Perspective* (Upper Saddle River, NJ: Prentice-Hall, 1997), chapter 2.

10. Joe R. Feagin, Hernan Vera, and Nikitah Imani, *The Agony of Education* (New York: Routledge, 1996), pp. 109–112.

11. National Advisory Commission on Civil Disorders, *Report of the National Advisory Commission on Civil Disorders* (Washington, DC: U.S. Government Printing Office, 1968), p. 1.

12. Nathan Glazer, *Affirmative Discrimination* (New York: Basic Books, 1975), pp. 6–7, 71–72.

13. George Gilder, *Wealth and Poverty* (New York: Basic Books, 1981).

14. Leon Wieseltier, "Scar Tissue," *New Republic*, June 5, 1989, pp. 19–20.

15. Elizabeth Ehrlich, "Racism, 'Victim Power,' and White Guilt," *Business Week*, October 1, 1990, p. 12.

16. Dinesh D'Souza, *The End of Racism: Principles for a Multiracial Society* (New York: Free Press, 1995), p. 113.

17. Anti-Defamation League, *Highlights from an Anti-Defamation League Survey on Racial Attitudes in America* (New York: ADL, 1993), pp. 18–25.

18. National Opinion Research Center, "1994 General Social Survey." Tabulation by author.

19. Ibid.

20. "Survey Finds Minorities Resent Whites and Each Other," *Jet*, March 28, 1994, p. 14.

21. Margery Austin Turner, Michael Fix, and Raymond J. Struyk, "Opportunities Denied: Discrimination in Hiring," Washington, DC, Urban Institute Report 91–9, August, 1991.

22. Lawrence Bobo and Susan A. Suh, "Surveying Racial Discrimination: Analyses from a Multiethnic Labor Market," unpublished research report, Department of Sociology, University of California, Los Angeles, August 1, 1995.

23. See Margery Austin Turner, Raymond J. Struyk, and John Yinger, *Housing Discrimination Study: Synthesis* (Washington, DC: U.S. Government Printing Office, 1991), pp. ii–viii.

24. Thomas Dye, *Who's Running America?* (Fourth edition; Englewood Cliffs, NJ: Prentice Hall, 1986), pp. 190–205.

25. Glass Ceiling Commission, *Good for Business: Making Full Use of the Nation's Human Capital* (Washington, DC: U.S. Government Printing Office, 1995), pp. 12, 60–61.

26. This section draws on Joe R. Feagin, "Old Poison in New Bottles: the

Deep Roots of Modern Nativism," in *Immigrants Out: The New Nativism and Anti-immigrant Impulse in the United States*, edited by Juan F. Perea (New York: New York University Press, 1997.

27. Peter Brimelow, *Alien Nation: Common Sense about America's Immigration Disaster* (New York: Random House, 1995), pp. 137–157.

28. Ibid., p. 10.

29. Ibid., p. 59.

30. Ibid., p. xv.

31. On these issues, see Bill Piatt, *Only English? Law and Language Policy in the United States* (Albuquerque: University of New Mexico Press, 1990).

32. Quoted in Clarence Page, "U.S. Media Should Stop Abetting Intolerance," *Toronto Star*, December 27, 1991, p. A27.

33. Quoted in John Dillin, "Immigration Joins List of '92 Issues," *Christian Science Monitor*, December 17, 1991, p. 6.

34. Allan Bloom, *The Closing of the American Mind* (New York: Simon and Schuster, 1987), p. 93.

35. Dinesh D'Souza, *Illiberal Education: The Politics of Race and Sex on Campus* (New York: Vintage, 1991), p. 257.

36. See Richard Bernstein, *Dictatorship of Virtue: Multiculturalism and the Battle for America's Future* (New York: Alfred A. Knopf, 1994), pp. 3–4, 206.

37. George Keller, "Black Students in Higher Education: Why So Few?" *Planning for Higher Education* 17 (1988–1989), pp. 50–54.

38. Sut Jhally and Justin Lewis, *Enlightened Racism* (Boulder, CO: Westview Press, 1992).

39. Joe R. Feagin and Hernan Vera, *White Racism: The Basics* (New York: Routledge, 1995), p. 146.

40. Brimelow, *Alien Nation*, p. 11; on no racists at higher levels, see Gilder, *Wealth and Poverty*.

41. Bloom, *The Closing of the American Mind*, pp. 89–90.

42. Doreen Carvajal, "A Career in the Balance; Rutgers President Starts a Firestorm With Three Words," *New York Times*, February 6, 1995, p. B1.

43. John Leo, "The Rutgers Star Chamber," *U.S. News & World Report*, February 20, 1995, p. 22.

44. Jonathan Alter, "White and Blue," *Newsweek*, October 16, 1995, pp. 66–67.

45. Martin Luther King, Jr., *Where Do We Go from Here? Chaos or Community* (New York: Bantam Books, 1967), p. 10.

46. Ibid., pp. 11, 13.

10

The Difficulty of Doing Good: Civil Rights Activism as Metaphor

Derrick A. Bell

Years ago, the *New Yorker* magazine published a short story about a group of black trash collectors and their unbearably arrogant white supervisor. In the story, Jake, one of the black workers, is always trying to give his boss good advice about how to run his business. The supervisor resents the unsolicited suggestions and finally dismisses Jake as a threat to his authority. The other black workers shake their heads. "Well, we knew it would happen. Ole Jake done gone and got his damn self fired trying to teach the white folks."

Jake's assertiveness-subservience dilemma will strike a familiar chord for many African Americans, including some holding positions far loftier than that of manual laborers. If he clowned around along with his co-workers and followed his boss's orders to the letter—even when they were stupid—Jake could have kept his job, though at great cost to his self-respect. The soul-saving alternative that he selected, candor and telling his boss what he thought, cost him his job and, unless he found another quickly—a difficult task his boss would not likely make any easier—he would not be able to care for his family and his self-respect would likely go along with everything else.

The moral contained in Jake's dilemma became an important touchstone during my thirty years of marriage to my late wife, Jewel, who died in 1990. Permanently ingrained in my memory is her predictable response whenever I sought her counsel before launching into some crazy protest that would likely jeopardize my job and outrage my colleagues. She would shake her head and sigh, "there you go again. After all these years, still trying to teach the white folks."

"Teaching the white folk" is both a manifestation of faith and an exercise in folly. Thus, while I might believe that I was doing what I thought "right," my wife's chiding was intended as a gentle reminder that I was not necessarily "doing good." That is, my good intentions might well translate into results that—at least in part—might be the very opposite of what I intended. The dichotomy between doing what we think "right" and doing "good" can be applied profitably to an assessment of civil rights efforts over the last dozen or so years. Few will deny that the racial equality goals that a few decades ago seemed in sight are now further away than ever. Equality, our experience tells us, did not follow the enactment of civil rights laws or winning cases in the courts. Similarly, the plight of the poor and the disadvantaged was not much eased by social programs that, no matter how ambitiously undertaken, seem able to deliver only food without nutrition, welfare without well-being, job training without employment opportunities, and legal services without justice. In fact, the minimum relief we provide to the needy serves mainly to drain away the revolutionary potential in their deprivations and thus ensures maximum status stability for the already well-off.

Subjected to scrutiny, I wonder how many civil rights programs and projects can be seen as sensible, even relevant, given both the ever-worsening status of an increasing number of poor blacks, Hispanics, and native Americans, and the powerful dynamics that transform even our social reform victories into new forms of disadvantage. That is, even those civil rights and civil liberties battles we think we won all too frequently were transformed before our eyes into new barriers for the ever-elusive equality, more rigid limits on liberties already too closely circumscribed. Consider that litigation intended to ensure fair trials, fair sentencing, and humane prison facilities has provided more semblance than substantive reform. Government entities respond to our hard-won procedural safeguards by cutbacks in services that worsen the plight of those trapped in the already beleaguered criminal justice system.

More than two generations of school desegregation efforts intended to bring about racially integrated school systems have mostly failed, particularly for the most needy black children. Now inner-city educators seeking to improve the schooling for poor black children through programs and policies focusing on race are advised that their efforts may run afoul of the *Brown* decision, a precedent that events have rendered irrelevant as a positive or protective value for these children. Affirmative action rules intended to improve hiring and admission opportunity for groups previously excluded on the basis of race and color are of principal benefit to whites, particularly white males who are able to take advantage of the publication requirements and fair selection criteria to apply for positions once awarded to those "in the know." Without affirmative action, far fewer minorities would be hired or promoted, but with affirmative action, all those minorities are deemed unqualified—save for color—a judgment that fits far better many of those whites who make the charge. Thus, for all its value in a society still predisposed to racial discrimination, affirmative action is diluted seriously by its symbolic status as a policy preference for unqualified blacks taking the jobs of worthy whites.

Despite the presence of fair housing laws at both state and federal levels, housing segregation and the willingness of the real estate industry to discriminate on the basis of race is as pervasive now as it was in the 1970s. Integrated developments like Starrett City in New York are possible only when the number of minorities admitted is limited by strict racial quotas, but these quotas are attacked as violating the basic non-discriminatory classification standard of the Fourteenth Amendment—a standard designed to protect "discrete and insular" minorities, but now applied to protect the majority from modest efforts to correct the effects of decades of discrimination that have disadvantaged members of discrete and insular minorities. In each of these areas—and many others as well—civil rights campaigns intended to further what we consider "good" have proven costly when they failed and counterproductive even when their original goals were achieved. If this is paranoia, it is a psychosis that is spurred and sustained by history. Nor is it limited to racial issues.

Social reformers worked for years to gain no-fault divorce laws. Now, at least according to some studies, those laws are working to disadvantage divorced women more than the old laws did. Unable to overturn death penalty statutes, civil liberties lawyers have evolved an endless series of appeal procedures that serve to maintain condemned persons on death row for ten to twenty years—sometimes against their will. One wonders whether such edge-of-death living is not as "cruel and inhuman" as the death penalty itself. Doing good in this racially charged, economically disparate environment is not simply difficult, it may not be possible. As my black laborer Jake's experience teaches, well-intended confrontations involving race are risky and always fraught with potential disaster . . . even when individuals are willing to make personal sacrifices in order to do good. Is it any wonder that so many racial and other social reform efforts fail?

Civil rights organizations are now floundering in part because they refuse to acknowledge that opposition to their racial equality goals is not the fault of a group of bad white people whose discriminatory propensities can be controlled by well-written civil rights laws, vigorously enforced. Even those blacks who through hard work and good fortune have experienced a measure of success become part of the problem rather than a slice of the solution. Our dilemma is expressed by a working-class black character in my book, one named for Langston Hughes's Semple. I had read him a passage from a book (*The Alchemy of Race and Rights*) by a former student, Patricia Williams. Semple was impressed:

"Maybe she can get beyond so many of our bourgeoisie black folks with all their degrees and fancy titles who still don't understand what we ordinary black folks have known for a very long time." "Which is?" I asked rather defensively. "Which is that the law works for the Man most of the time, and only works for us in the short run as a way of working for him in the long run." I had to laugh in spite of myself. Semple was a marvel. "You will be happy to know," I told him, "that some middle-class black professionals agree with you. Plus, Mr. Semple," I admonished, "you are too hard on those of us who managed to get degrees and what you call a bourgeois life style. I have to tell you that neither offers real protection from racial discrimination. We are both black—and, for precisely that reason, we are in the same boat."

"Not really, brother," Semple said. "I mean no offense, but the fact is you upper-income black folks hurt us everyday blacks simply by being successful. The white folks see you doing your thing, making money in the high five figures, latching on to all kinds of fancy titles, some of which even have a little authority behind the name, and generally moving on up. They conclude right off that discrimination is over, and that if the rest of us got up off our dead asses, dropped the welfare tit, stopped having illegitimate babies, and found jobs, we would all be just like you. It's not fair, brother, but it's the living truth. You may be committed to black people but, believe me, you have to work very hard to do as much *good* for black people as you do harm simply by being good at whatever you do for a living!"

Even Solomon with all his wisdom would be hard pressed to resolve the racial challenges facing our society. Deep down, most of us working in civil rights know that there is no real salvation in the racial field. With more faith in the law than in the lessons of our past experience, we continue to plan our civil right programs to conform to our romantic ideals about an integrated America. And, as with romance, we do so with a wild disregard for either logic or history. It is not that we civil rights advocates do not concede that racism is an enormous obstacle to our efforts to achieve racial justice. We know it exists and assert on every public occasion that no social fact in America is more salient than racial difference. But we underestimate the important connection between the economic subordination of blacks and the social and political stability of whites.

We underestimate when we do not entirely ignore the fact that there is a deeply held belief in white superiority that serves as a key, regulative force in an otherwise fragile and dangerously divided society. Indeed, it is difficult to think of another characteristic of societal functioning that has retained its viability and its value to social stability from the very beginning of the American experience down to the present day. Slavery and segregation are gone, but most whites continue to expect society to recognize an unspoken but no less vested property right in their "whiteness." This right is recognized and upheld by courts and society like all property rights under a government created and sustained primarily for that purpose. The result is that it is easy for opponents of social reforms needed by all, white as well as blacks, to build opposition to those reforms by painting them as somehow giving unfair advantage to blacks. Several years ago, some young white men in Dayton, Ohio, were arrested before they could carry out their plan to blow up the local museum. The men were outraged because the museum had presented an exhibit honoring the life of Dr. Martin Luther King, Jr. These young men, likely poor with even poorer prospects for a good life, had plenty of reason for outrage. But not at a museum honoring King's life.

They should have looked at what the redistribution of the wealth upward will mean to their life chances. Statistics show that U.S. wealth concentration in 1989 was more extreme than that of any time since 1929. Between 1983 and 1989, the share of the wealth held by the top half of one percent of the richest families increased by an almost unprecedented 4.6 percentage points. In dollar terms, of the 2.6 trillion dollars of increase in family wealth in that period, *55 percent* accrued to the top half of one percent of families. During the same period, 1983 to 1989, the lower-middle and bottom wealth class collectively (i.e., the bottom 40%) *lost* 256 billion dollars of wealth. And yet these young men viewed a museum honoring King as the enemy, not the local banks or the corporate headquarters in their area. Why don't whites wake up and see the real source of their disadvantage? Professor Kimberle Crenshaw suggests that:

To bring a fundamental challenge to the way things are, whites would have to question not just their own subordinate status, but also both the economic and the racial myths that justify the status quo. Racism, combined with equal opportunity mythology, provides a rationalization for racial oppression, making it difficult for whites to see the Black situation as illegitimate or unnecessary. If whites believe that Blacks, because they are unambitious or inferior, get what they deserve, it becomes that much harder to convince whites that something is wrong with the entire system. Similarly, a challenge to the legitimacy of continued racial inequality would force whites to confront myths about equality of opportunity that justify for them whatever measure of economic success they may have attained.[1]

Race consciousness makes it difficult—at least for whites—to imagine the world differently. It also creates the desire for identification with privileged elites. By focusing on a distinct, subordinate "other," whites include themselves in the dominant circle—an arena in which most hold no real power, but only their privileged racial identity. Consider the case of a dirt-poor, Southern white shown participating in a Ku Klux Klan rally in the movie *Resurgence*, who declared: "Every morning, I wake up and thank God I'm white." For this person, and for others like him, race consciousness—manifested by his refusal even to associate with blacks—provides a powerful explanation of why he fails to challenge the current social order.[2]

Novelist Toni Morrison provides a more earthy but hardly less accurate assessment of how the presence of blacks enables a bonding by whites that occurs across vast socioeconomic divides. Thus, when in a *Time* magazine interview Ms. Morrison was asked why blacks and whites can't bridge the abyss in race relations, she replied:

I feel personally sorrowful about black-white relations a lot of the time because black people have always been used as a buffer in this country between powers to prevent class war, to prevent other kinds of real conflagrations.[3]

If there were no black people here in this country, it would have been Balkanized. The immigrants would have torn each other's throats out, as they have done everywhere else. But in becoming an American, from Europe, what one has in common with that other immigrant is contempt for *me*—it's nothing else but color. Wherever they were from, they would stand together. They could all say, "I am not *that*." So in that sense, becoming an American is based on an attitude: an exclusion of me.

It wasn't negative to them—it was unifying. When they got off the boat, the second word they learned was "nigger." Ask them—I grew up with them. I remember in the fifth grade a smart little boy who had just arrived and didn't speak any English. He sat next to me. I read well, and I taught him to read just by doing it. I remember the moment he found out that I was black—a nigger. It took him six months; he was told. And that's the moment when he belonged; that was his entrance. Every immigrant knew he would not come at the very bottom. He had to come above at least one group—and that was us.[4]

The Toni Morrison observation gains in validity as Eastern Europeans—freed of the authoritarian domination of Communist control—engage in fierce and bloody ethnic conflicts. Those conflicts, and their violent counterparts in other parts of the world, give emphasis to the reason why Americans can boast that this nation is a melting pot of people from many origins. If immigrants from Europe, who are, after all, white, have seen the need to bolster their self-esteem by denigrating blacks, then what of the immigrants who are not European: those from Asia and those from Spanish-speaking nations? Can blacks expect these groups to reject the blandishments of quasi-white status and join in coalitions with blacks to fight the economic and social rejection suffered by both? At present, there is evidence pointing in both directions, but it will require great discipline and forbearance of self-interest for Spanish-speaking and Asian peoples to join in large numbers with blacks in a struggle that is not winnable in equal opportunity terms.

All of this is very difficult for one who, like most civil rights advocates, agreed with the philosophical underpinnings of Gunnar Myrdal's massive mid-century study *The American Dilemma*. Myrdal argued that racism was merely an odious holdover from slavery, "a terrible and inexplicable anomaly stuck in the middle of our liberal democratic ethos."[5] No one doubted that standard American policy making was adequate to the task of abolishing racism. White America, it was assumed, *wanted* to abolish racism. Forty years later, in *The New American Dilemma*,[6] Professor Jennifer Hochschild examined what she called Myrdal's "anomaly thesis," and concluded that it simply cannot explain the persistence of racial discrimination.[7] Rather, the continued viability of racism demonstrates "that racism is not simply an excrescence on a fundamentally healthy liberal democratic body, but is part of what shapes and energizes the body."[8] Under this view, "liberal democracy and racism in the United States are historically, even inherently, reinforcing; American society as we know it exists only because of its foundation in racially based slavery, and it thrives only because racial discrimination continues. The apparent anomaly is an actual symbiosis."[9]

Were there a solution or even a responsible theory to address the difficulty of doing good, the dilemma facing both individuals and groups seeking racial reform, it would have been discovered long before now. I can offer only a rationale for continuing the struggle even in the face of almost certain failure. This rationale is connected with the reason why some pursue and the rest of us persist in life—even with knowledge (albeit mostly suppressed knowledge) that the reasons we offer for our pursuits and persistence will not stand (and thus do not often receive) what we in the law refer to as "strict scrutiny." We struggle with ideological transformations in civil rights policy that are dictated by events rather than logic. Thus, many blacks now advocate public schools for black students only, despite the desegregation mandate of *Brown*; and black community leaders urge curbs on racist speech and curfews for teenagers in ghetto areas despite the strictures of the First Amendment. Even integration advocates support racial set-asides in public contracts and preferences in an array of government actions, without regard to seemingly contrary constitutional strictures or their own hopes for an integrated society.

Many of these policy proposals are made as an unconscious alternative to facing up to the fact that the "color-blind" ideal is a myth and that the society is unwilling and perhaps unable to treat persons without granting either privilege or disadvantage based on race and color. Programs of racial preference or separation are espoused despite their contradiction with earlier supported integration policies even though history gives little reason to believe these approaches will be more effective than the more idealistic integration-oriented measures they replace. We practice, even espouse, these contradictions in silent acknowledgment that what we hailed as progress has been a cyclical phenomenon in which legal rights are gained, then lost, then gained again in response to economic and political developments in the country over which blacks exercise little or no control. Civil rights law has always been a part of, rather than an exception to, this cyclical phenomenon.

Because the dimensions of this phenomenon remain uncharted, we who advocate on behalf of the nation's colored peoples seemed trapped in a giant unseen gyroscope. Even our most powerful efforts are unable to divert it permanently from its preplanned equilibrium, or alter its orientation toward dominance for whites over blacks. The symbols change and the society even accepts those symbols we civil rights advocates have urged on it, but our status remains fixed, its stability enhanced rather than undermined by the movement up through the class ranks of the precious few who too quickly are deemed to have "made it." The apparent contradictions in the constantly changing civil rights advocacy illustrate the harsh and disconcerting truth about racial progress. We prefer to ignore or rationalize rather than confront these contradictions because they disrupt our long-settled expectations of eventual racial equality. Civil rights advocates encourage us to suspend our disbelief and to continue to sing "We Shall Overcome" ever more fervently so as to drown out our doubts and theirs. The civil rights establishment is quite intolerant of those who express reservations about the possibility of achieving racial equality goals.

Protest has cost me my tenured position on the Harvard law faculty, as it cost me my deanship at the University of Oregon Law School. Neither loss was without trauma, misgivings, or remorse, but I have received far more public acclaim for my actions than I either expected or deserve. Candor, though, requires that I admit that my actions, like so many civil rights initiatives, may have harmed precisely the group I had hoped my protest might help. The fact is that a goodly number of black women law teachers do not thank me for "calling national attention to the plight of black women academics." As I inferred in announcing my protest leave, there is an element of the patriarchal in my protective feelings for the black women students whose calls for women faculty of color the faculty ignored. My protest, undertaken to support students, also had the effect of placing me in the spotlight of an effort that should be led by women of color. None of them elected me to this role.

Indeed, in one of those cruel tricks of fate that evade fiction because the truth would not be believable, I may inadvertently have placed women of color in law teaching in a position rather like the unfortunate young black women in one of my stories. In my earlier book, *And We Are Not Saved*, I invented an ailment that would place in a deep sleep an arbitrarily selected group of young, single, black women professionals. When they awakened after a few months, they found they had lost their professional skills—all because they had not received a bona fide offer of marriage from a black man. My thought was that so great a tragedy, one that only black men could prevent, would motivate us to shake off our societally imposed powerlessness with all its unhappy attributes and move us to function more responsibly *vis à vis* black women regarding marriage and everything else. My critics pointed out that the much-desired sense of power and responsibility for black men came at too high a price—the further subjugation of black women. Moreover, the facts in the allegory served to silence young black women and disabled them to participate in the healthier black man-black woman debate the chronicle was intended to promote.

In real life, we have women of color excluded from Harvard and many other law schools who, because they are outside the institutions, have no way of changing the exclusionary policies. The argument can be made that acting out of my own frustration and powerlessness to correct (cure?) this condition, I confronted the white establishment in a form that proves I am still willing to do battle, but in a fashion that virtually guarantees no women of color will be hired—according to some faculty members—for years to come. Even if they are wrong, the difficulties my critics saw in the story may come home to haunt women of color seeking law teaching jobs. In addition, my action makes it harder for these women to express their honest views on my protest. If they indicate their support, it will seem self-serving. If they express honestly held reservations, their opposition will tend to place them in the camp with the Shelby Steeles and other black beneficiaries of affirmative action who now deem such policies "demeaning" and in conflict with the great American principle of merit. The parallels are not precise, but if some women argue that I have harmed the cause I claim to support, I can hardly dismiss it as totally worthless.

My personal experience has public policy significance for social reform organizations, and perhaps for you as individuals. It is time that we face up to the difficulties of doing good in the area of racial reform. Those difficulties need not deter but should give us reason for humility as we pursue programs that no matter what we do are likely to fail. The key for those seeking justice is a determination to go forward with a full knowledge of the overpowering dilemmas they will encounter, dilemmas that can neither be avoided nor ignored. Each of us in our own way must be willing to face the dilemmas and make the sacrifices or take risks to do not only what we view as right but also what will prove to be good in some broader sense. It is difficult to act in the face of authority when the likelihood of failure, or harm to self or others, is so real. One must not expect much help from most of those who claim they share one's views. When I left the Justice Department, rather than give up my NAACP membership as my superiors were insisting I do, none of my young civil rights lawyer associates raised a word of protest—including at least one who earlier had boasted—privately—that he held an NAACP membership himself.

The larger burden though is to realize that in terms of meaningful reform, we have the potential of being our own worst enemies. I can illustrate this by repeating the advice I received from the Rev. Peter Gomes, minister to the Memorial Church at Harvard. As I was leaving

Harvard back in 1980 to become dean of the Oregon Law School, Peter told me:

Derrick, as a dean, you must look in the mirror each morning and say, "I am an evil." For you will have authority and sometimes you will be disappointing expectations you should reward and rewarding those expectations you should disappoint. So, you must remind yourself, "I am an evil." But then you must ask, "but am I a necessary evil?"

Challenging one's self as a necessary evil provides an appropriate foundation for the commitment to and involvement in good causes intended to serve others and gain salvation for yourself (in this world, not the next) that provides real, substantive, and lasting meaning for this existence we call life. This engagement and commitment is what my ancestors—slave and quasi-free—have been doing for centuries: Making something out of nothing. Carving out a humanity for themselves with absolutely nothing to help save imagination, will, and unbelievable strength and courage. Beating the odds while firmly believing in, *knowing* as only they could know, the fact that all those odds are stacked against them. As Nathan Huggins suggests in *Black Odyssey*, a book about slavery from the point of view of the slaves, "Uncertainty, the act of being engaged in an unknown and evolving future, was their common fate. In the indefinite was the excitement of the possible." The slaves, Huggins argues, knew there was no escape, no way out, and yet they continued to engage themselves. To carve out a humanity. To defy the murder of self-hood. Their lives were brutally shackled, certainly: but *not without meaning despite being imprisoned.*

Perhaps those of us who can admit that we are imprisoned by the history of racial subordination in America can accept, as slaves had no choice but to accept, our fate. This does not mean we legitimate the racism of the oppressor. Indeed, to the contrary: We can only delegitimate it if we can accurately pinpoint it. And racism lies at the center, not the periphery; in the permanent, not in the fleeting; in the real lives of black and white people, not in the sentimental caverns of the mind. Armed with this knowledge, and the enlightened, humility-based commitment that it engenders, we can accept the dilemmas of doing good. We can go forth to serve, knowing harm may come of it, but knowing as well that our failure to act will not change conditions and may very well worsen them.

In fact, once we recognize and acknowledge (at least to ourselves) that our actions are not likely to lead to transcendent change and, despite our best efforts, may be of more help to the system we despise than to the victims of that system we are trying to help, that realization and the dedication based on it can lead to policy positions and campaigns that are less likely to worsen conditions for those we are trying to help and more likely to remind the powers that be that there are persons like us who are not on their side and are determined to stand in their way.

Now there is more here than confrontation with our oppressors. Continued struggle can bring about unexpected benefits and gains that in themselves justify continued endeavor. We can recognize miracles we did not plan and value them for what they are rather than always measure their worth by their likely contribution to our traditional goals. As a former student, Erin Edmonds, concludes, it is not a matter of choosing between the pragmatic recognition that racism is permanent no matter what we do, or an idealism based on the long-held dream of attaining a society free of racism. Rather, it is a question of *both* the recognition of the futility of action—where action is more civil rights strategies destined to fail—*and* the unalterable conviction that something must be done, that action must be taken.[10] Underlying the ambivalence, the fear and misgivings, it is a philosophy very much like this that impels me to both live each day more fully *and* to examine critically the effectiveness of my actions. I hope beliefs that have served me well may prove of some help to you.

NOTES

1. Crenshaw, Kimberle. 1988. "Race, Reform, and Retrenchment: Transformation and Legitimation in AntiDiscrimination Law, 101." *Harv. L. Rev.* 1331, 1380–1381.

2. Ibid.

3. Ibid.

4. Tori Morrison, "The Pain of Being Black," *Time*, May 22, 1989: 120.

5. Myrdal Gunnar, *An American Dilemma: The Negro Problem and Modern Democracy* (New York: Harper, 1944, p. xix): "The Negro problem in America represents a moral lag in the development of the nation and study of it must record nearly everything which is bad and wrong in America . . . . However, . . . not since Reconstruction has there been more reason to anticipate fundamental changes in American race relations, changes which will involve a development toward the American ideals."

6. Jennifer Hochschild, *The New American Dilemma: Liberal Democracy and School Desegregation* (New Haven: Yale University Press, 1984).

7. Ibid., p. 203.

8. Ibid., p. 5.

9. Ibid., p. 5.

10. Erin Edmonds, *Civil Rights According to Derrick Bell* (unpublished manuscript).

11

Moving from Observation to Action: Addressing the New Politics of Race

Thomas S. Lyons and Gregg A. Lichtenstein

OBSERVATIONS ABOUT RACIAL DISCRIMINATION AND INEQUALITY

In his chapter entitled "The Difficulty of Doing Good," Derrick Bell paints a bleak picture of the outcomes of civil rights activism and affirmative action, culminating in his observation that African Americans must continue the struggle for their civil rights in the face of the fact that they will surely fail. Indeed, it is well documented throughout the chapters of this book that racial discrimination and inequality do not merely continue to exist, but may well be on the rise. Feagin and Vera assert that racism still exists in America and that whites today are actively trying to obfuscate or deny this fact. Jacob and Monges point out that economic anxiety has led to the rise of the "angry white men" of the 1990s, who are challenging affirmative action and other civil rights platforms. Logan and Alba document continued discrimination by race in housing markets. Collins finds racialized structures in private companies that obstruct job mobility, which are, ironically, the result of these firms' responses to affirmative action legislation. Herring, Horton and Thomas assert that inner-city persons (many of them African Americans) are forced into entrepreneurship because they lack access to jobs, and, once they start their own businesses, they are impeded by racial isolation. The result is often that they are nominally self-employed.

All of this is, at best, discouraging and, at worst, cause for dark despair over the possibility that the race problem in America may never be resolved. However, we also find reasons for hope within the pages of this book. Among these is Morris's observation that social activism and upward mobility can overcome oppression. Another is Cunnigen's discussion of W.E.B. Du Bois's ideas about African Americans forming cooperative relationships that are based on their social-historical commonalities. This mutualistic perspective can be extended to all Americans through an emphasis on education that explores cultural diversity and reduces the "psychological separation" between races. Still another wellspring of hope is Durr's finding that cross-ethnic ties can help occupational mobility. Finally, Denton's observation that not working together for African-American progress merely enables those who would block such progress is a challenge to continue the good work that has gone on before. The cross-cutting message here is that relationship building across races and ethnicities may well be our best hope for ending racial discrimination and inequality. This is an important message, emanating from Du Bois himself, and it deserves further attention. But what kind of attention exactly?

MOVING FROM OBSERVATION TO ACTION

It is clearly important to bear witness to the racial discrimination that permeates our society and to document it in ways that preclude denial of its existence and fuel the desire to act to eliminate it. Our colleagues who have authored the preceding chapters have done this admirably. They have energized us to act. Yet, the question remains, what should we do? While affirmative action and other civil rights policies appear to be moving us forward, it has become apparent that they have not been institutionalized in the way that their architects had hoped. They can be, and in many ways have been, too easily subverted. Current nostrums for action, fostered by an increasingly conservative worldview, tend to focus on responsibilities at the expense of rights. This has led to the advocacy of bootstrapping policies for effecting economic and social mobility for minorities. As Morris pointed out in his introduction to this book, however, these are "Band-Aid" or "feel good" strategies that are not adequate to the task. Should it be concluded, then, that the antidote is the liberal tendency to advocate for rights at the expense of responsibilities? We think not. The bedrock of effective, efficient, and equitable democracy is a healthy balance between rights and responsibilities.

We contend that neither the focus on rights nor the focus on responsibilities is capable of producing the kind of societal transformation necessary to end racism. Rights and responsibilities are simply two sides of the same coin—they are necessary but insufficient to produce a truly systemic solution to this societal problem. An end to racism would not simply require a change in humanity's behavior, but a change in how we humans view ourselves and our relationships to each other. Change is a multilevel process (Dilts 1996). We can make changes in:

- our *environment* (in things external to ourselves)
- our *behaviors* through which we interact with our environment
- our *capabilities* and the *strategies* by which we direct and guide our behavior
- our *beliefs* and *value systems* by which we motivate and reinforce our guidance systems and maps
- our *identity* of which we select the values and beliefs we live by
- our *relationship to those things that are bigger than us* (those things that most people would call the spiritual)

By emphasizing rights and responsibilities, current proposals to address racism are trying to legislate behavior (that is, why they can only have limited effect); such attempts ignore the more fundamental and powerful levels of capabilities, beliefs, identity, and spirit—the deeper places from which people act. For human beings to truly treat each other with genuine respect, changes *at all of these levels* are required.

These changes will involve both personal and societal transformations. A transformation represents a leap to a higher (and very different) level of functioning, not just more of the same. It is a qualitative, not a quantitative change. Whereas the process of *in*forming takes place within an existing structure and set of skills, *trans*forming involves a change in the structure of the individual or group and the creation of some new possibility.

There are reasons to believe that humans are capable of making these kinds of changes. Over the last thirty years, the field of developmental psychology has demonstrated that human beings are capable of evolving to higher and more sophisticated levels of cognitive, emotional, and moral functioning (Alexander and Langer 1990; Fisher and Torbert 1995; Fowler 1981; Kegan 1994). These higher levels involve the ability to integrate differences that are physical, emotional, and cognitive in nature.

There is remarkable consistency among the findings of researchers about the nature of these levels of development as well as their sequence.

There are also many thinkers who argue that society itself must proceed through these levels of development if the human race is to survive (Beck and Cowan 1996; Fisher and Torbert 1995; Wilber 1995). These theorists maintain that differentiation must precede integration (a principle that is consistent with theories of biological evolution). In cognitive development, for example, the ability of an individual to recognize differences must precede the ability to integrate those differences. If this is true, then the challenges we face as a society need not be seen as something cast in stone without the possibility for change, but rather as representing a natural stage (although quite a difficult one to exist in) of human and social development that we must pass through, if we have the courage to follow the path. At this point, the discussion may appear to be highly theoretical and nonactionable. For this reason, we would like to describe a specific example of an approach that utilizes these principles to achieve individual and social transformation in the more specific arena of enterprise development.

AN EXAMPLE: THE ROLE OF ENTERPRISE DEVELOPMENT IN BUILDING MINORITY ECONOMIC MOBILITY

The assault on racial discrimination and inequality in this country must be multipronged. One of those prongs is the fight for economic mobility. One strategy that is being advocated extensively these days is minority self-employment or entrepreneurship. In Chapter 6, Herring, Horton, and Thomas raise major doubts about the ability of this approach to alleviate poverty. They point out that inner-city entrepreneurship is impeded by denial of credit, racially segregated industries, and isolation from the rest of the metropolitan economy.

We agree with Herring, Horton, and Thomas's assessment. As it is currently practiced, enterprise development is not widely effective in enhancing the economic mobility of inner-city minority entrepreneurs. However, we cannot be satisfied with leaving it at that. Part of the problem, we believe, lies in the fact that we, as a nation, still do not fully understand the needs of minority groups in the United States. By "needs" we mean the obstacles that minority individuals face in obtaining and utilizing the resources they require for economic mobility. Americans tend to look at these needs superficially or assume that we already know what they are, based on ethnically or racially skewed perspectives. Superficial diagnosis begets superficial treatment, which, in turn, perpetuates the illness.

Effective diagnosis is an extremely difficult activity. The problems of economic mobility are complex and systemic in nature; they are co-produced by many different factors working in combination. They cannot be understood nor addressed by methodologies that examine a single factor at a time. However, most analyses are univariate; that is, they focus on only a single dimension or factor. The issue is how all of these factors relate and interact with each other to collectively produce the obstacles that we observe. If we are to *change* those results (not merely understand them), we must look at all of them and how they work in combination.

We advocate a very deep and multidimensional diagnosis of minority needs that allows for treatments specifically tailored to individual needs that can be strategically assembled into a holistic plan for the economic mobility of minority individuals and groups (see Lichtenstein and Lyons 1996). Helping minorities to overcome the obstacles they face requires skill building. But, such skill building cannot take place in a vacuum. It cannot be a matter of the majority "treating" the ills of the minority. This is an insensitive approach that has been tried, and continues to be attempted, without any real success. True skill building, to be consistent with the developmental perspective described above, must involve the mutual development of skills by all groups in our society, interacting and learning from one another—Du Bois's mutualistic perspective in action.

Any economic or social solution to these issues must focus on strengthening all of the parts that have become differentiated in our society—both minority and majority—and then work to integrate (or re-integrate) these parts into a stronger, healthier, and more effective whole. We must address the developmental needs of minorities. But at the same time, a parallel process must be taking place with "established" groups (i.e., the majority) on their developmental issues (e.g., prejudice, intolerance, lack of recognition of and respect for differences) in ways that will make it possible for integration to occur.

OUR PROPOSAL: THE ENTREPRENEURIAL DEVELOPMENT SYSTEM

Through our own research, we have concluded that the current local and regional enterprise development apparatus is incapable of producing the level of entrepreneurial activity necessary to truly transform a community's economy and bring economic mobility to all its residents, because it is highly fragmented and engages its clients in largely arms-length transactional relationships. What is needed is a system that eliminates the fragmentation and fosters developmental and transformational relationships that can be accessed by all entrepreneurs in the region. We have developed a model for such a system, which we call the Entrepreneurial Development System (EDS).

The first step in establishing an EDS in any community is a diagnosis of local entrepreneurial need, as we describe our discussion of minority needs above. This permits a determination of the entrepreneurial skill of each entrepreneur entering the system. This information is used to assign entrepreneurs to "leagues," which are levels at which entrepreneurs share a common degree of skill. The EDS employs the terminology of baseball in labeling these levels as Rookie, Single A, Double A, Triple A and the Majors. The purpose of identifying levels is multifold: (1) to ensure that entrepreneurs receive the proper type and intensity of assistance at each skill-building plateau; (2) to permit entrepreneurs with similar degrees of skill to interact with one another to facilitate learning, problem-solving, resource and risk pooling, etc.; (3) to enhance the identification and development of mentor-protégé relationships between levels; and (4) to create a skill-building ladder from the earliest stages of entrepreneurship to the most advanced. In this way, the EDS transforms entrepreneurs and their businesses, and, in turn, the local economy.

The EDS addresses the fragmentation in the current enterprise development "system" found in any given community by organizing service providers in a way that eliminates overlap and fills gaps in service. It also focuses service providers on doing what they do best and operating at the league level(s) where they can create the most value. In so doing, the EDS also creates a seamless web of service provision that ensures participating entrepreneurs that they can find appropriate skill-building help at any rung on the ladder.

Underlying this enterprise development infrastructure is a very important concept—entrepreneurship skills. The business literature on entrepreneurship focuses on the traits or characteristics of successful entrepreneurs (Huefner and Hunt 1994; Schumpeter 1991). We find this to be a very limiting approach. There is little or nothing that can be done about traits. An individual either has them or does not have them. Thus, enterprise development based on this assumption can only "cream" the people with the "right stuff" for entrepreneurship and leave others by the wayside. Furthermore, it assumes that because these entrepreneurs already have the necessary traits for success, their interaction with the

Enterprise Development System will be self-guided, self-regulated, and short term. Indeed, this is the way in which most assistance to entrepreneurs is provided. This helps to explain why programs such as microenterprise development, community development venture capital, and empowerment business incubation, which are focused on low-income and minority entrepreneurship, are unable to help most of their clients to escape poverty or marginal self-employment, as Herring et al. note. Only those with the right characteristics are harvested, and there is no ladder for advancing the rest.

It seems to us that it is much more accurate and useful to view successful entrepreneurship as a set of learned skills. Those who have the desire to obtain these skills can get help in mastering them and thereby enhancing their chances for entrepreneurial success. This is not only a more democratic approach to entrepreneurship, but it changes the focus of enterprise development assistance provision as well. Now, assistance can be made available to anyone who wants it and for as long as they need it.

What are the skills necessary for successful entrepreneurship? Using the work of Gerber (1995) and our own research findings (Lichtenstein and Lyons 1996), we have identified four dimensions of relevant skills: technical skills, managerial skills, entrepreneurial skills, and personal maturity skills. Technical skills are those that have to do with the specific techniques required for the given business in which one is engaged (e.g.: knowledge of the use of word processing software for a word processing business). Managerial skills include skills necessary to administer the day-to-day activities of operating the business (e.g., bookkeeping, marketing, managing people, etc.). The skills essential to developing innovative solutions to business problems are termed "entrepreneurial skills." Personal maturity skills are probably the least understood and most neglected skill set of the successful entrepreneur. They include self-awareness, emotional stability, accountability, and creativity, among others. This latter skill set may well be the most difficult to teach and to master; yet, it is arguably the most important for ultimate success.

The Entrepreneurial Development System creates the skill-building ladder that allows a self-employed minority individual who may come to entrepreneurship at the Rookie League level to work her way up to the point where she possesses the entrepreneurial skills to compete successfully in the regional (and perhaps national and international) economy and gain access to the resources that were previously available only to those entrepreneurs who started out at a higher skill level. In this way the EDS eliminates most, if not all, of the barriers to inner-city entrepreneurship identified by Herring et al. in Chapter 6. It makes entrepreneurship a viable tool for breaking out of poverty and building wealth. Furthermore, it does so by creating the kinds of linkages discussed by Morris, Cunnigen (on Du Bois), Durr, and Roschelle in this book—the social capital necessary for transformation. In doing so, it connects inner-city minority entrepreneurs to the resources and markets of the larger economy.

WHERE DO WE GO FROM HERE?

The Entrepreneurial Development System is a transformational model for effecting change in the enterprise development arena, an admittedly small part of the racial equality picture. However, its key elements are suggestive of a transformational approach to combating racial discrimination and inequality.

What is truly needed in America is a societal transformation. This is a massive and very long-term process. It requires highly intensive network-building efforts, both within the African American community and between that community and the rest of society. This must be social capital building at its highest level (Coleman 1988; Putnam 1993).

It must start with a deep diagnosis of where society stands now with regard to issues of race. What are our strengths? What are our weaknesses? Where do individuals and groups stand on the ladder to interracial acceptance and harmony (hate, intolerance, indifference, tolerance, acceptance, complete mutuality)? What kind of help will these individuals and groups need in building the civic skills required to advance rung by rung up the ladder? Who is helping now and at what level? Where are there gaps in assistance? How might we fill those gaps?

Just as the EDS creates opportunities for entrepreneurs to interact and learn from each other within and across skill levels, so should our system for societal transformation. It is much more difficult to hate someone you truly come to know and understand. Cultural geographers have a term for instances where peoples of a nation become physically separated from one another and lose their common bonds. They call it "distance decay." Segregation has had a similar effect on the people of the United States. By remaining emotionally and physically separate as races, we allow ourselves to entertain myths about one another, to develop negative attitudes, and to forget that we are all Americans and all part of the human race.

The EDS also emphasizes the role of mentors. These individuals must play a major part in our system for societal transformation as well. They must lead by word and by example. They must be teachers and role models. They must represent all races and ethnicities. Within the EDS there is also the role of relationship broker. This is an individual who works to connect entrepreneurs within and across league levels, helping them to identify and consummate joint ventures and other business partnerships. As an example, minority and women entrepreneurs are often not taken seriously as business people by majority firms. The relationship broker can bring these parties together, affording them an opportunity to get to know one another and the products/services in which they trade. Experience has shown that this helps to explode myths that stand in the way of productive business relationships. Similarly, a relationship broker in the system for societal transformation could bring people together in cross-racial relationships that break down barriers caused by ignorance or false perception.

In many cases, people already exist who undertake these roles in society, but their efforts are not well coordinated and their interventions are not strategic, much like the enterprise development service providers mentioned above. A societal transformation system is needed to address the issue of race relations systemically and consistently. Without this, our efforts to end racial discrimination and inequality can never be transformational.

We all have a role to play in this societal transformation system. As scholars, we can contribute to the analysis required for deep diagnosis of need. However, our contributions should not stop there. Rather than merely acting as observers, policy critics, and chroniclers of racial discrimination and inequality in the United States, we need to "roll up our sleeves" and engage in action research in this arena. We need to test our theories and use our knowledge in the field in an effort to build and perfect the societal transformation system. The practical issue confronting us in academia is not just how to build an awareness of the need for development and racial harmony, for example, but rather how to help people live according to these values.

This action research should be coordinated as well. A consortium of universities from around the country could be established to take the lead and to coordinate efforts. A pilot community could be chosen for developing and testing the societal transformational system. A charter organization made up of community leaders from the public, private, and nonprofit sectors could be established to support the system and oversee its activities. The possibilities for innovation in effecting this transformation are virtually limitless.

We have only scratched the surface in our discussion of a societal transformation system designed to change the way in which the races in America interact with one another. Our intention here is to continue a thought process that leads to action—a thought process that was begun by the Du Bois–Washington debates.

REFERENCES

Alexander, C. N. and Langer, E. J. (Eds.). 1990. *Higher Stages of Human Development*. New York: Oxford University Press.

Beck, Don Edward and Christopher C. Cowan. 1996. *Spiral Dynamics*. Cambridge, MA: Blackwell Press.

Coleman, J.S. 1988. "Social Capital in the Creation of Human Capital." *American Journal of Sociology*, 94 (Supplement): S95–S119.

Dilts, R. B. 1996. *Visionary Leadership Skills*. Capitola, CA: Meta Publications.

Fisher, D. and Torbert, W. R. 1995. *Personal and Organizational Transformations*. New York: McGraw-Hill.

Fowler, James W. 1981. *Stages of Faith: The Psychology of Human Development and the Quest for Meaning*. New York: Harper Collins.

Gerber, M. E. 1995. *The E-Myth Revisited: Why Most Small Businesses Don't Work and What to Do About It*. New York: HarperCollins.

Huefner, J.C. and H.K. Hunt. 1994. "Broadening the Concept of Entrepreneurship: Comparing Business and Consumer Entrepreneurs." *Entrepreneurship Theory and Practice*, Spring, 61–75.

Kegan, R. 1994. *In Over Our Heads*. Cambridge, MA: Harvard University Press.

Lichtenstein, G. and Lyons, T. S. 1996. *Incubating New Enterprises: A Guide to Successful Practice*. Washington, DC: Aspen Institute.

Putnam, R.D. 1993. "The Prosperous Community: Social Capital and Economic Growth." *Current*, October, 356: 49.

Schumpeter, J. 1991. "Comments on a Plan for the Study of Entrepreneurship." In Swedberg, R. (Ed.). Joseph A. Schumpeter, *The Economics and Sociology of Capitalism* (pp. 406–428). Princeton, NJ: Princeton University Press.

Wilber, Ken. 1995. *Sex, Ecology and Spirituality*. Boston, MA: Shambhala Publications.

Index

Abbott, A., 55
Access, equal, 71, 72, 78. *See also* Housing
Activism, 175–86
Adaptive perspective, 114
Adarand v. Pena, 31
Advancement. *See* Mobility
Advisory Board on Race, 32
AEI. *See* American Enterprise Institute
Affirmative action, 2; administration of, 47; failure of, 177, 189, 190; and housing, 72, 87; and managers, 39, 40, 41, 48; and Proposition 209, 23–36; and women, 55; and work, 30, 31, 39–52, 55, 56, 63, 177
Affluence. *See* Wealth
African Americans: and corporations, 39–52; and diversity, 147–50; and education, 5–7, 24, 25, 26, 35; and entrepreneurship, 94, 98, 99, 100, 101, 102, 103, 104, 105, 106, 108; and family structure, 114; and housing, 72, 73, 75, 76, 77, 78, 81, 82, 83, 84–85, 146; and income, 79, 80, 83; and New York City, 72, 73, 74, 75, 76; and Proposition 209, 24, 25, 26, 35; and Republican party, 30, 31; and segregation, 2, 75, 76, 77, 78, 146; and Texas, 27; and ties, 62, 64; and United States population, 137–38; and work, 39–52, 55–67. *See also* Blacks
Afro-Caribbeans, 74, 75, 76
Age, and entrepreneurship, 95, 100
Albany Study, 58
Aleuts, 138
Alter, Jonathan, 170–71
American Civil Liberties Union, 23
American Enterprise Institute, 161, 163
Ancestry, 73, 82–83
Anderson, James D., 9
Anomaly thesis, 181

and entrepreneurship, 192–93; and equality, 10; and family, 117; and Puerto Rican support networks, 122–24, 126, 128; and Puerto Rican women, 118, 120, 130; and racism, 161–62; and Washington, 11; and whites, 161–62. *See also* Income

Edmonds, Erin, 186

Education: and affirmative action hiring, 42; and African Americans, 5–7, 8, 9; bilingual, 32, 166; and Bloom, 170; classical liberal, 12; and Du Bois, 12, 14–15; and Du Bois-Washington debate, 5–7, 12; and Entrepreneurial League System, 194, 195; and entrepreneurship, 95, 100, 104, 106; and equality, 9–10; and failure of desegregation, 176–77; and industry, 10, 13; and knowledge, 19; liberal cultural, 9–10; and mentor, 194, 196–97; and multiculturalism, 167–68; primary and secondary, 26–27, 28; and Proposition 209, 23–36; and race, 19–21; and racism, 162; and segregation, 182; and South, 9; and Washington, 5–7, 10, 11, 12, 13, 14; and whites, 8; and women, 183, 184; and work, 131. *See also* Skill; Training

Ehrlich, Elizabeth, 163

Elite, 17, 159, 160, 161, 162

Enclave, ethnic, 97, 100, 102, 103, 104, 105, 107, 108

Enemy, identification of, 150, 152–53

Ensel, W., 59

Entrepreneurial League System, 193–96

Entrepreneurship, 89–108, 192–93; theories of, 91–95

Equality: economic, 10; and education, 9–10; failure to achieve, 176; and gender, 183; and King, 171–

72; and missionary philanthropists, 9–10; political and legal, 10. *See also* Civil rights

Eskimos, 138

Ethnicity, 91, 142

Exchange reciprocity, 113, 119, 126, 127, 128

Executive. *See* Manager

Familism, 114, 117–18, 121, 122, 126, 129

Family, 93, 101, 103, 113–31, 129. *See also* Community

Feminism, 115–16. *See also* Women

Fertility, 141

First Amendment, 182. *See also* Civil rights

Frey, William, 144

Gary, 146

Gender: and entrepreneurship, 97, 100, 103; and equality, 183; and family, 115; and oppression, 116; and Puerto Rican women, 118; and racially defined network, 58; and ties, 65–67; and work contacts, 59. *See also* Men; Women

Gilder, George: *Wealth and Poverty*, 163

Gitlin, Todd, 36

Glazer, Nathan, 163; "Why I No Longer Think Affirmative Action Is Unjust," 29–30

Gomes, Peter, 184–85

Government, 55, 67; and entrepreneurship, 89, 90, 105; and housing, 71–87; and Puerto Rican support networks, 124; and work, 41, 52

Grandparents, 101, 103, 104, 107, 108

Granovetter, M., 57

Greenwald, P., 58, 65

Greve, Michael, 34

Values, universal, 8
Vanguard, 16
Victim, 143

Washington, Booker T., 5–6, 10, 12,
13, 14; Atlanta Cotton Exposition
speech, 11
Washington, D. C., 165
Watts, J. C., 30
Wealth, 79, 161, 179–80
Weber, Max, 91
Welfare, 129, 131, 158
Wells-Barnett, Ida, 15
West, 144, 145, 146
West Indies, 73
White Man's Burden, 169
Whites: and affirmative action, 42;
and Brimelow, 166; and care networks, 117; and change, 2; and co-
lonialism, 160; and *Dances with
Wolves*, 167–68; and denial of racism, 151; and discrimination, 169;
and diversity, 149; and Du Bois,
12, 15; and Du Bois-Washington
debate, 14; and economy, 161–62;
and education, 8; and entrepreneurship, 98, 99, 100, 101, 102, 103,
104, 105, 106; and family structure, 114; and housing segregation,
75, 76, 77, 78; images of, 168–70;
and immigration, 140; and income,
79, 80, 83; and King, 171–72; and
migration, 145; and New York
City, 73, 75, 76; non-Hispanic, 78,
138, 139, 140–41; and politics,
149; and population, 139–41, 142,
161; and power, 165; and
Proposition 209, 25, 26, 27, 33;
and Puerto Rican women, 124, 131;
and racism, 151, 157–72, 164; and
stereotypes, 164; as superior, 167,
170, 179, 180; and support net-

works, 119; as victims, 169; *vs.*
minority, 72; and Washington, 10,
14; and *White Man's Burden*, 169;
and work, 42, 161
Wieseltier, Leon, 163
Wilkins, Roger, 29–30, 33
Wilson, Pete, 23, 31
Wilson, William Julius, 84–85, 115
Women: and affirmative action, 55;
and African American family, 114;
and care networks, 117; and education, 183, 184; and entrepreneurship, 100, 103, 104, 106; and
exchange reciprocity, 113; and
family, 115; and Puerto Rican support networks, 117, 118, 119, 120–
27, 128, 129, 130, 131; and Republican party, 30, 31; and ties, 65–
67; and work, 65–67. *See also*
Gender
Work: and affirmative action, 30, 31,
39–52, 55, 56, 63, 177; and African Americans, 39–52, 55–67; and
blacks, 164, 168; denial of, 94,
102, 103, 104, 107, 108; and discrimination, 39, 165; and education, 131; and entrepreneurship, 89–
108; and housing, 85; and men,
65, 66, 67; and minorities, 55–67;
and politics, 67; and Puerto Ricans, 124, 128, 130; and race, 59;
racialized, 98, 102, 103, 107, 108;
racialized *vs.* mainstream, 41, 42–
43, 44–45, 46, 48, 50, 51, 52, 56;
and racism, 189; and segregation,
39, 48; support, 46; and support
networks, 118; and Washington, 11;
and women, 65–67
Working class, 12, 161. *See also*
Class

Xenophobia, 166

About the Contributors

RICHARD D. ALBA is currently the Vice-President of the American Sociological Association and Professor of Sociology at SUNY-Albany. He has taught at Lehman College and the City University Graduate Center in New York City and at Cornell University. His teaching and research focuses mainly on race-ethnicity and international migration in the United States and in the Federal Republic of Germany, where he has twice been a Fulbright Scholar. His books include *Ethnic Identity: The Transformation of White American* (1990); *Italian Americans: Into the Twilight of Ethnicity* (1985), and *Right versus Privilege: The Open Admissions Experiment at the City University of New York* (with David Lavin and Richard Siberstein, 1980). He has published numerous articles in major journals of sociology.

DERRICK A. BELL is the author of *And We Are Not Saved, Faces at the Bottom of the Well, Confronting Authority*, and *Gospel Choirs*. Currently he is serving as a Visiting Professor at New York University Law School after being dismissed from Harvard University for protesting the failure of the institution to tenure women of color.

SHARON M. COLLINS is an Associate Professor in the Department of Sociology at the University of Illinois at Chicago. Among her recent publications are *Black Corporate Executives: The Making and Breaking of a Black Middle Class* (1997); "Black Mobility in White Corporations: Up the Corporate Ladder But Out on a Limb" (*Social Problems*, 1996); and "Retreat form Equal Opportunity? The Case of Affirmative Action" in *The Bubbling Cauldron* (1995), edited by Michael Peter Smith and Joe R. Feagin.

DONALD CUNNIGEN is an Associate Professor of Sociology at the University of Rhode Island. He has published in the *Annual Review of Sociology, Southern Studies, Journal of Mississippi History*, and *Western Journal of Black Studies*. Presently, he is co-editor of a monograph on the intellectual contributions of Booker T. Washington and on the contributions of second-generation African American sociologists.

NANCY A. DENTON is an Associate Professor at the University at Albany (SUNY-Albany) and is the co-author of *American Apartheid*, which won the 1995 Otis Dudley Duncan Award by the American Sociological Association. She has participated on many panels on housing.

MARLESE DURR is an Associate Professor of Sociology in the Department of Sociology and Anthropology and the Director of Women's Studies Program at Wright State University. She is the co-author of "Racial Submarkets in State Government: African American Professionals in New York State" with John R. Logan in *Sociological Forum*, "Does Race Matter?: The Determinants and Consequences" with Cedric Herring, Hayward Derrick Horton, and Melvin E. Thomas in *Race & Society*, "Social Cost and Enterprise Development within African American Communities" with Thomas S. Lyons in *National Journal of Sociology*, and "Examining the Unique Needs of Urban Entrepreneurs: A Research Note" with Thomas S. Lyons and Gregg A. Liechtenstein in *Race & Society*. Professor Durr is currently completing a Guest Edited Issue for *Gender & Society* with Shirley A. Hill of the University of Kansas entitled "African American Women: Gender Relations, Work, and the Political Economy in the 21st Century" to be in print June 2002. Her areas of research are small business development in inner-cities and the outcome of affirmative action policies within large-scale organizations management structure.

JOE R. FEAGIN, President of the American Sociological Association, is a Graduate Research Professor at the University of Florida and the Lynd Distinguished Professor of Sociology. For thirty years he has done extensive research on racial and gender discrimination issues. His recent books include *Modern Sexism* (Second Edition 1995), *Racial and Ethnic*

Relations (Fifth Edition, 1996), *Living with Racism: The Black Middle Class Experience* (1994), *White Racism: The Basics* (1995), and *The Agony of Education: Black Students at White Colleges and Universities* (1996). Feagin has published thirty-two scholarly books and 130 research articles in his research specialties and is currently working on a book on the social costs of racial discrimination. He has served as Scholar-in-Residence at the U.S. Commission on Civil Rights. His earlier book, *Ghetto Revolts* (1973), was nominated for a Pulitzer Prize and his recent books, *Living with White Racism* and *White Racism: The Basics*, have won the Gustavus Myers Center's Outstanding Human Rights Book Award. Feagin has served as Chair of the American Sociological Association's section on Racial and Ethnic Minorities and is currently a member of the governing council of that association.

CEDRIC HERRING is currently the Interim Director of the Institute for Research on Race and Comparative Public Policy at the University of Illinois at Chicago. He is also Professor in the Department of Sociology at the University of Illinois at Chicago and in the Institute of Government and Public Affairs at the University of Illinois and a Faculty Associate at the Irving B. Harris Graduate School of Public Policy Studies at the University of Chicago. He has published three books, three research monographs, and more than thirty-five journal articles and book chapters on subjects such as racial inequality, social policy, labor force issues and policies, and politics. He has also received support for his research from the National Science Foundation, the Ford Foundation, the Mac Arthur Foundation, and the Joyce Foundation. In addition, he has shared his findings in community forums, at press conferences, in newspapers, magazines, on radio and television with community groups, and before legislators and other government officials. Dr. Herring is the past President of the Association of Black Sociologists.

HAYWARD D. HORTON's research areas are racial-ethnic demography and population theory. Resent research has focused on the demography of race and entrepreneurship, demographic analysis of racial differentials in home ownership and housing values, rural-urban differences in poverty within the black population, the impact of sex ratios on the black community and black male marriability over time. He is currently conducting research on the impact of cohort differentials on black socioeconomic status and patterns of mortality. Finally, he is also conducting research on the demography of HIV/AIDS within the Puerto Rican population. Dr. Horton is an Associate Professor of Sociology at the University at Albany.

JAMES E. JACOB is the former Dean of the College of Social Sciences at the University of California, Chico. In 1992 he was the recipient of the Jose Antonio Aguirre Prize, an international competition sponsored by the Fundacio'n Sabino Arana of Spain for the best manuscript on Basque nationalism. Dr. Jacob is author of numerous publications in the field of ethnic politics, language conflict, and nationalism, among them: *The Hills of Conflict: Basque Nationalism in France* (1994) and co-editor along with William Beer of *Language and National Unity* (1985). He is a nationally recognized speaker in the area of cross-cultural communications,

GREGG A. LICHTENSTEIN is the President and CEO of Collaborative Strategies in Margate, New Jersey, and is co-author of *Incubating New Enterprises* with Thomas S. Lyons.

JOHN R. LOGAN is a Professor of Sociology and Public Policy at the University at SUNY-Albany. He is co-author of *Urban Fortunes* with Harvey Molotch (1987), *Beyond City Limits* with Todd Swanstrom (1990) and *Family Ties* with Glenna Spitze (1996). He is the author of more than thirty-five journal articles on suburbanization and won the 1990 Distinguished Book Award form the American Sociological Association for Urban Fortunes.

THOMAS S. LYONS is Associate Professor of Management of Urban Policy and the Director of the Center for Research on Entrepreneurship and Enterprise Development at the University of Louisville. He is the co-author of three books on economic development: *Creating an Economic Development Action Plan* (2001), *Incubating New Enterprises*, and *Economy Without Walls* (1996). His principal research interests lie in the area of small business incubation and the creation of community-based enterprise development systems.

MIRIAM MA'AT-KA-RE MONGES is an Associate Professor in the Department of Sociology/Social Work and Coordinator of the African American Studies Program at California State University at Chico. She is the author of *KUSH: The Jewel of Nubia* (forthcoming). She has also written "Reflections on the Role of Female Deities and Queens in Ancient Kemet" in the *Journal of Black Studies*, "I've Got a Right to the Tree of Life," in *The Black Panther Revisited*, edited by Charles Jones (forthcoming), and "Beyond the Melting Pot: Values Clarification Exercise for Teachers and Human Service Professionals" in *Teaching About Culture, Ethnicity, and Diversity: Exercises and Planned Activities*, edited by Ted Singelis (forthcoming). Dr Monges has directed programs involving a wide range of social issues including services to homebound elderly, youth, welfare recipients, recovering substance abusers, and sexually active adolescents.

ALDON MORRIS is a Professor of Sociology at Northwestern University whose areas of interest include social movements, theory, the Civil Rights Movement, race, religion, social inequality, and political sociology. His book, *Origins of the Civil Rights Movement*, won the 1986 Distinguished Contribution to Scholarship Award of the American Sociological Association, the Gustavus Myers Award, and honorable mention for the C. Wright Mills Award of the American Sociological Association. He is the author of over thirty-seven articles and three books.

ANNE R. ROSCHELLE is an Assistant Professor and the Director of the Women's Studies Program at the University of San Francisco. Her teaching and research focus on racial and ethnic minorities, gender inequality, and poverty. She is the author of *No More Kin: Exploring Race, Class, and Gender in Family Networks* (1997) and is on the editorial board of *Race, Gender, and Class in the World Cultures*. Her article "Declining Networks of Care: Ethnicity, Migration, and Poverty in a Puerto Rican Community" appeared in the special issue on Latinos in the journal *Race, Gender, Class in World Cultures*. Her current research is a qualitative analysis of homeless and formerly homeless families in the San Francisco Bay area.

MELVIN E. THOMAS is a Professor in the Department of Sociology and Anthropology at North Carolina State University. His areas of specialization include race, inequality, religion, and social psychology. He is currently involved in research on the relative impact of race and class on the lives of African Americans. His recent publications include "Racial and Gender Differences in Returns from Education" with Cedric Herring and Hayward D. Horton in *Race and Ethnicity in America: Meeting the Challenges of the 21st Century*, edited by Gail Thomas, "Race, Class, and Occupation: An Analysis of Black and White Earning Differences for Professional and Non-Professional Men, 1940–1990" in *Research in Race and Ethnic Relations, 1995*, edited by Rutledge Dennis, "Race, Class, and Personal Income: An Empirical Test of the Declining Significance of Race Thesis, 1968–1988" in *Social Problems*; "The Continuing Significance of Race: A Study of Race, Class, and Quality of

Life in America, 1972–1985," *American Sociological Review*; and "Determinants of Satisfaction for Blacks and Whites" with Bernadette Holmes in *Sociological Quarterly*.

HERNAN M. VERA, a native-born Cuban, is an Associate Professor at the University of Florida at Gainesville and has co-authored several books and articles with Joe R. Feagin. Like Feagin, his work examines issues of race and ethnicity for Latinos in the United States.